Transportation, Energy, and Environment: How Far Can Technology Take Us?

ACEEE Books on Energy Policy and Energy Efficiency

Series Editor: Carl Blumstein

Transportation, Energy, and Environment: How Far Can Technology Take Us?

edited by
John DeCicco
Mark Delucchi

American Council for an Energy-Efficient Economy
Washington, D.C.
1997

Transportation, Energy, and Environment: How Far Can Technology Take Us?

Published by the American Council for an Energy-Efficient Economy, 1001 Connecticut Avenue, N.W., Suite 801, Washington, D.C. 20036

Cover design by Chuck Myers
Printed in the United States of America

Library of Congress Cataloging-in-Publication Data

Transportation, energy, and environment : how far can technology take us? / edited by John DeCicco and Mark Delucchi.
    p.290   cm.
    "Based on presentations given at the 1995 Asilomar Conference on Sustainable Transportation Energy Strategies, held in Pacific Grove, California, on July 31 through August 3" — Ackn.
    Includes bibliographical references and index.
    ISBN 0-918249-28-7
    1. Transportation — United States — Planning — Congresses.
2. Transportation — Environmental aspects — United States — Congresses.
3. Sustainable development — United States — Congresses. 4. Energy conservation — United States — Congresses. I. DeCicco, John M.
II. Delucchi, Mark A. III. American Council for an Energy-Efficient Economy. IV. Asilomar Conference on Sustainable Transportation Energy Strategies (1995 : Pacific Grove, Calif.)
HE206.2.T683 1997
338'.0973 — dc21   97-36757
                                                    CIP

NOTICE

 Printed on recycled paper.

Acknowledgments

This book is based on presentations given at the 1995 Asilomar Conference on Sustainable Transportation Energy Strategies, held in Pacific Grove, California, on July 31 through August 3, 1995. Acknowledgments are gratefully given to the organizations that supported the conference and enabled the publication of this volume. The conference was organized by the Energy and Alternative Fuels Committees of the National Research Council's Transportation Research Board (TRB) along with the Institute of Transportation Studies of the University of California at Davis (ITS-Davis). Conference sponsors were the U.S. Department of Energy (DOE), the Federal Highway Administration (FHWA), and the University of California Transportation Center. Co-sponsors include Argonne National Laboratory (ANL), Oak Ridge National Laboratory (ORNL), and the American Council for an Energy-Efficient Economy (ACEEE).

We take the liberty to thank, on behalf of the conference organizers and attenders, the individuals who helped carry out the 1995 conference program. Daniel Sperling of ITS-Davis, Larry Johnson of ANL, David Greene of ORNL, Barry McNutt and Lew Fulton of DOE, and John De-Cicco of ACEEE comprised the conference steering committee. Special acknowledgment is due to Barry McNutt for proposing the theme and orienting the conference toward a productive focus. Daniel Sperling, along with staff and graduate students of ITS-Davis, hosted the conference and provided the numerous logistical and administrative services needed to make it a success. Larry Johnson chaired the opening session, which included presentations by Dan Santini, also of ANL, and Jim Sweeney of Stanford University. The topical sessions were chaired by David Greene; Roberta Nichols, consultant, formerly with the Ford Motor Company; Steve Plotkin, then of the Office of Technology Assessment and now with ANL; Robert Sawyer of the University of California at Berkeley; and Al Sobey, consultant, formerly with General Motors. An "open-mike" session was organized and moderated by Barry McNutt. Jananne Sharpless of the California Energy Commission, assisted by David Greene and Barry McNutt, chaired the closing session.

We also thank a number of individuals who contributed to the publication of this book. A set of anonymous reviewers provided comments and suggestions that helped strengthen the revised papers collected here. At ACEEE, Glee Murray managed the production process, Renee Nida and Mary Rubin assisted with editing, and Martin Thomas handled graphics production. Mary Anne Stewart performed copyediting; Karen Stough proofread the manuscript; Marc Savage created the index; and Chuck Myers provided layout and design.

The information and opinions expressed in this volume are the sole responsibility of the individual authors and should not be construed as reflecting the views of the sponsoring organizations associated with the conference or the production of this book.

Contents

Transportation, Energy, and Environment: How Far Can Technology Take Us?

Chapter One

Introduction and Overview

JOHN DECICCO AND MARK DELUCCHI

Throughout history, the technology of transportation has influenced where we live and what we do. From ancient times to the present, major cities have been located at the crossroads of important trade routes and on coasts and inland waterways accessible by boat. In the last century, transcontinental railroads expanded the frontiers and opened large tracts of the interior of continents for settlement. At the beginning of this century, trolley lines made it economical to live on the outskirts while commuting to work in a central city and thereby helped engender the modern suburb.

The technology of transportation has evolved rapidly since the beginning of the twentieth century. Automobiles and roads became ubiquitous and a major force in shaping urban and regional landscapes. Airplanes soon connected the far corners of the globe and expanded our economic and cultural horizons. Most recently, and perhaps most profoundly for the future, advances in electronic communication now allow us to transport information without transporting ourselves and may alter our geography in unforeseen ways as the twenty-first century unfolds.

As transportation systems and the economies they support have grown, so too have the undesirable impacts of transportation on the environment, both locally and globally. Although these problems have been with us from the beginning, the collective desire to mitigate them is relatively recent. Indeed, we began to seriously address the local and regional environmental impacts of transportation less than thirty years ago; the security of our supplies of transportation energy, only

1

twenty years ago; and the global environmental impacts of transportation, only a decade ago. Today, the U.S. transportation sector is almost totally dependent on oil, remains a major source of urban air pollutants, and is the nation's fastest-growing source of greenhouse gas emissions. The situation is substantially similar throughout the world and, with present transportation policies and plans, is not likely to change any time soon.

Decisions that we make today, including the default choice of not significantly altering the present course of petroleum-intensive motorized transport, will influence the transportation systems used by our descendents. Applied to transportation energy use, the question of sustainability impels us to consider how our choices—of infrastructure, vehicles, and fuels—will impact the future welfare of humanity. Do today's transportation systems incur costs and risks in ways that jeopardize the future? If so, today's systems are not sustainable. As a society, we may not agree on the answer to this question. Nevertheless, this book and the conference that generated it grew from a shared realization that many energy-related aspects of today's transportation systems are unlikely to be sustainable.

The 1995 Asilomar Conference

Policymakers, along with the industries, interests, and academic community associated with transportation energy use and its impacts, have been grappling with the question of sustainability since at least the time of the 1970s energy crises. From July 31 through August 3, 1995, a conference on sustainable transportation energy strategies was held at the Asilomar Conference Center in Pacific Grove, California. This conference was the latest in a series of meetings held since the late 1980s to discuss alternative fuels for transportation. The scope of these meetings has broadened to include more general ways of addressing the economic and environmental impacts of transportation energy use in the United States. Since 1991, conferences have been held every other year and have included representatives from federal and state agencies, national laboratories, industry, universities, and public interest groups active in research and policy analysis regarding the energy and environmental aspects of transportation systems.

As an analytical convenience, the organizers of the 1995 conference distinguished two general means to make the transportation system more sustainable with regard to energy use and environmental impacts. One is to change the technology of transportation—that is, to make the physical systems cleaner and more energy-efficient. The other is to change how the system is used—for example, by inducing people to switch from dirty modes to clean ones. Of course, the characteristics of technology and the use of technology interact strongly and cannot be separated perfectly. Nevertheless, engineering analysis differs enough from behavioral analysis to make the distinction useful. The organizers sought to explore the limits of the "tech fix" by examining how far technology changes could take the United States toward a more sustainable transportation system with minimal changes in how technologies are used. Thus, the conference theme was posed as a question: "Is Technology Enough?"

Enough for what? Here the organizers sought to stimulate pragmatic discussions rather than political debates. They did not want to become bogged down with questions such as what level of carbon emissions, what level of nitrogen oxide emissions, and so forth, might be sustainable. Therefore, to provide a framework for the presentations, the conference organizers suggested the following set of sustainability targets for the transportation sector:

- Reduce on-road criteria pollutant emissions to the low-emission-vehicle (LEV) level over the full life of vehicles and to lower levels in severely polluted areas.

- Reduce sector oil use 10 percent by 2005 and further thereafter.

- Return sector greenhouse gas emissions to their 1990 level by 2015.

- Increase renewable fuels to 15 percent of total transportation fuel use by 2015 and further thereafter.

These targets were not derived from formal analysis. Rather, they were offered as quantifiable indicators of a trend toward a more environmentally sustainable system. Presenters were asked to examine aspects of the U.S. transportation system and to assess the extent to which known or expected technology developments could help achieve the posited targets.

An opening session gave the conferees an opportunity to criticize these goals, not so much in terms of the specific values, but rather in terms of concept. Agreement was nearly unanimous on the desirability of defining policy goals in terms of emissions reductions, both for criteria air pollutants and for greenhouse gases. (It was acknowledged that disagreement still exists on the need for near-term action to curtail greenhouse gas emissions.) Less agreement existed on the goals of reducing oil use per se and increasing the use of renewable fuels. Some participants felt that such changes in fuel use and mix would likely result from pursuing emissions reduction targets but were not valid as stand-alone targets. In any case, the invited presenters were free to interpret the targets as they felt appropriate for their particular topics. Thus, presentations ranged from analyses that addressed the goals quantitatively to perspectives on the technological challenges and issues that would arise in attempting to reach them.

Overview

The 1995 conference had four main topical sessions, addressing various aspects of vehicle and fuels technology in the transportation sector. Sessions were organized under the following topics, the first and third of which focused on light-duty vehicles (passenger cars and light trucks):

1. Incremental Vehicle Efficiency Improvements: How Far Can We Go?

2. Alternative Fuels: Small Benefits, Small Costs?

3. The Potential of Leap-Forward Vehicle Technology

4. Trucks, Trains, and Planes: Can Technical Improvements Offset Growth?

Chapters based on eleven of the seventeen presentations made during the topical sessions are included here. Chapters 2 through 10 are papers given at the conference that were subsequently revised in response to peer review. Chapters 11 and 12 were not peer reviewed and are included here as received so that the authors' views would be incorporated in this volume. On the final day of the conference, a wrap-up session was held to see how much consensus had emerged from the presentations and discussions. The Epilogue presents a brief summary of that discussion.

The remainder of this chapter provides a summary of the contributions included here, with synopses of each of the chapters.

Incremental Improvements to Light Vehicles

Today's mass-produced light vehicles (passenger cars and light trucks) are almost exclusively based on an established design paradigm of steel bodies with petroleum-fueled engines. Although this technology is quite mature, automotive engineering continues to advance. Ongoing refinements in both emissions control and energy efficiency offer clear near-term progress toward meeting some of the sustainability goals. Questions involving how much progress, how quickly, and at what cost were examined at the first topical session of the conference, chaired by Robert Sawyer of the University of

California at Berkeley. The three papers presented at this session are included here as Chapters 2, 3, and 4.

An important sustainability goal is reducing emissions of regulated air pollutants: carbon monoxide (CO), reactive hydrocarbons (HC), nitrogen oxides (NO_x), sulfur oxides (SO_x), and particulate matter (PM), especially fine particulates. The target posed for the 1995 conference was to reduce such emissions to LEV levels over the life of vehicles. (LEV standards, which are specified by vehicle class, are among the more stringent now being applied in California.) The "life of vehicles" clause alludes to one reason—emissions control degradation as a vehicle ages—why actual emissions levels exceed the standards to which new vehicles are certified by laboratory testing. A number of regions are struggling with ways to effectively inspect vehicles for in-use emissions and to ensure the maintenance needed to keep emissions from degrading too severely. Emerging knowledge indicates, however, that much more can be done to ensure that new vehicles are designed to more carefully and robustly control emissions during real-world driving.

Real-World Emissions

In Chapter 2, "Real-World Emissions from Conventional Passenger Cars," Marc Ross and Tom Wenzel draw on extensive emissions measurements to provide an overview of the sources of CO, HC, and NO_x emissions in actual in-use conditions over the life of vehicles. They estimate grams-per-mile emissions for contemporary late-model cars (represented by model year 1993) and project the reductions achievable from known, feasible emissions control improvements by the years 2000 and 2010. It is often heard—sometimes from parties who should know better—that "today's new car emissions are 90 percent lower than those of two decades ago." This statement is false. The emissions that matter are those coming from vehicles on the road in *real-world driving*, not those indicated by the simulated driving tests used to satisfy the emissions standards (which are indeed about 90 percent more stringent than preregulatory emissions levels). Ross and Wenzel estimate that an average model-year 1993 car has CO and HC emissions four to five times higher than the standards and NO_x emissions about twice as high as the standards. They identify the major sources of these excess emissions and pay particular attention to those due to malfunctions of a vehicle's emissions control systems (including the catalytic converter, air/fuel intake controls, and associated components).

In contemporary cars, Ross and Wenzel find that malfunction emissions often occur because of poorly designed emissions control

systems. Their analyses of remote-sensing data and realistic dynamometer test data show that certain models have distinctly higher
emissions attributable to control system malfunction. Just as particular
models may be prone to, say, transmission problems, bad brakes, or
unreliability in other components, breakdowns of emissions controls
are also model-dependent. This insight challenges the conventional
wisdom that malfunction emissions are mainly the fault of individual
car owners or repairmen (a view dating from the days of simpler control systems, carburetors, and leaded gasoline). Unfortunately, the current regulatory approach is largely premised on this misunderstand-
ing. Inspections are designed on the assumption that individual
owners are responsible. Little attempt is made to identify particular
model lines that are prone to malfunction. Inspection and maintenance programs aimed at individual vehicles, as well as ongoing
tightening of tailpipe standards, do not address the most important
sources of real-world emissions and so are likely to be but marginally
effective.

Ross and Wenzel's analysis does indicate important opportunities
for cutting real-world emissions. New information technologies, such
as remote sensing and on-board diagnostics, as well as carefully obtained test data, can be applied to identify malfunction-prone models.
Emissions certification test procedures can be reformed to reduce "off-
cycle" emissions (further discussed in Chapter 3). If such developments are used to motivate automakers to design more robust emissions control systems, substantial emissions reductions can be reliably
achieved. Ross and Wenzel project achievable reductions in real-world
emissions of HC by 50 percent, NO_x by 56 percent, and CO by 60 percent for model-year 2010 cars. Such cuts would be an impressive
achievement but still leave emissions considerably above the LEV
level. Thus, the authors conclude, longer-term efforts are also needed
to induce substantial improvements in vehicle efficiency and encourage shifts to alternative drivetrain and fuel technologies.

Off-Cycle Emissions

In Chapter 3, "Federal Test Procedure Revisions and Real-World
Emissions," John German of the U.S. Environmental Protection
Agency (EPA) summarizes recent analyses revealing the extent of, and
major factors contributing to, emissions that occur "off-cycle"—that is,
during driving modes encountered in real-world, in-use situations
that are not accounted for during the standard emissions tests. He also
discusses likely vehicle emissions control techniques and their implications for vehicle efficiency. Light vehicles are certified to meet U.S.

federal and state (namely, California) emissions standards on the basis of measurements taken during standardized driving cycles, in what is known as the Federal Test Procedure (FTP). EPA, the California Air Resources Board (CARB), and the auto industry have been conducting research in support of proposals to revise the FTP so that it better reflects real-world driving. This research forms the basis of German's chapter.

German presents his results with a rich set of graphs showing the magnitude and causes of off-cycle emissions. Analyses of the data behind these graphs indicate how the current FTP significantly under-represents emissions during high-speed driving, rapid accelerations, and air conditioner use. Other factors causing off-cycle emissions include throttle fluctuations, the distance a vehicle travels before being shut off, and how long it stays off before being restarted. A key cause of off-cycle CO and HC emissions is "command enrichment," wherein a vehicle is designed to inject extra fuel (a "rich" mixture) during certain operating conditions. This enrichment appears to be necessary at times to protect the catalytic converter from overheating, generally under high-power conditions such as high-speed driving and high rates of acceleration. However, opportunities exist to reduce unneeded command enrichment, thus avoiding substantial excess CO and HC emissions.

German also discusses factors that affect estimates of the total emissions inventory (as opposed to per-mile vehicle emission factors) for mobile sources. One such factor is the average trip length. Generally, two 5-mile trips will produce more emissions than one continuous 10-mile trip because emissions are relatively high during the first few miles of a trip, before the catalyst is fully warmed up. German also points out the association of air conditioner use with increased NO_x emissions for many vehicles. Other causes exist for excess NO_x emissions, which are quite complex to analyze and not yet fully understood.

Combining Efficiency and Renewable Fuels

To reduce oil consumption and greenhouse gas (GHG) emissions in the transportation sector, one must either (1) use less fuel per mile, (2) switch to fuels that emit fewer GHGs per mile, or (3) switch to modes of transportation that emit fewer GHGs per mile. These three areas—fuel economy, alternative fuels, and travel demand—typically have been treated separately by separate groups of researchers. This division is unfortunate, because the areas are in fact complementary. For example, to the extent that alternative fuels are expensive or require expensive fuel-storage systems, the energy efficiency of alternative-fuel vehicles must be increased in order to reduce the costs of fuel consumption and fuel storage.

In Chapter 4, "Combining Efficiency and Renewable Fuels to Cut Oil Use and CO_2 Emissions," John DeCicco and Lee Lynd analyze the synergy between improved fuel economy and the use of wood-derived (cellulosic) ethanol in light-duty vehicles as one approach to meeting the conference's sustainability targets for oil use, greenhouse gas emissions, and renewable-fuels use. Drawing on previous analyses of the potential to improve fuel economy, they project the changes in fleet-average efficiency as improved vehicles replace older ones on the road. They review Lynd's analyses of the cost of biomass ethanol (see Chapter 5) and project potential production levels. Their analysis examines three rates of fuel economy improvement (0 percent, 3 percent, and 6 percent per year), plus a low and a high scenario of expansion in ethanol production capacity.

The authors find that improvements in fuel economy, combined with the use of cellulosic ethanol, can reduce oil use by 10 percent in 2005 and return greenhouse gas emissions to their 1990 level in 2015. However, no scenario results in 15 percent renewable-fuels use by the year 2015. DeCicco and Lynd point out that both efficiency improvement and renewable-fuels use are constrained by time lags, but that the periods of constraint are staggered. With allowance for the time needed to put more efficient vehicles into widespread production, substantial energy savings are achievable in two decades. Longer lead times are needed to bring new cellulosic ethanol production capacity on-line, so that considerable benefits from an efficiency-plus-renewables synergy would evolve over three decades. The combined scenario of 6 percent/yr efficiency improvement and a high rate of cellulosic ethanol capacity expansion projects light-vehicle greenhouse gas emissions 21 percent below the 1990 level and a 24 percent renewable-fuels share of light-vehicle energy use by 2025.

DeCicco and Lynd doubt that market forces alone will drive the transitions they delineate, even given considerable research and development of fuel-economy and ethanol-production technologies. Accordingly, the authors identify a range of regulatory and incentive mechanisms aimed at improving fuel economy and reducing the cost of ethanol from wood. They also note, appropriately, that their transition scenarios are only schematic and that a much more detailed analysis of capital availability, infrastructure expansion, consumer acceptance, and other factors is necessary. (Such transition issues are discussed in Chapter 6 of this volume.) In the end, the combination of improved fuel economy and renewable ethanol has considerable promise but also faces serious hurdles.

Alternative Fuels

Alternative fuels have been the subject of much deliberation and a focus of numerous policy developments over the years. These policy developments have culminated most recently in programs authorized by the 1992 Energy Policy Act (EPACT). However, the questions of which fuels to pursue, how to economically and effectively advance them, and what progress can be expected are far from resolved. Roberta Nichols, who for many years led Ford Motor Company's alternative-fuel activities and is now a private consultant, chaired the conference session addressing these questions. Her presentation is included here as Chapter 12. Lee Lynd's presentation on cellulosic ethanol and Margaret Singh and Marianne Mintz's paper on transition issues are included here as Chapters 5 and 6, respectively. Other presenters at this session, whose papers do not appear in this volume, included John Russell of the U.S. Department of Energy (DOE), who summarized his agency's alternative-fuels deployment programs, and Mark Delucchi, who discussed preliminary findings from his recent study of the full costs of various fuel options.

Cellulosic Ethanol Technology

Many researchers believe that in the long run, the transportation sector will have to switch from fossil fuels to renewable fuels (hence the inclusion of a renewable-fuels target among the conference discussion goals). Although there are a variety of renewable fuels and feedstocks, most research has focused on either hydrogen derived ultimately from solar power or liquid fuels derived from renewable biomass. In Chapter 5, "Cellulose Ethanol Technology in Relation to Environmental Goals and Policy Formation," Lee Lynd makes the case for ethanol derived by converting the lignocellulosic content of woody biomass.

In the United States, much reformulated or oxygenated gasoline already contains ethanol or an ethanol derivative, ethyl tertiary butyl ether (ETBE). This ethanol, however, is derived from the fermentation of corn, a process that converts only the sugar and starch content of the crop to alcohol. The corn-to-ethanol cycle is therefore rather inefficient and requires substantial input of fossil fuels. As a result, using corn-derived ethanol results in as much greenhouse gas emission as using petroleum-derived gasoline. For this and other reasons, corn (and other sugar- or starch-based crops, such as cane) are unlikely to be desirable feedstocks for producing biofuels in the long run.

However, ethanol also can be made from the lignin and cellulose (the lignocellulosic content) in plants, by processes that convert a much higher portion of the plant material into fuel. Lignocellulosic conversion permits much higher fuel production efficiencies than corn-based conversion and involves little or no fossil fuel input. Though not discussed here, biomass gasification processes also permit efficient conversion of plant materials into high-quality fuels. Lynd focuses on one of the most promising lignocellulose-to-ethanol conversion technologies, enzymatic hydrolysis. He discusses the likely cost and efficiency of advanced conversion processes, which he believes can be developed successfully given sizable and sustained support. He projects ethanol production costs as low as $0.50/gallon ($0.76/gallon on a gasoline energy-equivalent basis), for mature, advanced, highly efficient technologies.

If Lynd's projections of low cost and high efficiency prove correct, the benefits will be considerable. The wood-to-ethanol cycle will emit virtually no greenhouse gases and will consume very little petroleum. Ethanol internal-combustion-engine (ICE) vehicles probably will emit fewer criteria pollutants than will gasoline engines, although the reductions typically will be moderate. Further pollution reduction is likely with hybrid vehicles, and in the long run, ethanol could be reformed to supply hydrogen to fuel cells, which are nonpolluting. As Lynd argues, the transition to ethanol—a liquid fuel—may be easier than the transition to other renewable fuels, such as gaseous hydrogen. Although one reasonably might not be as optimistic about the future of biomass ethanol as Lynd is, his arguments for a substantial research and development effort are compelling enough to warrant serious consideration.

Alternative-Fuel Transition Issues

Over the past twenty or so years of research on alternative fuels and vehicles, analysts have identified several technologies that have the potential to compete successfully with conventional gasoline and diesel vehicles. To realize this potential, however, vehicle and fuel production levels must achieve a scale sufficient to yield acceptably low costs (financial costs, time costs, reliability costs, and so forth) to the consumer. Thus the challenge to even the most promising of alternatives: to gain a foothold in a market dominated by, and structured to foster the continued use of, petroleum fuels. Few if any detailed analyses of the early transition to alternative-fuel vehicles (AFVs) have been conducted to date. In Chapter 6, "Alternative Fuels and Vehicles: Transition Issues and Costs," Margaret Singh and Marianne Mintz begin to address this gap by reporting on the results of a preliminary assessment of the transition issues and costs facing alternatively fueled vehicles and alternative fuels.

Singh and Mintz review the many market and institutional barriers faced by the producers, distributors, and consumers of new fuels and vehicles and present an initial estimate of the magnitude of some of the transition costs. Their quantitative analysis examines five transition costs: the cost of fuel production, the cost of fuel retailing, the time cost of refueling trips, the cost of vehicles, and the cost of servicing the vehicles. During a transition period, all of these items will likely entail incremental costs over and above the corresponding long-run equilibrium costs for an AFV technology. In the long run, for example, the refueling time for a liquid alternative fuel may be little different from that for gasoline today. However, during the transition period, filling stations providing the new fuel initially will be few and far between, so that it will take extra time to find them. This additional time represents an incremental cost to vehicle users. Such costs are estimated for one of the AFV market penetration scenarios developed for a DOE study that examined the feasibility of displacing 30 percent of transportation petroleum use by 2010, in which AFVs number over 90 million by 2010.

Singh and Mintz also estimate the benefits of a transition to alternative fuels. These benefits include reduced oil imports, lower crude oil costs, increased consumer satisfaction due to the availability of new fuels and vehicles, and environmental benefits. Comparing the trajectory of costs with the trajectory of benefits during the transition, the authors find that in the early years, the costs exceed the benefits. After about six years, benefits begin to exceed the costs, and within ten years the benefits greatly exceed the costs.

Singh and Mintz caution that theirs are initial, first-cut, order-of-magnitude estimates. Ongoing work at DOE should help reduce the uncertainties in likely transition costs. Nevertheless, the general conclusion—that early in the transition to alternative fuels and vehicles, the costs will be high but the benefits low—is sound. Such a result is, of course, expected; the value of their work is that it begins a systematic, quantitative assessment of the transition cost issue, providing information that will be most crucial in informing the ongoing debate about the up-front investments needed to achieve a transition to a more sustainable transportation system. A key implication is the need for a concerted effort, involving costs incurred a number of years before comparable or greater benefits are seen, to address the transition barriers facing alternatives to petroleum if the long-run promise is ever to be realized.

Leap-Forward Technology for Light Vehicles

In September 1995, with what can be characterized as a self-inflicted lobotomy, the U.S. Congress eliminated its Office of Technology Assessment (OTA). For more than two decades, OTA had produced some of the nation's best in-depth studies of scientific and technical issues confronting policymakers. One of OTA's last published reports was an analysis of the costs and performance of advanced automotive technologies. K. G. Duleep's summary of that work, presented here as Chapter 7, examines prospects for "leap-forward" or "next-generation" vehicles, referring to designs using technologies that go beyond the steel-bodied ICEs of today's mass market. The session was chaired by Steve Plotkin of OTA (now with Argonne National Laboratory), who was project director for the OTA advanced vehicle technologies report. The session also featured remarks by Linda Lance, from the Office of the Vice President, who described the administration's approach to vehicle issues and the context for policy development and research efforts. Vernon Roan of the University of Florida presented views on fuel cells. Dick Kinsey of Ford Motor Company provided an auto industry perspective on advanced vehicle technologies, which is included here as Chapter 11.

Evolutionary and Revolutionary Technologies

As director of engineering for the firm of Energy and Environmental Analysis Inc. (EEA), K. G. Duleep has performed numerous studies of vehicle technology for government agencies and other clients. In Chapter 7, "Evolutionary and Revolutionary Technologies for Improving Fuel Economy," he provides estimates of the fuel economy and incremental retail price (IRP) of several passenger car technology combinations, ranging from advanced conventional designs to various battery-only and hybrid electric designs. The reference vehicle is a 1995 midsize car, such as a Ford Taurus. His analysis controls for vehicle performance, so that the advanced designs maintain grade-climbing and acceleration capabilities comparable to those of the reference vehicle (except for range with battery-electric vehicles). Generally, Duleep finds that advanced-technology vehicles will offer only modest gains in efficiency over advanced gasoline vehicles but will cost several thousand dollars more. For example, he estimates that a battery-only EV will have about the same fuel economy as an advanced conventional gasoline vehicle (when the efficiency of the generating plant is taken into account) but will cost almost $3,000 more at the retail level.

Duleep concludes that there may be niche markets for advanced-technology vehicles. However, his findings are tempered by several considerations. First, as he properly acknowledges, considerable uncertainty exists in the estimates, and cost and performance could be quite a bit higher or lower than in his base case. For example, he estimates that in the most optimistic scenario, a battery-electric vehicle (EV) will cost only $400 more than the comparable advanced gasoline vehicle. Second, as he points out, it may be desirable to sacrifice some performance in advanced-technology vehicles in order to reduce cost. Third, he estimates only the incremental retail price, not the life-cycle cost. The more efficient advanced technologies may have lower fuel costs, which will at least partially offset the higher incremental retail prices. Duleep's estimates are based on extensive discussions with experts at automobile companies, national laboratories, and product development companies, and he appropriately shuns hype and unproven assertions (especially regarding the cost and performance of batteries). However, in our view, he appears to treat the claims of independent researchers and developers of advanced technologies more skeptically than he treats the claims of automobile companies.

Trucks, Trains, and Planes

Although light vehicles dominate energy use and emissions in the transportation sector, the role of freight vehicles and aircraft has been growing. Because of fuel economy improvements, the light-vehicle share of transportation energy use dropped from 69 percent in 1975 to 60 percent in 1995. Similarly, pollution controls have progressed more for light vehicles than for heavy vehicles. Given the relative technological optimism regarding further potential improvements in light vehicles, greater attention will need to be paid to commercial transport, particularly the energy-intensive modes of freight trucks and aircraft. One session of the conference, co-chaired by Al Sobey and David Greene, examined what we know about the technological opportunities for reducing emissions and energy use from trucks, trains, and planes. In addition to the three contributions described below, this session also had a presentation by Stephanie Williams of the California Trucking Association. She focused on the progress that industry has been making in reducing its emissions and, notably, presented encouraging perspectives regarding opportunities for the trucking and railroad industries to collaborate on intermodal shipping.

Keep On Trucking—Sustainably?

In Chapter 8, "Keep On Trucking—Sustainably?" K. G. Duleep examines freight transport, in which energy use and emissions are dominated by trucking, particularly by the larger, over-the-road tractor-trailer combination trucks (18-wheelers and the like). Quantifying the link between freight movements and economic activity, Duleep projects a growth of 49 to 64 percent from 1990 to 2015, as measured in ton-miles of annual freight traffic by all modes. Since trucking's share of total freight shipments is also growing, the number of truck ton-miles could more than double over this period. Duleep develops two scenarios based on recent trends in, and the future potential for, higher efficiency. Efficiency can be raised by truck technology improvements and operational changes, including a shift of some long-haul trucking to intermodal shipping by rail. His "expected" scenario, based on what might occur absent new policy initiatives, suggests a net 29 to 42 percent increase in freight truck energy use between 1990 and 2015. His "optimistic" scenario, which would probably require policies to accelerate the efficiency improvements, sees truck energy use in 2015 held to the 1990 level or perhaps 10 percent lower. Duleep did not examine fuel substitution in freight trucking, and thus, with nearly exclusive use of petroleum fuels, greenhouse gas emissions track energy use. Tighter truck emissions standards already are planned under the 1990 Clean Air Act Amendments. Duleep projects that the total amount of NO_x and particulate matter (PM_{10}) from freight trucks might be cut by half or more, even accounting for the growth in truck travel.

It seems, then, that U.S. freight trucking can see significant progress toward sustainability goals for greenhouse gas and criteria emissions. However, goals for oil displacement and use of renewable fuels remain unaddressed, and we have several other reservations about Duleep's guardedly optimistic conclusions. In-use emissions data (especially for PM) are nearly totally absent for freight trucks. Much usage of medium- as well as heavy-duty trucks—many of quite old vintages—is concentrated in urbanized areas with large, exposed populations. Evidence has mounted that current particulate standards do not adequately protect public health. Such concerns make it clear that many questions remain open regarding the environmental sustainability of the U.S. trucking system as currently operated and regulated.

Moreover, looking beyond 2015 and considering the extent to which Duleep's analysis pushes petroleum-based diesel technology toward its limits, continuing growth in truck use will conflict with the likely need for additional constraints on greenhouse gas emissions. Further research and policy development are needed regarding new propulsion technologies, fuel substitution, and intermodal alternatives before the country can "keep on haulin'" sustainably.

Steel Wheels in Sustainable Transportation

Rail freight transport traditionally has received little attention in the energy literature, except for the recognition that it can be much more energy-efficient than trucking for certain shipments and distances. Perhaps because the inherent efficiency of rail freight transport is taken for granted, energy analysts have felt less need to scrutinize the opportunities for improving rail efficiency or to elicit the industry's own knowledge of the subject. In Chapter 9, "Integrating Steel Wheels into Sustainable Transportation," Dick Cataldi provides a welcome review of the recent progress of railroads in reducing energy consumption as part of broader efforts to improve their overall efficiency of operation.

In 1993, railroads moved 38 percent of all U.S. freight ton-miles—more than any other mode—while consuming 12 percent of freight energy use. Even though rail movement has always been relatively efficient, marked efficiency improvements have been realized in the past decade and a half since the industry was deregulated. Cataldi notes that since 1980, competitive forces have motivated higher productivity, including energy productivity (for example, ton-miles/Btu), helping railroads decrease shipping prices while increasing profits. Technological improvements that have raised (and continue to raise) efficiency include lighter-weight, higher-capacity freight cars; more powerful and more efficient locomotives; lower-resistance axle bearings; wheel-rail lubrication; and computer-assisted train dispatch. Other improvements include better freight car and locomotive utilization; improved track quality; enhanced training of locomotive engineers and dispatchers; and coordination with trucking and steamship firms for efficient intermodal container and trailer movements.

Although Cataldi does not present statistics on implementation rates and estimates of the remaining potential for these measures, he reports that these steps are far from fully implemented. For the future, railroads are researching more advanced energy savings options, including flywheel storage for regenerative braking and load leveling as well as further refinements in diesel engine efficiency. Railroads are also investigating the feasibility of fuel cells and alternative fuels, such as natural gas. Beyond the various means of improving efficiency within the current scope of rail and intermodal operations, Cataldi also points out the opportunities for expanded shifting of truck to rail freight. He notes that barriers now exist to greater rail use and that government action may be needed to help overcome them. Further study is needed to identify ways in which this potential can be exploited.

Commercial Air Transport

Air travel is, after light vehicles and freight trucks, the third largest subsector of U.S. transportation energy use and emissions. In terms of activity (measured in passenger miles of travel per year), it has been the most rapidly growing. In Chapter 10, "Commercial Air Energy Use and Emissions?" David Greene reviews recent trends, examines future opportunities to reduce energy use and emissions in air travel, and identifies the challenges that this subsector poses for sustainable transportation goals in the United States and worldwide.

Over the past two decades, U.S. air travel has increased at an average rate exceeding 6 percent per year and yet has had the highest rates of efficiency improvement among all transportation modes. As a result, growth in air transportation energy use was held to 2 percent per year over this period. Looking ahead, Greene reviews several projections, which indicate only a modest decline in air travel growth over the next two decades. However, even optimistic estimates of future efficiency improvement rates are still lower than air travel growth rates, so that it does not appear possible to stabilize air energy use and greenhouse gas emissions for the foreseeable future.

Greene identifies the spectrum of technological and operational efficiency improvements that could help restrain energy use and emissions associated with air travel. Fuel costs are a significant fraction of airline operating costs, motivating investments to improve efficiency even at relatively low and stable fuel prices. Airlines have strong incentives to adopt improvements that yield cost-effective fuel savings. Technological options include more efficient jet engines, advanced aerodynamics, and airframe weight reduction. Operational improvements include various ways to increase aircraft load factors. Greene also addresses criteria emissions, noting that the bulk of emissions occur in the upper atmosphere and are not yet subject to regulation. Improvements in jet turbine combustor design offer potential NO_x reductions. However, an efficiency trade-off can be involved, since NO_x formation rises with the higher temperatures and pressures involved in more efficient turbines. In addition, the use of alternative fuels—such as liquified natural gas, hydrogen, or synthetic fuels—in aircraft appears to remain a distant, largely speculative prospect.

Greene provides a range of projections for U.S. air travel, energy use, and emissions through 2015. A "low-efficiency" scenario, based on consensus travel growth forecasts (4.0 percent/yr in the United States between 1999 and 2015) with a lower rate (0.7 percent/yr) of fuel efficiency improvement, implies a doubling of air energy use by 2015. A "high-efficiency" scenario, based on travel growth of 3.6 percent/yr between 1999 and 2015 and a 2.5 percent/yr efficiency improvement, implies a 25 percent increase in U.S. air energy use by 2015. Greene notes that global air travel growth rates are even greater. World air travel energy use could rise 55 percent to 150 percent over the next two decades, assuming the higher and lower levels of efficiency improvement, respectively. Thus, Greene answers the question posed by his title with a clear negative. Even in the best cases, technological and operational improvements will not even keep pace with growth in demand, let alone actually reduce emissions and energy use from their 1990 levels. Nevertheless, the difference in outcomes between the low- and high-efficiency scenarios is substantial, amounting to 1.75 Quads, or 34 million metric tons of carbon, for the United States in 2015. It will be crucial to examine ways to ensure an outcome closer to the high-efficiency scenario, which would reduce the burden on other modes and sectors to compensate for the apparently inevitable growth in air travel. Further work is also needed to explore other options, such as intermodalism and fuel substitution, that can help offset the energy-related impacts of air travel over the long run.

Other Contributions

Chapters 11 and 12 are papers as delivered at the time of the conference and, unlike the other chapters, were not revised in response to peer review. We include them because they provide perspectives from conference participants affiliated with the auto industry. Automakers have, in response to energy, environmental, and public safety policies established in the past, made technological improvements resulting in vehicles that are substantially cleaner, more efficient, and safer today than they were in the early 1970s. The industry is being challenged to advance technology yet further in order to make vehicles even cleaner and more efficient.

In the long run, because of the enormous expected growth in automobile use worldwide, the challenge to develop a sustainable transportation system will be formidable. The growth is at once a product of two factors. One is the seemingly insatiable consumer demand for automobility. The other is the industry's own aggressive drive to expand its markets. Growth in travel and energy demand is encouraged by the occasionally punctuated but historically declining trend in oil prices, as well as road-oriented infrastructure and pricing policies that both foster and follow from travel demand. To meet such challenges over the long run is likely to require changes that are far more profound than those identified by most chapters of this book.

Potential of Leap-Forward Technology

In Chapter 11, "Potential of Leap-Forward Technology: Automotive Industry Perspective," Dick Kinsey reviews the Partnership for a New Generation of Vehicles (PNGV), a joint U.S. government and industry research and development venture with a long-term goal of tripling average passenger car fuel economy. PNGV was announced in September 1993 and is by now well known to most observers of U.S. transportation and energy issues. So too are the technology options for attaining PNGV's "Goal 3" of tripled fuel economy. Kinsey provides some insight into the industry's thinking since the partnership was formed. Propulsion system options center on direct-injection diesel engines, turbines, or fuel cells deployed in a hybrid electric drivetrain. All-electric vehicles recharged from the grid are not considered contenders under the PNGV. The electrical energy storage devices needed for hybrid vehicles span the full range of known options: various advanced batteries, ultracapacitors, and flywheels. Kinsey reiterates the crucial need to cost-effectively reduce vehicle mass while maintaining crashworthiness and improving recyclability.

Whatever new designs are needed for next-generation vehicles, Kinsey notes the need for phase-in schedules that make business sense, in accord with the industry's ongoing refurbishment and updating of its plants. We are left, however, with no guidance about how to relate these schedules to measurable progress toward sustainability goals such as those posed for the conference.

Although the PNGV program is most noted for its goal of tripling fuel economy, it also has another, more modest objective ("Goal 2") that calls for improvements in efficiency and reductions in emissions for conventional gasoline and diesel vehicles. This goal certainly is consistent with the sustainability targets offered for discussion at the Asilomar conference. Unfortunately, Kinsey fails to offer specifics as to how goal 2 might be realized. Thus, although the partnership has laudable objectives, important questions remain unanswered about how to get from here to there.

Transition to New Sources of Energy

In Chapter 12, "The Transition to New Sources of Energy Using Sustainable Energy Strategies," Roberta Nichols, one of the pioneers in the development of alternative-fuel vehicles, reflects on her years of experience with Ford Motor Company and offers some observations regarding the best ways to introduce such vehicles. She advocates a gradual transition from petroleum fuels, which, as she points out, are finite, to nonpetroleum fuels such as methanol, compressed natural gas, and perhaps in the long run, hydrogen. Nichols argues that market incentives, such as tax exemptions, investment tax credits, and Corporate Average Fuel Economy (CAFE) credits, are needed to help alternative fuels and vehicles overcome the substantial barriers to entry into the marketplace.

However, Nichols's years in the auto industry make her cautious. She believes that consumers are inherently conservative and unlikely to buy vehicles or fuels that are radically different from those to which they have become accustomed. In her view, the transition to alternative fuels must be slow and methodical, and driven by consumer preferences. She is wary of mandates, such as California's zero-emission-vehicle (ZEV) mandate, on the grounds that they might prematurely force the adoption of unproven and unpopular technologies. Nichols reviews some of Ford's efforts and experience in introducing methanol and natural gas vehicles. However, she does not provide details about cost, performance, and emissions, or to support her views about consumer acceptance of new technologies. Thus, many questions remain regarding effective approaches for bringing about a transition to alternative-fuel-vehicle technologies.

Epilogue

In the Epilogue, "Is Technology Enough? A Synthesis of Views Expressed at the Conference," Barry McNutt, Lew Fulton, and David Greene present the results of a consensus-seeking exercise conducted as the final, wrap-up session of the conference. The session was structured to allow the participants to see, after the formal presentations and discussions of the prior two days, whether they could agree on (1) the types of questions they felt would be best addressed and (2) what the answers to the questions might be. The exercise included voting on a numerical scale to indicate the level of agreement with the various propositions that were proffered, discussed, and refined. The session thus allowed some inferences to be made regarding answers—by the attending group of experts, stakeholders, and interested individuals—to the central question of the conference, Is technology enough?

The results of the wrap-up session as summarized in the Epilogue are much richer than our brief synopsis. However, we are struck by the sense of technological optimism—the belief that technologies such as those examined here have the potential to move U.S. transportation toward sustainability, at least in terms of goals for reduced energy use and emissions. This optimism was counterbalanced by the near-unanimous agreement with the proposition that "current programs and policies will not bring these technologies into use to the degree needed to achieve the goals." Moreover, McNutt et al. report how a majority at the wrap-up session called for increased attention to consumer requirements, education, perceptions, and behavioral issues regarding policies and technologies, as well as to the need for greater public concurrence that transportation-related energy and environmental problems are pressing enough to warrant significant change.

In the end, the answer to the question of whether technology improvements can lead us to a sustainable transportation remains mixed. Yes, technological solutions can be found, but no, they may not come to fruition without new programs and policies. In any case, the feasibility of technologies, programs, and policies rests greatly on nontechnological issues of perception and behavior. This ambiguous answer would be no surprise, of course, to behavioral scientists, who might find it bemusedly heartening that it was reached at a conference dominated by technologists.

Chapter Two

Real-World Emissions from Conventional Passenger Cars

MARC ROSS AND TOM WENZEL

The history of automotive emissions regulation reveals remarkable success in reducing emissions from new automobiles as measured in certification tests. The grams-per-mile (gpm) standards for these tests are stringent, with 96 percent reductions in carbon monoxide (CO) and hydrocarbon (HC) mandated in respect to the estimated precontrol levels of the mid-1960s. Powerful new technologies have been developed and incorporated into every new vehicle to accomplish these reductions. Most noteworthy are the catalytic converter and closed-loop engine controls; the latter include sensors before and after the engine proper and computer analysis of the information, leading to real-time control of fuel injection and spark timing with a principal objective being to maintain the optimal chemical balance of fuel and air.

During this same period, the real-world gpm emissions of CO and HC were reduced by roughly 75 percent. Since vehicle-miles of travel (VMT) increased by about a factor of two during this period, total automotive emissions declined by a national average of roughly 50 percent. If real-world exhaust emissions had matched the standards, a reduction of total automobile exhaust emissions of roughly 90 percent would have been achieved over the past 30 years. Nevertheless, the 50 percent reduction in total automobile exhaust emissions is an important achievement, quite noticeable in some metropolitan areas where pollution is dominated by cars and light trucks.

Ambient air quality measurements confirm that our nation's air is improving. For the 10-year period from 1983 to 1992, the national average of the "second highest nonoverlapping eight-hour average CO concentration" (an Environmental Protection Agency measure of ambient air quality) dropped by 34 percent. Since emissions of CO are usually dominated by cars and trucks, we must agree with EPA (1992) that "this indicates that the Federal Motor Vehicle Control Program has been effective on the national scale, with controls more than offsetting growth during this period."

The effect of auto emissions regulations on ambient HC, nitrogen oxides (NO_x), and ozone concentrations is less clear because of the more complex atmospheric chemistry of these species and because the contribution of motor vehicles to overall HC and NO_x emissions is proportionally less than it is for CO. However, EPA (1992) has reported a 21 percent decrease in the national average "second highest daily maximum one-hour ozone concentration" from 1983 to 1992. In addition, over the same period, the population exposure to unhealthy levels of ozone in Los Angeles was cut in half (Lents & Kelly 1993).

In spite of this important progress, air quality is far from satisfactory in many major metropolitan areas. Moreover, vehicle travel continues to grow, so unless gpm emissions are further reduced, the progress will be eaten away—about as rapidly as it was achieved. The large discrepancy between the regulatory tests, called the Federal Test Procedure (FTP), and real-world emissions is well known (Calvert et al. 1993) and is a focus of the Clean Air Act Amendments of 1990 (CAAA90). Although manufacturers have been able to meet the strict certification test standards in the FTP, limitations in the current regulatory approach are permitting the much higher emissions in the real world. Most of these excess emissions come from two regulatory loopholes: off-cycle driving (essentially, driving at higher power than required in the FTP) and malfunction of emissions control systems (ECSs).

The current driving cycles in the FTP were developed over 20 years ago and were based on driving conditions in downtown Los Angeles. The initial cycles had rather low maximum speed and acceleration since vehicles could not be driven at high accelerations on the first generation of dynamometers without slipping. Technical improvements in dynamometer design, as well as EPA's study of real-world driving behavior (the FTP Revision Project, or FTP-RP), have resulted in a new regulation to expand the FTP to better represent real-world conditions, thus reducing much of the emissions from off-cycle driving. The supplemental FTP will come into full effect in 2002 (EPA 1996).

Special regulatory initiatives aimed at reducing emissions from ECS malfunction have long been on the books: in-use vehicle testing

with recalls, and emissions control system inspection and maintenance (I/M) programs. Broadly speaking, these efforts have not been
successful; the emissions reductions they have achieved are a small
fraction of the emissions addressed. More particularly, in-use testing is
largely unsuccessful because the law states that manufacturers are responsible only for the emissions performance of vehicles that have
been "properly maintained and used." In response to this wording,
the vehicle recruitment and screening procedures of the in-use tests
make the observation of malfunctioning ECSs unlikely. The I/M programs are also severely flawed in many ways. Efficient identification
of malfunctioning vehicles through smog inspections has proved difficult. Making lasting and effective repairs is even more difficult: diagnosis is difficult, and it is much easier to make a temporary fix than to
identify and repair the underlying cause of malfunction.

Largely as a result of the CAAA90, new policies are being developed to close these two regulatory loopholes and reduce real-world
emissions. We project that the supplemental certification tests will reduce much of the off-cycle emissions and that new information technologies may lead to better identification and diagnosis of ECS malfunctions. However, even these new policy directions will not
eliminate such emissions entirely.

This chapter analyzes real-world emissions from model-year (MY)
1993, 2000, and 2010 passenger cars. For the MY1993 analysis, we
break down the emissions from recent-model cars into six physical
sources. On the basis of that analysis, we then project the average lifetime emissions for model-year MY2000 and MY2010 vehicles. We examine in some detail one of the largest emissions sources not measured in the certification tests: CO and HC tailpipe emissions in
warmed-up driving by cars with severely malfunctioning ECSs. Finally, we draw some conclusions regarding the effectiveness of policies to reduce in-use emissions. John German's contribution in Chapter 3 of this volume presents further analysis on off-cycle emissions
and strategies for reducing them.

Overall Results

Six sources of in-use emissions have been established—all are exhaust emissions except (3) and (6):

1. Properly functioning warmed-up (hot-stabilized) cars in moderate
   on-cycle driving (*on-cycle* being defined as driving represented in
   the FTP)

2. Cold start for cars with properly functioning emissions controls

3. Evaporation from the vehicle, including malfunctioning evaporation control

4. Off-cycle operations of cars with properly functioning emissions controls (with the focus on driving that involves higher power than occurs in, or is emphasized in, the FTP)

5. Malfunctioning emissions control systems affecting tailpipe emissions

6. Upstream emissions (from fuel extraction, transportation, refining, and distribution)

We have examined in some detail the two largest sources not measured in the certification tests: (4), off-cycle operation of properly functioning cars, especially high-power driving (Goodwin & Ross 1996), and (5), malfunctioning ECSs (Wenzel & Ross 1996). The public-domain measurements analyzed for off-cycle emissions are extensive dynamometer tests on small sets of vehicles, as well as surveys of driving patterns using instrumented vehicles, both conducted as part of the FTP-RP (Haskew et al. 1994). For malfunction emissions, we analyze a large-scale remote-sensing survey (Stedman et al. 1994) supplemented by dynamometer surveys of vehicles tested in the condition in which they were received (the California Air Resources Board's Light-Duty Vehicle Surveillance Program, or LDVSP) (CARB 1994). In both cases, accurate analysis is difficult because the incidence of the problems is small, whereas the emissions per affected vehicle/event are large. We derive estimates of hot, on-cycle emissions and cold-start emissions from the FTP-RP; we rely primarily on EPA's emissions factor model MOBILE5a for estimates of evaporative emissions (EPA 1994b); and we exploit a new model created by one of us to predict the upstream emissions (Wang 1996). More detail on the analysis of all the sources can be found in Ross et al. (1995).

Our estimates of lifetime emissions from MY1993 vehicles are shown in Table 2-1. The projections for MY2000 and MY2010 vehicles are given in Table 2-2. Figure 2-1 presents the estimates for MYs 1993 and 2010 graphically. The numbers are weighted by their relative occurrence in total driving, so that the sum of emissions from all sources equals our estimate for total lifetime emissions for the average car.

Table 2-1 shows that total emissions of CO and HC are four to five times the tailpipe standards and that those for NO_x are about twice the federal standard and four to five times the California standard. These totals are consistent with those of MOBILE5a. The 1993 tailpipe standard (bottom row) legally applies only to the emissions shown in row (1) plus two times those in row (2a). Evaporative HC emissions (row 3) are subject to a separate standard and are determined by a separate

Table 2-1

Lifetime Emissions for a Model-Year 1993 Car, Weighted Average over Vehicle Life

Source	CO (g/mi)	HC (g/mi)	NO$_x$ (g/mi)
(1) Hot moderate driving[a,b]	0.983	0.090	0.201
(2) Cold start			
(a) 70° F[a,b]	0.663	0.071	0.070
(b) 20° F[a,b]	1.658	0.178	0.091
SUBTOTAL	3.304	0.339	0.362
(3) Evaporation[c]	0	0.5	0
(4) Off-cycle[a,b]	7.9	0.12	0.3
(5) Malfunction[a]	6	0.6	0.8[d]
(6) Upstream	0.063	0.098	0.315
TOTAL	17	1.7	1.8
1993 tailpipe standard	3.4	0.41	1.0

Note: Sources are weighted by relative occurrence in total driving so that average per-car emissions are shown.
[a]Exhaust emissions.
[b]Properly functioning cars.
[c]MOBILE5a estimate.
[d]The NO$_x$ malfunction estimate is simply the difference between the total exhaust NO$_x$ emissions estimated by MOBILE5a and our estimate of sources (1), (2), and (4).

test procedure. Upstream emissions (row 6) are regulated in part by evaporative controls on fueling hoses and on-board vehicles. For example, for CO, 0.98 + [2 × 0.66] = 2.3 gpm should be compared for compliance with the 3.4 gpm standard. Thus, certification emissions from the average MY1993 car are well within the current tailpipe certification standards. (Manufacturers actually design vehicles to test at roughly half the standard to allow themselves a cushion.) As shown in Table 2-2, we predict that vehicles will continue to be able to meet increasingly strict standards for on-cycle tailpipe emissions (hot-stabilized plus cold start), based on the current FTP. The exception is that average MY2010 vehicles will not meet the California low-emissions vehicle (LEV) HC nonmethane organic gases (NMOG) tailpipe standard. This standard would apply only to vehicles in states that adopt the California LEV standards.

High-power driving leads to high emissions of CO and NO$_x$. CO emissions are high because at high power, vehicles are designed

Table 2-2

Sources of Emissions for Model-Year 2000 and 2010 Cars, Weighted Average over Vehicle Life

Source	CO MY2000 (g/mi)	CO MY2010 (g/mi)	HC MY2000 (g/mi)	HC MY2010 (g/mi)	NO$_x$ MY2000 (g/mi)	NO$_x$ MY2010 (g/mi)
Hot-stabilized + cold start[a]	2.9	1.4	0.22	0.11	0.26	0.13
Evaporation[b]	0	0	0.37	0.37	0	0
Off-cycle[a]	2.4	2.4	0.036	0.036	0.1	0.1
Malfunction	5	2	0.4	0.2	0.6	0.3
Upstream	0.063	0.055	0.097	0.085	0.31	0.25
TOTAL	10	6	1.1	0.8	1.1	0.8
Tailpipe standards:						
Tier I 2000, Tier II 2010	3.4	1.7	0.25[c]	0.125[c]	0.4	0.2
Tier I 2000, CA LEV 2010	3.4	3.4	0.25[c]	0.075[d]	0.4	0.2

[a]Properly functioning car.
[b]MOBILE5a prediction.
[c]Nonmethane hydrocarbons (EPA Tiers I & II).
[d]Nonmethane organic gases (CA LEV).

to override their ECS, and a rich fuel-air ratio is commanded. One consequence is that low-power vehicles, when one attempts to drive them like high-power cars, are among the worst polluters on the road. EPA's new rule for emissions certification, involving the supplemental FTP cycle, will limit command enrichment. Considering the types of driving in which command enrichment occurs and the rationales for command enrichment, we predict substantial reductions in off-cycle emissions, particularly for CO. NO$_x$ emissions are high during high-power driving because they are sensitive to the high temperatures in the cylinder. EPA's new rule also addresses these NO$_x$ emissions.

Vehicles with malfunctioning ECSs are currently the source of almost half of each of the pollutants. (Degradation, as distinct from malfunction, of properly functioning ECSs beyond laboratory aging of the catalyst is not considered, so the on-cycle emissions—(1) and (2) in Table 2-1—are probably underestimated.) The data on CO associated with malfunction from the 1991 CARB remote-sensing survey (Stedman et al. 1994) are far superior to those on the other pollutants. Our analysis of these data shows that malfunction emissions are strongly dependent on the vehicle model. Interpretation of this result will be

Figure 2-1

Estimated Contribution of Off-Cycle and Malfunction Emissions to Total Lifetime Emissions in Model-Year 1993 and 2010 Cars

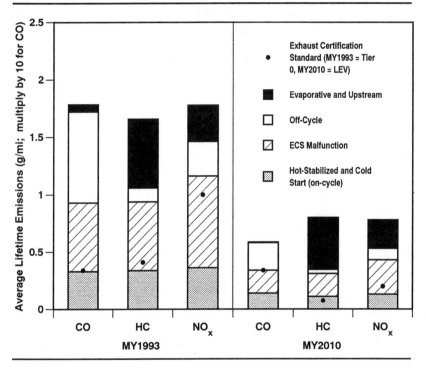

highly controversial because the emissions community has embraced the concept (from study of 1970s and early-1980s model-year cars) that ECS failures are due to improper maintenance by individual owners and mechanics. The data on more modern models do not support this concept and call for an entirely different regulatory approach. For example, with two- to five-year-old popular cars of Asian manufacturers, malfunctions are rare to moderately frequent in midprice models, but frequent in some less expensive models of each of the manufacturers. Different ways of examining these data support our view that the responsibility is fundamentally that of the manufacturers, not that of the individual car owner or mechanic.

The impact of ECS malfunctions is large. In the 1991 survey, roughly one-fourth of the vehicle models from MY1987 through MY1989 had a high probability for malfunctioning ECSs; some 16 percent to 30 percent of the cars in these models were malfunctioning. For these models, the average car (averaged over malfunctioning and properly functioning cars) polluted more than ten times as much as a properly functioning car. Other popular models were found to have extremely low malfunction rates. Our prediction that manufacturers could meet a tough standard for robustness of ECSs is based on these results. Our prediction that they will meet such a standard is based on the assumption of continued progress in the development and implementation of new technologies to identify malfunctions, remote sensing, and on-board diagnostics (OBD). The capabilities of these technologies are being rapidly improved, and in a few years they should be flooding us with good information.

Of particular importance for reducing ozone smog are summertime emissions of NO_x and HC. The totals in Table 2-1 are the weighted average of both summer and winter conditions. In addition to the seasonal cold-start emissions assumptions, we account for two additional special factors on hot summer days that affect the gpm emissions:

1. *NO_x associated with heavier-than-average loads on the engine (air conditioning, construction, vacation travel).* We estimate extra emissions of 0.2 gpm at these times with MY1993 cars. This excess should be reduced to about one-third that level with MY2000 cars as a result of EPA's rule involving a supplemental FTP.

2. *HC associated with higher-than-average evaporation.* Evaporative emissions are estimated to increase 0.3 gpm on a day when the high temperature is 95° F rather than the 86° F we assumed. New instrumentation for measuring vehicular evaporation and more realistic evaporative tests in the proposed rulemaking may help reduce this excess, but we do not predict major reductions. On the other hand, fuel vapor pressure regulation has been fairly effective. The vapor pressure could be reduced further in the summer in the Northeast, to values now mandated in California and some southern states.

As percentages of real-world MY1993 emissions, the predicted reductions for MY2000 are 40 percent for CO, 35 percent for HC, and 28 percent for NO_x. These reductions are relatively modest because the time period for changes affecting lifetime emissions for MY2000 is short. The reductions could well be even smaller. As percentages of real-world MY1993 emissions, we project that for MY2010, lifetime emissions of CO will be reduced by 65 percent, those for HC by 50 percent, and those for NO_x by 56 percent. However, in-use emissions for MY2010 will substantially exceed LEV tailpipe emissions standards, by factors of nearly 2 for CO, 11 for HC, and 4 for NO_x. The results for MYs 1993 and 2010 are also presented graphically in Figure 2-1.

We stress that both the breakdown of MY1993 emissions and the prediction of emissions reductions involve substantial uncertainties.

The greatest uncertainties are associated with lack of data on: (1) the extent and nature of the NO_x emissions we have attributed to malfunctioning ECSs; (2) CO and HC cold-start emissions from vehicles with malfunctioning ECSs; and (3) emissions from real-world, properly functioning cars in on-cycle driving. For (1), we simply show NO_x malfunction emissions as the difference between the emissions we are able to estimate and the total predicted by MOBILE5a. However, evidence for large NO_x malfunction emissions is weak in the CARB (1994) LDVSP-12 dynamometer survey. For (3), our data are for very clean cars; the LDVSP-12 suggests that average in-use vehicles emit about twice as much of each of the pollutants as our estimates indicate (because of ECS degradation, as distinguished from ECS malfunction) (CARB 1994).

Because of a lack of accurate data, the predicted reductions in all three pollutants associated with ECS malfunction are based on our analysis of CO alone. Moreover, the prediction of CO malfunction emissions is based on remote-sensing data for MY1987 through MY1989 fuel-injected cars taken in 1991 (that is, two- to five-year-old vehicles). This dataset is far from ideal; data from high-mileage (that is, older) cars with modern fuel and emissions control technologies that are no longer under warranty would be preferable. Another prediction, for evaporation, is not based on new information, but is simply taken from the nominal forecast in MOBILE5a. Of course, all predictions are uncertain; the ones we have singled out here appear to us to have the largest uncertainties.

What influence might these uncertainties have on our predictions? In spite of the serious data problems, we believe the predictions of relative reductions for 2010 to be fairly robust because the physical opportunities are fairly well defined and the reductions are similar in percentage terms for all major sources except evaporative HC. (The reductions for 2000 could, however, be much smaller than shown.) The policy uncertainty is probably the most critical. If the application of improved information technologies—counted on here to detect ECS failures and to cause adoption of robust ECSs—is not vigorously pursued, the progress is likely to be much smaller.

Malfunctioning Exhaust Emissions Controls

Vehicles whose emissions controls are not properly functioning (as distinguished from normal degradation) comprise the largest and the least understood source of emissions. Two important examples of malfunctioning emissions controls are (1) substantial damage to the catalyst and (2) failure of the oxygen sensor that provides feedback for control of the fuel-air ratio. The catalyst can be damaged, for example, by exposure to the prolonged high temperatures (and reducing atmosphere) associated with prolonged high-power driving—for example, in mountain driving or trailer pulling. They can also be the secondary result of inadequate performance of fuel-air ratio controls or of engine misfire. The oxygen sensor can fail if it becomes disconnected or is operating improperly.

It has been well documented that a substantial portion of CO and HC emissions is due to a small number of high-emitting vehicles with malfunctioning emissions controls (Beaton et al. 1995, Lawson 1993, Stedman et al. 1994, Stephens 1994). There appear to be at least five possible causes of ECS failure:

- extensive high-power driving of a vehicle
- outright tampering with the ECS—deliberate disabling of emissions controls or related parts (by owner or mechanic)
- inadequate maintenance (by owner)
- improper repairs (by owner or mechanic)
- poor initial ECS design or manufacture

Current Vehicles (MY1993)

Malfunctioning emissions controls lead to very high emissions. For example, a properly functioning catalyst controls all but a small percentage of engine-out CO emissions; catalyst failure would allow nearly all engine-out emissions to exit the tailpipe uncontrolled, resulting in an order-of-magnitude increase in tailpipe emissions. Failure of fuel-air controls also increases CO emissions by an order of magnitude. The emissions of vehicles with malfunctioning emissions controls are roughly comparable to those of the preregulation era (before the late 1960s), estimated to be 84 gpm for CO, 11 gpm for HC, and 4 gpm for NO_x (AAMA 1994). By this rule of thumb, if 11 percent of cars are malfunctional in regard to CO (Table 2-3), the CO emissions due to malfunction would be about 7 gpm, which compares well with our estimate of 6 gpm in Table 2-1.

One way to estimate the role of emissions from malfunctioning cars is from the MOBILE5a model, which is based on extensive comparisons with emissions from in-use vehicles, even though it—and all in-use emissions data—must be questioned in terms of how representative they are in terms of the kinds of driving and vehicles involved. Although malfunctioning vehicles are not identified as such within

Table 2-3

Occurrence of CO Malfunctions in Model-Year 1987–1991 Fuel-Injected Cars

	MY1991 (%)	MY1990 (%)	MY1989 (%)	MY1988 (%)	MY1987 (%)	MY1987–1989 (%)
Average CO concentration, all cars	0.22	0.25	0.30	0.32	0.36	0.33
Malfunctioning cars						
Percentage	4.9	5.6	7.3	7.2	8.4	7.6
Average CO concentration	2.65	2.52	2.61	2.63	2.79	2.67
Percentage of total CO	59.0	57.0	63.0	59.0	64.0	62.0
Properly functioning cars						
Percentage	95.1	94.4	92.7	92.8	91.6	92.4
Average CO concentration	0.09	0.11	0.12	0.14	0.14	0.13
Percentage of total CO	41.0	43.0	37.0	41.0	36.0	38.0

MOBILE5a, since we independently project the emissions from properly functioning vehicles, we can project the incremental malfunction emissions by simple subtraction. The malfunction emissions for NO_x shown in Table 2-1 are calculated by this method. The malfunction emissions for CO and HC shown in Table 2-1 are estimated from direct remote-sensing measurements. The two methods roughly agree.

We estimate the incremental malfunction emissions using remote-sensing data collected by the University of Denver for CARB in 1991 (Stedman et al. 1994). . In that study, an infrared beam was directed across a single lane of traffic, at the height of an automobile's tailpipe. As a vehicle passed the beam, the instrument measured the absorption of infrared light to determine CO, HC, and CO_2 concentrations in the exhaust. The vehicle was identified by videotaping its license plate, later cross-checking license plate numbers with vehicle identification numbers (VINs), and then decoding VINs to obtain technical information on individual vehicles. The sites were primarily expressway ramps and an urban boulevard closed down to one lane by the police. The sites were selected to minimize the number of readings taken from vehicles operating off-cycle (with cold catalysts or under fuel enrichment).

Figure 2-2 illustrates a sample dataset for CO that includes approximately 18,000 observations of MY1987 through MY1989 cars. The distribution shown is the cumulative fraction of cars observed per unit interval of CO concentration. The key to the distribution is that it has two parts. The first is a central peak, with about 90 percent of the cars,

Figure 2-2

Cumulative Distribution, Remote-Sensing Measurements of CO in Model-Year 1987–1989 Cars

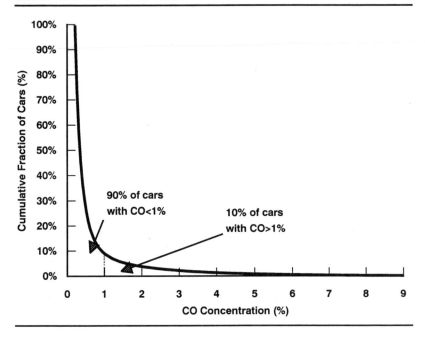

whose average CO concentration agrees essentially with the dynamometer data for properly functioning cars. The second part is the tail at high CO concentrations, with about 10 percent of the cars, whose average CO concentration is about 40 times that for properly functioning cars. These are the cars assumed to have malfunctioning ECSs. There are uncertainties about the remote-sensing data, but checks, such as restricting the analysis to cars observed at least three times, show that our essential results are valid.

Our criteria for malfunctioning vehicles are 1 percent for CO and 0.2 percent for HC concentration. These criteria are lower than the cutpoints used in most previous analyses of remote-sensing data. I/M programs use higher remote-sensing cutpoints to reduce the probability of misidentifying an individual vehicle as a high emitter. Our malfunctioning vehicle cutpoints are essentially 15 to 20 times those expected for clean, properly functioning cars, based on Bag 2 emissions from the FTP-RP dynamometer tests. Representative results for emissions by fuel-injected cars with malfunctioning emissions controls are shown in Table 2-3.

For cars of average lifetime mileage (at an age of about four years), the incremental CO emissions from vehicles with malfunctioning emissions controls is over four times the emissions from properly functioning cars, even though only about one-tenth of the cars are malfunctioning. This factor is based on an average CO FTP Bag 2 emissions rate of 0.054 gpm for properly functioning cars, from FTP-RP measurements [(2.79 − 0.14) × 0.084/0.054]. The factor of four is for warmed-up moderate driving; we estimate that the fraction of emissions from malfunctioning cars in cold start is about one-fifth as large, although we have very limited information. We take the incremental malfunction emissions to be 4.1 times emissions for moderately driven properly functioning cars (0.98 gpm from Table 2-1) plus one-fifth the annual average cold-start rate (2.32 gpm), which results in 6 gpm [4.1 × (0.98 + 0.2 × 2.32)] for CO malfunction (see Table 2-1).

For HC, we determine the incremental malfunction emissions in moderate driving by using the same factors applied to CO, times the HC emissions from properly functioning cars, resulting in 0.6 gpm [4.1 × (0.09 + 0.2 × 0.25)] for HC malfunction (see Table 2-1).

Future Vehicles (MY2000 and MY2010)

The emissions due to malfunctioning vehicles are the product of the probability that vehicles malfunction and the level of emissions per malfunctioning vehicle. As can be seen in Table 2-3, the second factor does not vary strongly with the age of the vehicle or emissions control technology. Perhaps the most important finding of this analysis is that the probability for vehicles to have severely malfunctioning ECSs, rather than the emissions rate of malfunctioning vehicles, is the most important factor in the relative contribution to total malfunction emissions. Therefore, how malfunction probability may depend on vehicle design (fuel system or emissions control technology) or manufacture and how it may be affected by policy becomes critical.

The Probability of Malfunctions

We examine remote-sensing measurements taken in the 1991 CARB study (Stedman et al. 1994) to determine if malfunction probability is related to particular vehicle characteristics (as noted above, the study included videotaping of the license plates of cars passing roadside sensors, which permitted identification of VINs and, in turn, engine and other characteristics of individual vehicles). In analyzing the data for CO, we find that the probability of malfunction is strongly

Figure 2-3

CO Malfunction Probability and Average Concentration in 76 Model-Year Models, Model-Year 1987–1989 Cars

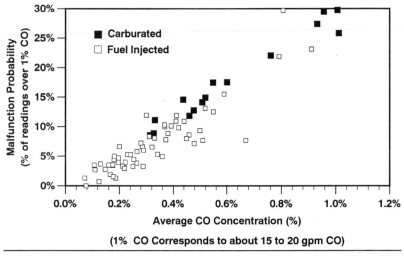

Note: Over 50 cars observed for each point.

correlated with vehicle model. We look in detail at 76 MY-models from MY1987 through MY1989, for which at least 50 vehicles were observed by the remote sensor (for vehicles of each domestic manufacturer, we group individual vehicles by engine family, based on engine displacement, number of cylinders, and fuel system). Since the measurements were made in the summer of 1991, the cars were then two to five years old. Figure 2-3 shows the probability for malfunction (CO concentration greater than 1 percent) for the 76 MY-models against the average CO concentration for all cars of the model.

Previous studies (Stephens et al. 1994) indicate that on-road emissions, and therefore remote-sensing measurements, for an individual vehicle can be highly variable. Averaging multiple remote-sensing readings for a particular vehicle improves the characterization of that vehicle as properly functioning or malfunctioning. For vehicles with multiple readings, we calculate the average reading per vehicle before calculating the average concentration for each model.

The spread in malfunction probability is very large, with six MY-models in the sample having none or only one high-emitter (see bottom left of Figure 2-3) and five having more than 25 percent high-emitters (see upper right of Figure 2-3). The apparent intercept on the

Figure 2-4

Average CO C0ncentration and Standard Error in
76 Model-Year Models

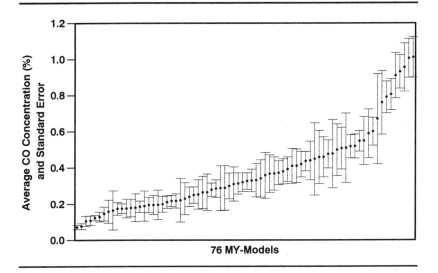

x-axis, at about 0.07 percent, is consistent with expectations for properly functioning cars (0.05 percent), based on the FTP-RP dynamometer data.

Figure 2-3 demonstrates that average CO concentration for a MY-model correlates well with the malfunction probability for that MY-model. This correlation is due to the fact that the fraction of high-emitters have a large effect on the average concentration for the entire group of vehicles. The relationship allows us to test the statistical significance of our malfunction probabilities by calculating standard errors for the average concentration for each MY-model. Figure 2-4 shows the average CO concentration and error for each MY-model, from cleanest to dirtiest, and indicates that the average CO concentration between the best and worst models is statistically significant.

Of the MY-models shown in Figures 2-3 and 2-4, five less expensive models (14 MY-models) of Asian manufacture had especially high malfunction rates. The average malfunction rate of this group was 22 percent, whereas only 6 percent of all other MY-models were malfunctioning. Cars from these five models represent nearly 60 percent of the malfunctioning cars from all of the 76 MY-models analyzed, and nearly 30 percent of the malfunctioning cars from the entire dataset of

Figure 2-5

Malfunction Probability and Average CO Concentration by Fuel System in Model-Year 1987–1989 Nissan Maximas and Sentras

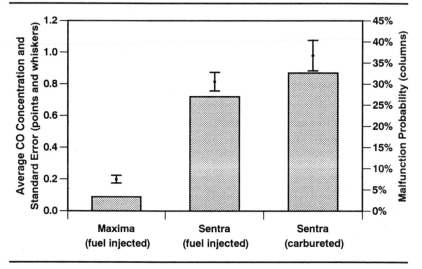

MY1987 through MY1989 cars. Corresponding popular midprice models of these manufacturers tend to have lower malfunction rates—and for some models, very low malfunction rates.

Figure 2-5 demonstrates that this result is quite dramatic for two models manufactured by Nissan. (We use the Nissan Maxima and Nissan Sentra simply for purposes of illustration—we have no reason to believe that current Nissans are any better or worse than current models of other manufacturers.) The columns in Figure 2-5 represent the probability of malfunction, whereas the point and whisker plots give the average CO concentration and standard error. MY1987 through MY1989 Nissan Maximas show extremely low ECS malfunction rates, while corresponding Nissan Sentras show very high rates. The difference in the average CO concentration between the two models is statistically significant, suggesting that the difference in the malfunction probability is as well. Figure 2-5 suggests that carbureted versions of the Sentra are higher emitters than fuel-injected versions. Most of the vehicles of the five worst models use carbureted fuel systems (two models are exclusively carbureted and one model is predominantly carbureted; the remaining two models switched to exclusively fuel-injected vehicles in MY1988).

There are three major possibilities for the strong relationship between vehicle model and malfunction probability:

1. The result is wrong because of inadequate sample sizes, model-dependent driving behavior, or some difficulty associated with the remote-sensing methodology.

2. Owners of less expensive cars do not take proper care of them, whereas owners of midprice cars do take care of them.

3. Flaws in design or manufacture are much more probable in certain models than in others.

1. *The result is wrong because of inadequate sample sizes, model-dependent driving behavior, or some difficulty associated with the remote-sensing methodology.* We have looked at these possibilities and find the evidence to be strongly against them. Remote-sensing surveys to date have been criticized as too uncertain for identifying individual cars with malfunctioning ECSs for the purpose of requiring those vehicles to be inspected more thoroughly and repaired. In-use emissions from even a properly functioning vehicle are highly variable; off-cycle events leading to command enrichment can increase CO emissions rates by as much as three orders of magnitude (Ross et al. 1995). However, events leading to very high increases in emissions are rare, on the order of 1 percent of the time in FTP-style driving (EPA 1994a).

Vehicles observed at the road sites in the remote-sensing survey were probably under less power than typical in FTP driving, whereas vehicles observed at some of the ramp sites may have been operating at higher power levels. For this reason we examine the malfunction probability by site. In general, the malfunction probabilities were indeed higher at ramp sites. Nevertheless, the malfunction probabilities of the high-emitting Asian models remained substantially higher than those of other models at the road sites, with 5 of the 14 Asian MY-models at 19 percent and over, and 12 of the MY-models at 10 percent and over.

The dispute over the accuracy of remote sensors is of less concern here: our use of the remote-sensing data is completely different, and less demanding. For our research purposes we need to determine reliable statistical ratios, not to assure the accuracy of individual identifications of vehicles as high-emitters.

For example, one of our critical results is that the data show that 21 percent of 3,440 individual readings from the five worst MY1987 through MY1989 models had CO concentrations in excess of 1 percent. Because in-use emissions concentrations of even a properly functioning vehicle are highly variable, a single remote-sensing measurement may not accurately describe a vehicle as a properly functioning or malfunctioning vehicle. If we average all readings for individual cars with more than one reading, the malfunction probability is virtually unchanged at 22 percent for the 2,356 individual cars in this group of five models. When we consider only the 182 cars for which three or more remote-sensing measurements were obtained, the probability of malfunction is again essentially the same, at 21 percent. This indicates that the 21 percent malfunction rate for a fairly large group of models based on the average of individual readings is robust, even though an individual measurement may not be accurate.

We do note a site effect on average emissions rates and the number of malfunctioning cars. Figure 2-6 shows that average CO emissions rates were greater at sites where vehicles were observed accelerating (predominantly ramp sites) than at sites where the average vehicle was cruising at a constant speed (road sites). This site effect could be due to properly functioning vehicles undergoing enrichment; alternatively, malfunctioning vehicles may have higher emissions rates when operating under higher load at the ramp sites.

Another issue is the use of emissions data in terms of concentrations in the exhaust rather than mass (grams). National tailpipe emissions standards are expressed in grams per mile, rather than grams per gallon of fuel or exhaust concentration (although regional I/M

Figure 2-6

Average CO Emissions by Model Year, Ramp Site, and Road Site

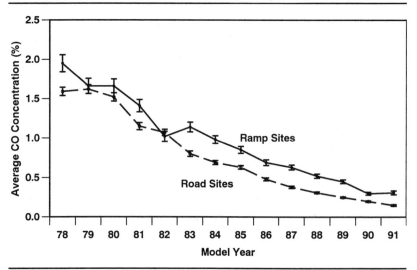

standards are based on exhaust concentration). Since total exhaust volume decreases as fuel use decreases, a fuel-efficient vehicle may have a high CO exhaust concentration, but its low total exhaust volume allows it to meet the gpm standard. In other words, comparing emissions rates based on exhaust concentration, rather than the gpm standard that cars are designed to meet, will make fuel-efficient cars appear dirtier than less efficient cars. The five models with high malfunction probability do tend to have higher fuel economy ratings than the other models; however, we have no measurement of fuel use at the time the remote-sensing measurement was made. We calculate CO gpm for each CO concentration reading from the calculated CO grams per gallon figures in the dataset and the average fuel economy for each model, from EPA's Fuel Economy Guide (EPA 1995). Although this adjustment reduces the spread between the five worst models and other cars, there is still a clear distinction. However, without instantaneous fuel use measurements, this calculation is a crude approximation of actual grams emitted.

The most powerful argument that high model-specific malfunction probabilities are not caused by enrichment events, and are not a result of the measurement units, is the agreement between remote-sensing measurements and dynamometer measurements. We analyze high-emitters from four sets of dynamometer data, including the LDVSP-12 (CARB 1994). The same models that were identified by remote sensing as having a high malfunction probability tend to fail dynamometer tests as well. Fourteen percent of all cars tested in the LDVSP had CO emissions in excess of 10 gpm, whereas seven of the nine cars from the five Asian models identified as high-emitters by the remote-sensing analysis exceeded 10 gpm CO (Wenzel & Ross 1996). When the four sets of dynamometer data are combined, 21 percent of the five Asian models are high-CO-emitters, whereas only 3 percent of all other models are high-emitters. The dynamometer data therefore confirm our finding from the remote-sensing data: that cars from a few models have over four times the malfunction probability as all other cars (further discussion of the analysis of dynamometer data can be found in Wenzel & Ross 1996).

2. *Owners of the less expensive cars do not take proper care of them, whereas owners of the midprice cars do take care of them; thus over 20 percent of the former have malfunctioning ECSs in two to five years, whereas almost none of the latter do.* In the past, there has been evidence to support this concept—surveys of models older than those under discussion showed extensive tampering—and one might believe that tampering or lack of maintenance is more likely in low-price vehicles,

especially after the original owner sells the vehicle and voids the manufacturer's warranty. Unfortunately for this argument, vehicles and their ECSs have become much more sophisticated since most of the published tampering surveys, making deliberate tampering unlikely.

Insufficient maintenance remains a possibility. However, we find that, among the five relatively inexpensive Asian models, MY1989 cars (only two to three years old) have a high malfunction rate (21 percent), similar to that of MY1988 (21 percent) and MY1987 (25 percent) models. It is our conclusion that tampering or insufficient maintenance does not explain the striking differences observed between the less expensive and midpriced Asian models. Two of the six domestic-engine families for which there are sufficient data show large decreases in malfunction rates between MY1987 and MY1989; the remaining engine families show small, or inconsistent, changes in malfunction rates over time. In view of these results, we believe that tampering or insufficient maintenance is not important for most two- to five-year-old cars of these model years. On the other hand, we have not studied even-older cars; for them, tampering or insufficient maintenance might be an important factor in ECS malfunction.

3. *Flaws in design or manufacture are much more probable in certain models than in others.* This relationship may be associated with the fuel system employed in a particular model. Most of the high-emitting models use carburetors rather than fuel injectors, although some fuel-injected models have a high probability of malfunction, whereas some carbureted models have a low probability. As suggested by Figure 2-5, within a given vehicle model, vehicles with carbureted engines tended to be high-emitters more often than vehicles with fuel injection.

Figure 2-7 shows the anomaly of the Honda Civic. In MY1987, a carbureted and a fuel-injected Civic were available; only the fuel-injected version was available in MY1988 and MY1989. However, Figure 2-7 demonstrates that average emissions and malfunction probability increased with the introduction of fuel injection in all Civics. It is likely that Honda had some initial problems with its fuel-injected Civic engine. This isolated case bolsters our argument that flaws in design or manufacture, rather than poor maintenance or outright tampering, explain a large portion of ECS malfunction.

Figure 2-7 also demonstrates that vehicles equipped with manual transmissions have higher emissions than vehicles with automatic transmissions. This difference may be due to transients associated with closing and opening the throttle in manual shifting. Unfortunately, only a few manufacturers identify transmission type in their

Figure 2-7

Malfunction Probability and Average CO by Fuel System and Transmission Type in Model-Year 1987–1989 Honda Civics

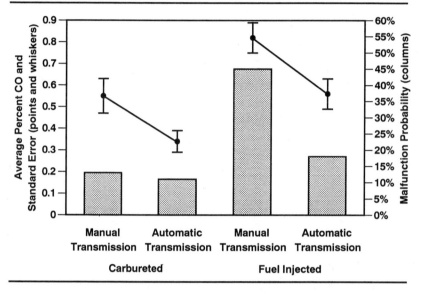

Figure 2-8

Malfunction Probability and Average CO by Fuel System and Site in 76 Model-Year 1987–1989 Models

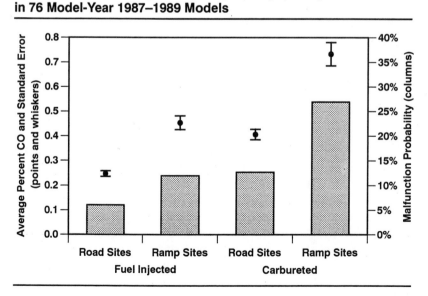

VINs, so we are not able to determine if this effect is widespread among vehicle manufacturers and models.

Figure 2-8 shows the combined effect of remote-sensing site and fuel system on emissions. Clearly, vehicle operation has a larger impact on emissions from carbureted cars than on those from fuel-injected cars.

Finally, the notion of model-dependent component failures is well established for vehicle components other than ECSs. We conclude that ECSs suffer the same kind of difficulty.

Approaches to Reduce Malfunction Emissions

Roughly half of CO, HC, and NO_x emissions are due to malfunctioning emissions controls. EPA (1993) has claimed that these failures are in large part due to tampering. This claim is important, as much of the analysis and policy discussion has presumed tampering. Without making a judgment as to the validity of the tampering claim for earlier models, we conclude that the claim is, in any case, out of date. We have not seen any evidence that computer-controlled vehicles of the postcarburetor, post-leaded-gasoline era suffer from a substantial amount of deliberate disabling of emissions controls.

Regulators are trying three basic approaches to reduce malfunction emissions: (1) identification of vehicles with malfunctions, (2) repair of malfunctions, and (3) reduction in the frequency of malfunctions in future vehicles—that is, through more robust emissions controls. By far the largest efforts are currently devoted to identification of individual malfunctioning vehicles. Attempts to enhance vehicle I/M programs using a more thorough dynamometer test (the IM240) in areas where ambient pollution exceeds standards have been in the news a great deal (for example, see Wald 1994). Installation of on-board diagnostic technology is another major program for identifying malfunctions. In addition, remote sensing of malfunctioning vehicles is being introduced for identification of individual malfunctioning vehicles.

Even though EPA is retreating on requiring IM240 tests as part of enhanced I/M, strong technological progress is being made with the other two identification technologies. The new generation of OBD instrumentation will be effective in identifying malfunctions and has been formally implemented in MY1996, although it may take time to work out bugs. The information provided by remote sensing is also being strikingly improved. By the late 1990s, identification of malfunctioning vehicles with these two technologies will be a powerful tool. But will identification of problems lead to progress in repairs or in robustness of emissions controls?

At present, there is no reason for optimism about repair of malfunctioning emissions controls. The record is poor. This situation is not surprising, because even after proper identification, many of the required repairs are neither easy nor cheap. Often it is easier to make a superficial repair, which yields satisfactory test results at the time but does not endure. As an extreme example, replacing a failed catalyst often yields good temporary results, but if the failure was caused by another faulty component, the catalyst will fail again later. Unlike the situation with performance repairs, the driver does not know whether emissions control work has been successful because cars usually perform adequately even when emissions controls do not. Faulty repairs, and sometimes fraud, may result. Moreover, large-scale success on repairs is made unlikely by the complexity of the system: there are about 60,000 general automotive repair shops, including 26,000 auto and truck dealers.

We are much more optimistic about the eventual role of more robust ECSs in reducing malfunction emissions. Up to the present, a barrier to reducing malfunctioning emissions controls has been the weakness, in the regulations, of manufacturer responsibility with respect to malfunction. Current regulations require manufacturers to avoid excessive deterioration of components only in "properly maintained and used" vehicles. Regulatory tests in this area of concern (50,000- or 100,000-mile certification tests and in-use tests) are not designed to identify models with failed ECSs.

Existing ECS technology can be designed to reduce the probability of malfunction of all vehicle models. For example, the best quartile of MY-models in Figures 2-3 and 2-4 has an average malfunction rate of less than 3 percent. The robustness of emissions controls in essentially all vehicle models is likely to reach a high standard in the future because the new instrumentation technologies—remote sensing and on-board diagnostics—will provide much information about malfunctions to all parties. Well-disseminated results by vehicle model would likely change manufacturer priorities. We recommend, in addition, modifications in regulations to help this change occur (see below). With this move to increase manufacturer priority in one area, we recommend reduced priorities in other emissions-related areas.

Prediction for MY2000 and MY2010

In our view, the probability and consequences of ECS malfunction will be affected by the utilization of remote sensors and OBD, not to identify individual vehicles for further testing and repair, but to identify vehicle models that can benefit from improved ECS design and manufacture. Our predictions of future malfunction emissions of all three pollutants are based on the incidence of CO malfunctions in MY1987 through MY1989 models. We have found that many of these models are already rather robust against malfunction. Manufacturers can, and in our opinion will, improve the ECS durability of all their models to the level already met by the best of their models.

We assume for MY2000 that all models will be as robust as MY1987 through MY1989 fuel-injected models that had malfunction frequencies of 16 percent or lower. (Of the 76 MY-models with adequate statistics, 54 are fuel injected.) This assumption reduces the average frequency of malfunction for the 54 fuel-injected MY-models from 7.4 percent to 5.7 percent, a 23 percent reduction. (Although we are working from actual data on the incidence of ECS malfunctions, the progress we predict for MY2000 is simply a judgment.) We assume that the average emissions of a car with malfunctioning ECS will be the same as for those from MY1987 through MY1989, essentially the emissions rates for precontrol cars. Therefore, a 23 percent reduction in malfunctions will lead to a 23 percent reduction in malfunction emissions by MY2000.

For MY2010, we predict that the average frequency of malfunction will correspond to that of the best quartile of MY1987 through MY1989 fuel-injected models studied, those with a frequency of malfunction of 3.5 percent or lower. (This assumption is made because all six of the highest-selling manufacturers have at least one model or engine family in the best quartile.) This reduces the average frequency of malfunction found for the 54 fuel-injected MY-models from 7.4 percent to 2.6 percent, a 65 percent reduction in malfunctions and malfunction emissions from that estimated for MY1993.

An increased incidence of successful repairs is not taken into account in these predictions. Although we believe that OBD will improve mechanics' ability to properly diagnose the causes of ECS malfunction, in the overall picture we believe repair will be much less important than making ECS more robust.

Although substantial progress in reducing malfunction emissions is technically possible, continued improvements and applications of the remote-sensing and OBD technologies are necessary to ensure that our predicted reductions are achieved. Without such improvement, reduction of malfunction emissions will take much longer.

Policy Implications

In light of our analyses, we draw a number of conclusions about policies to reduce real-world emissions.

- In connection with the core of the regulatory program, compliance testing of new vehicles, we stress the importance of developing instrumentation and information to support any effort of this kind. The failure to make an adequate effort in the 1980s badly served manufacturers, regulators, and the public. Better information can lead not only to more effective regulation but to simpler regulation.

- Although we have not studied I/M programs in detail, we believe that the potential for effective I/M programs is dubious because they are based on two doubtful assumptions: that most ECS failures are caused by the individual user or the individual mechanic, and that essentially all malfunctioning cars can be repaired effectively at a moderate price.

- The remote-sensing and OBD technologies now in development are highly promising as tools to achieve a sharp reduction of malfunction emissions at relatively low cost. Their use should be focused not on identifying individual vehicles for repair, but on identifying entire models or engine families that suffer from poor design or manufacture.

- Although the public information that should become available from these two new technologies may well bring about changes in design and manufacture that greatly reduce ECS malfunction, a recall program based on real-world observation of excessive numbers of high-emitters is needed to spur manufacturers to act on that information. It may be appropriate to balance changes in other regulations against the new regulations aimed at closing the loopholes.

- Engine-out emissions are roughly proportional to fuel use. When emissions controls are essentially circumvented (during off-cycle driving) or malfunction, tailpipe emissions also are roughly proportional to fuel use. As a result, policies to dramatically increase fuel economy (such as the Partnership for a New Generation of Vehicles' goal of tripling fuel economy) would likely have major emissions benefits and should therefore be supported.

- As an alternative to the increasing variety of regulatory initiatives, we suggest that manufacturers try a more proactive approach. For instance, they could commit to reducing real-world, and not just certification, emissions, as determined through high-statistics measurements with the new instrumentation now becoming available.

There are two broad, and controversial, policy approaches to the reduction of vehicular emissions in the near term. The emphasis of the official approach, nationally and in California, is to require new vehicles to perform better—that is, with lower gpm—in the laboratory-like tests to which they now are subject for emissions certification. In addition, vehicles are required to meet various emissions standards, such as Tiers I and II nationally and the low-emission-vehicle (LEV) and ultra-low-emissions-vehicle (ULEV) standards in California. These new vehicle standards are complemented by I/M programs and in-use testing aimed, in principle, at keeping ECSs functional, or repairing them if necessary. The justification for this approach is that the regulatory structure of the past two decades has led to substantial emissions reductions and the various players are used to it, so it should be continued in a strengthened version. In the strictest sense, this program has failed in meeting its gpm emissions goals. However, certification tests can be seen as a means to reduce real-world emissions. In this view, real-world emissions will continue to be substantially higher than the test limits but are acceptable as long as progress is made.

The second approach is based on new regulatory initiatives (required or proposed for further study in the CAAA90) that have not yet received wide attention among nonspecialists. This approach emphasizes closing the loopholes in the old approach, rather than further tightening the standards based on the original certification test. The new initiatives are (1) EPA's supplement to the new-vehicle certification test aimed at sharply reducing off-cycle emissions and (2) radically improved information technologies to identify and reduce ECS malfunctions through changes in manufacturing. The argument for this change in emphasis is that the emissions associated with the loopholes discussed above are larger than those measured in the certification test (see Tables 2-1 and 2-2 and Figure 2-1). Moreover, the causes of the loophole emissions are different so that, in the absence of effective targeted measures, little further reduction in emissions will be achieved by stricter standards under the old certification tests.

These two approaches are not necessarily in conflict with each other, so why not pursue them simultaneously? We are concerned that there may be high costs to an unfocused campaign that includes some relatively ineffective policies. The regulations may be poorly carried out because of the lack of focus and the limited budgets of the regulatory agencies. In addition, very strict NO_x certification test standards may inhibit rather than encourage technical development on some promising technologies, such as lean-burn engines. Perhaps most importantly, there might be political penalties from trying to implement so many different policies, especially ineffective policies.

Our analysis suggests emphasizing the second approach. Policies aimed at closing the two loopholes will reduce the emissions associated with those loopholes by about two-thirds. We recommend that these policies be vigorously pursued, including strong support for development and use of instrumentation to create better publicly available information on real-world emissions. To help assure these reductions, we suggest that the manufacturers and regulators discuss basing future emissions regulations on real-world data rather than laboratory test results.

In contrast, the policies of the first approach, increasingly strict new car standards and I/M programs, either do not directly address the loopholes or have been found to be only marginally effective against them. In addition, they are costly. In terms of conventional-vehicle emissions, we suggest that these policies be deemphasized. This conclusion is our opinion; the analyses we report do not directly address these conventional policies.

However, although we are impressed with the progress we estimate for conventional cars, the second approach will not fully close the loopholes. Would this partial success be good enough for 2010? A third approach, aimed at reduction of vehicular emissions over the longer term, is required. This policy focuses on creating and marketing vehicles of substantially higher fuel efficiency and with new propulsion technologies that run on fuels that are intrinsically cleaner (for example, electric vehicles, hydrogen fuel-cell vehicles) or potentially cleaner (for example, superefficient hybrid drivetrains or alternative fuels such as natural gas or methanol). Some of these long-term technologies undoubtedly will have lower test emissions, as well as lower uncontrolled emissions, if not lower ECS malfunction probabilities. Under this long-term strategy, dramatically lower test standards are one policy to push manufacturers to develop and sell alternative new vehicle technologies, particularly in areas that suffer from especially poor air quality, such as southern California. We hope that our prediction of real-world emissions from conventional vehicles manufactured at that time will help in the evaluation of potential new propulsion technologies and alternative policies to encourage their development and use.

References

American Automotive Manufacturers Association (AAMA). 1994. *Motor Vehicle Facts and Figures 94*. Detroit: American Automobile Manufacturers Association.

Beaton, S., G. Bishop, Y. Zhang, L. Ashbaugh, D. Lawson, and D. Stedman. 1995. On-Road Vehicle Emissions: Regulations, Costs, and Benefits. *Science* 268: 991–993.

California Air Resources Board (CARB). 1994. *Test Report of the Light-*

Duty Vehicle Surveillance Program, Series 12 (LDVSP-12). MS-94-04. El Monte, Calif.: Mobile Source Division, California Air Resources Board.

Calvert, J., J. Heywood, R. Sawyer, and J. Seinfeld. 1993. Achieving Acceptable Air Quality: Some Reflections on Controlling Vehicle Emissions. *Science* 261: 37–45.

Goodwin, R., and M. Ross. 1996. *Off-Cycle Emissions from Modern Passenger Cars with Properly Functioning Emissions Controls*. SAE Technical Paper 960064. Warrendale, Penn.: Society of Automotive Engineers.

Haskew, H., K. Cullen, T. Liberty, and W. Langhorst. 1994. *The Execution of a Cooperative Industry/Government Exhaust Emission Test Program*. SAE Technical Paper 94C016. Warrendale, Penn.: Society of Automotive Engineers.

Lawson, D. 1993. "Passing the Test": Human Behavior and California's Smog Check Program. *Journal of the Air and Waste Management Association* 43 (12): 1567–1575.

Lents, J., and W. Kelly. 1993. Clearing the Air in Los Angeles. *Scientific American*. October: 32–39.

Ross, M., R. Goodwin, R. Watkins, M.Q. Wang, and T. Wenzel. 1995. *Real-World Emissions from Model Year 1993, 2000, and 2010 Passenger Cars*. Washington, D.C.: American Council for an Energy-Efficient Economy.

Stedman, D., G. Bishop, S. Beaton, J. Peterson, P. Guenther, I. McVey, and Y. Zhang. 1994. *On-Road Remote Sensing of CO and HC Emissions in California*. Contract No. A032-093. Sacramento: California Air Resources Board, Research Division.

Stephens, R. 1994. Remote Sensing Data and a Potential Model of Vehicle Exhaust Emissions. *Journal of the Air and Waste Management Association* 44 (11): 1284–1292.

Stephens, R., M. Giles, P. Groblicki, R. Gorse, K. McAlinden, D. Hoffman, R. James, and S. Smith. 1994. *Real-World Emissions Variability as Measured by Remote Sensors*. SAE Technical Paper 940582. Warrendale, Penn.: Society of Automotive Engineers.

U.S. Environmental Protection Agency (EPA). 1992. *National Air Quality and Emissions Trends Report*. EPA 454-R-93-031. Research Triangle Park, N.C.: Office of Air and Radiation, U.S. Environmental Protection Agency.

———. 1993. *Motor Vehicle Tampering Survey—1990*. EPA 420-R-93-001. Washington, D.C.: Office of Air and Radiation, U.S. Environmental Protection Agency.

———. 1994a. *Federal Test Procedure Review Project: Preliminary Technical Report*. EPA 420-R-93-007. Washington, D.C.: Office of Air and Radiation, U.S. Environmental Protection Agency.

_____. 1994b. *User's Guide to MOBILE5 (Mobile Source Emission Factor Model)*. Ann Arbor: Office of Mobile Sources, U.S. Environmental Protection Agency.

_____. 1995. *Fuel Economy Guide Database*. Ann Arbor: Office of Mobile Sources, National Vehicle Emissions Laboratory.

_____. 1996. Final Regulations for Revisions to the Federal Test Procedure for Emissions from Motor Vehicles. *Federal Register* 61, no. 205 (22 October 1996): 54852.

Wald, M. 1994. EPA to Allow Flexibility in Auto Emission Testing. *New York Times*, Dec. 10.

Wang, M.Q. 1996. *Development and Use of the GREET Model to Estimate Fuel-Cycle Energy Use and Emissions of Various Transportation Technologies and Fuels*. ANL/ESD-31. Argonne, Ill.: Center for Transportation Research, Argonne National Laboratory.

Wenzel, T., and M. Ross. 1996. *Emissions from Modern Passenger Cars with Malfunctioning Emissions Controls*. SAE Technical Paper 960067. Warrendale, Penn.: Society of Automotive Engineers.

Chapter Three

Federal Test Procedure Revisions and Real-World Emissions

JOHN GERMAN

The 1995 Asilomar Conference on Sustainable Transportation Energy Strategies addressed the question of whether technological improvements could, by 2015, stabilize greenhouse gas emissions from vehicles to 1990 levels while reducing criteria pollutant emissions to low-emissions-vehicle (LEV) levels. Calculation of vehicle emissions and fuel efficiency are traditionally based on the U.S. Environmental Protection Agency's test procedures. Thus, implicit in analyses of the conference questions is the assumption that EPA's test procedures accurately reflect real-world operation.

Among the provisions of the 1990 Clean Air Act Amendments was a paragraph directing EPA to examine the Federal Test Procedure (FTP) used to test automobile and light-duty truck emissions to determine whether the FTP adequately represents actual current driving conditions. Since little information was available about actual driving behavior, EPA conducted a research program in cooperation with the California Air Resources Board (CARB) and vehicle manufacturers to investigate driving behavior and the related emission impacts.

This chapter presents a summary of the driving behavior and potential impacts on emissions and fuel consumption found during the FTP revision study. For the convenience of the reader, we first summarize the driving behavior and emission test results previously reported in EPA technical papers (Enns et al. 1993; EPA 1993). We then turn to a discussion of the potential implications of off-cycle driving behavior and emission control on fuel consumption and fuel efficiency technology.

Description of Driving Surveys and Vehicle Testing

Driving Surveys

With support from the American Automobile Manufacturers Association (AAMA) and the Association of International Automobile Manufacturers (AIAM), EPA conducted surveys of driving behavior in Baltimore, Maryland, and Spokane, Washington, from February through April of 1992. Two methods of data collection were employed. In an instrumented vehicle study, 113 Baltimore vehicles and 102 Spokane vehicles were equipped with three-parameter data logger packages that recorded second-by-second speed and two other variables during seven to ten days of operation. As part of the same survey, the manufacturers recruited another 79 vehicles for study using six-parameter instruments designed to measure additional variables. A separate chase car study collected similar speed data in the two cities using a laser device mounted on a patrol car that tracked in-use target vehicles. About 250 routes were driven by the chase car in each city.

The Baltimore and Spokane surveys were supplemented by data collected in two other cities. EPA's Office of Research and Development sponsored an instrumented vehicle study on 101 vehicles in Atlanta, Georgia, and CARB sponsored a chase car study over 102 routes in Los Angeles similar to the chase car studies in Spokane and Baltimore.

In May 1993, EPA published the *Federal Test Procedure Review Project: Preliminary Technical Report* (EPA 1993). This report presented a detailed discussion of the driving survey methods, data collection, and preliminary analyses of the driving survey data. For reasons relating to representativeness, availability, and precision of the survey data, most of the discussion in the report and the summary presented below under "Driving Behavior and Emission Impacts" is confined to driving observed in the Baltimore three-parameter instrumented vehicle study.

Cycle Development

The next step after analysis of the driving patterns data was to assess the exhaust emissions during such driving. Such an assessment required reduction and synthesis of the driving data into representative driving cycles for use in vehicle testing. To develop such driving cycles, EPA selected actual segments of in-use driving from the Baltimore driving survey data and the Los Angeles chase car data that matched the joint distribution of in-use speed and acceleration. The following three cycles were developed to represent different types of driving:

- *Start cycle:* Driving occurring during the first four minutes after the start of the vehicle (excluding the initial idle).

- *High-speed/acceleration cycle:* In-use distribution of speed and accelerations outside the boundary of the FTP.

- *Remnant cycle:* That portion of in-use driving not represented by the high-speed/acceleration cycle or the start cycle.

In addition, two other cycles were developed for testing purposes:

- *CARB cycle:* Developed by CARB to represent the high-speed acceleration distribution and to include some of the most aggressive driving behavior found in the driving surveys.

- *High-load cycle:* Designed to test vehicles under relatively long, steady high-load conditions.

A description of the cycle development methodology is contained in a report on the potential emission implications of non-FTP driving behavior published by EPA in November 1993 (Enns et al. 1993).

Vehicle Emission Test Programs

A number of test programs have been conducted in coordination with industry and CARB. An updated assessment of overall emission impacts of non-FTP driving behavior was presented jointly by EPA and AAMA/AIAM at the March 1994 Society of Automotive Engineers (SAE) meeting in Washington, D.C. Extensive analyses of the data are also contained in the support documents to EPA's Notice of Proposed Rulemaking on FTP Revisions (EPA 1995).

EPA conducted the initial testing for off-cycle emission impacts on eight vehicles representing a range of vehicle and engine types. A wide variety of tests were conducted, including the FTP and all of the cycles described above. Testing was also conducted on a subset of vehicles to evaluate the emissions impact of soak times (the period between when a vehicle's engine is turned off and when it is restarted), start-up driving behavior, air conditioning operation, and road grades.

The manufacturers have conducted four test programs to date, and a fifth is in progress. Two of the programs concentrated on emissions from high-speed and high-acceleration driving. Although this testing was conducted on only a subset of the cycles and thus cannot be used for a complete assessment of in-use emissions, it has several valuable features. A relatively large sample of vehicles was tested (twenty-six 1992–1994 vehicles in the first program and twenty-eight Tier I vehicles in the second); modal (that is, second-by-second) emissions were gathered; and most of the vehicles were retested using special calibrations designed to eliminate commanded enrichment during high-load events. The original industry test program is described by Haskew et al. (1994), and the data are available on CD-ROM.

The rest of the manufacturers' test programs focused on emissions during actual air conditioning operation (the current FTP simulates air conditioning load with dynamometer loading, and poorly at that). All the testing was conducted in a full environmental chamber, which accurately reflects actual wind conditions, sun load, temperature, humidity, and heated pavement. Each of the three programs assessed air conditioning emissions on six to eight vehicles at 95° F and under bright sunshine conditions.

Because of the limited cycles tested by the manufacturers, the emission impacts of high-speed and high-acceleration driving and different soak times presented below are based on EPA's testing. The air conditioning impacts are based on the manufacturers' testing. The fuel economy implications of off-cycle emission standards are largely inferred from the modal data generated by the manufacturers.

Driving Behavior and Emission Impacts

Extensive analyses of the driving surveys and emission test data have identified three principal areas of concern: aggressive driving (that is, high speeds and accelerations), air conditioning operation, and soak times and trip lengths. The actual driving behavior and emission impacts of these areas of concern are summarized here. A more extensive discussion, including issues likely to be important for calculating state and regional emissions inventories, is given by Enns et al. (1993). In addition, an assessment of overall emission impacts of non-FTP driving behavior was presented jointly by EPA and AAMA/AIAM at the March 1994 SAE meeting in Washington, D.C. Finally, extensive analyses of the data are contained in the support documents for the Notice of Proposed Rulemaking on FTP Revisions (EPA 1995).

Speed and Acceleration

The speeds observed in Baltimore were much higher than are represented on the FTP. A comparison of the Baltimore and FTP speed

Figure 3-1

Comparison of Observed Driving Speeds with Speeds Assumed by the Federal Test Procedure (FTP)

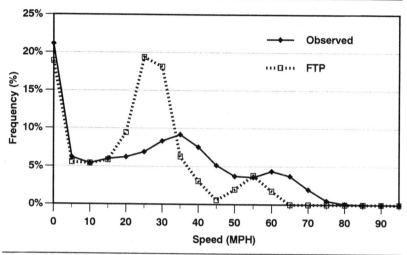

Source: Data from 1992 Baltimore instrumented vehicle driving survey.

Note: Speed distributions are in 5 MPH ranges, plotted by the top of the range. For example, the 30 MPH point represents the proportion of all driving spent between 25 and 30 MPH. The 0 speed point reflects the portion of idle operation.

distributions by 5 MPH increments is presented in Figure 3-1. The average speed in Baltimore was 24.5 MPH (median speed was 23.7 MPH). The speeds observed ranged to almost 95 MPH; 6.4 percent were above 60 MPH, and 2.6 percent were above 65 MPH. By comparison, the FTP has an average speed of 19.6 MPH with a maximum of 56.7 MPH. About 8.5 percent of all speeds in Baltimore exceeded the FTP maximum. Only the Baltimore data are reported here. Speeds observed in Spokane were lower than those in Baltimore, but both Los Angeles and Atlanta had substantially larger amounts of high-speed (that is, above 60 MPH) driving.

Acceleration rates in Baltimore were also significantly higher than those on the FTP. Observed acceleration rates ranged up to 15 MPH/sec, whereas the FTP has a maximum acceleration rate of only 3.3 MPH/sec. However, acceleration rates are really only half the story. For a given acceleration rate, the power required from the engine goes up linearly with vehicle speed. The joint distribution of speed and acceleration is the best measure, but it must be examined in three dimensions, which is difficult to visualize and comprehend.

Figure 3-2

An Index of Engine Power Requirements, Observed Versus Federal Test Procedure (FTP)

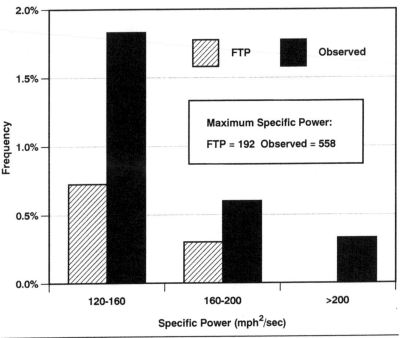

Source: Data from 1992 Baltimore instrumented vehicle driving survey.
Note: For a given acceleration rate, the power required from the engine goes up linearly with vehicle speed. Thus, power requirements are roughly proportional to the specific power. Forty percent more small-scale speed deviations were observed in-use than are represented by the FTP.

While not as good as the joint distribution of speed and acceleration, the best two-dimensional measure is specific power, which is roughly equivalent to 2 × speed × acceleration. This measure also indicates that the observed driving behavior was more aggressive than on the FTP. Specific power for the Baltimore sample ranged up to 558 MPH^2/sec and averaged 46.0 MPH^2/sec, with a median of 34.7 MPH^2/sec. The FTP has a maximum specific power of 192 MPH^2/sec, an average of 38.6 MPH^2/sec, and a median of 21.6 MPH^2/sec. A comparison of the amount of time spent in the higher specific power ranges is presented in Figure 3-2. An analysis was also done of the scatter of speed acceleration points occurring in the Baltimore sample outside the FTP envelope of speed and accelerations. These points represent about 18 percent of total Baltimore driving time. Although driving in Spokane was

Figure 3-3

Comparison of Federal Test Procedure (FTP) Driving Emissions with Simulated In-Use Driving Emissions

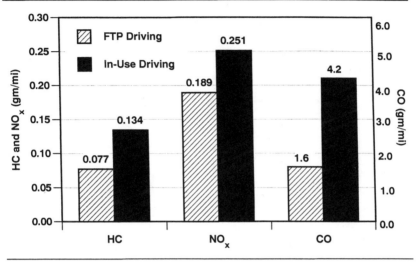

Source: Data from EPA 1993.

less aggressive than in Baltimore, both Los Angeles and Atlanta had higher specific power averages. It should also be noted that the survey contained a substantial number of older, low-performance vehicles. It is possible that the amount of time spent in high power operation may be larger for newer or higher-performance vehicles.

Figure 3-3 presents a summary of the emission results for the eight vehicles in the FTP test program. All the tests were run with the vehicle in a hot stabilized condition, including the baseline FTP results (that is, the impacts of the cold start and the hot start on the FTP have been removed). The in-use emissions are the weighted result of the start, high-speed/acceleration, and remnant cycles. The weighted in-use emissions (hot, stabilized) are significantly higher than the weighted FTP emissions. Hydrocarbons (HC) increased by 0.05 gm/mi, carbon monoxide (CO) jumped by 2.6 gm/mi, and nitrogen oxides (NO_x) rose by 0.06 gm/mi. Evaluation of the high-speed/load test results on the larger manufacturer dataset (the start and remnant cycles were not run by the manufacturers) indicates that the NO_x impact may be substantially larger than estimated from the eight vehicles tested by EPA.

Whereas the causes of the NO_x increase on the in-use cycles are relatively complex, the HC and CO increases are due primarily to

Figure 3-4

Impact of Removing Enrichment at Wide-Open Throttle on Catalyst Temperature

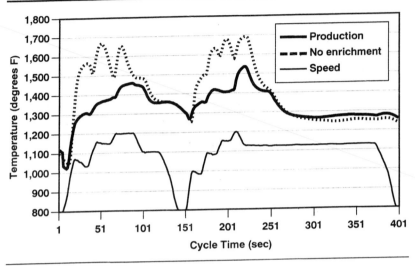

Source: Data from EPA Test Program.

commanded enrichment. The primary concern with elimination of commanded enrichment is elevated engine and catalyst temperatures. The catalyst temperature concern is illustrated in Figure 3-4. Each of the rapid temperature increases on the "No Enrichment" line corresponds with an 8-second wide-open throttle (WOT) event. The problem is that, unlike the production calibration, which uses enrichment during the high-load events, temperatures with the "no enrichment" calibration show no sign of leveling off during extended WOT events. The temperature rise is about 30° F per second during WOT. Thus, elimination of all commanded enrichment could lead to excessive deterioration of the catalyst during extended WOT operation.

Analyses were also conducted of small-scale speed variations, which are reflective of the amount of in-use throttle movement. The in-use data contained about 40 percent more speed variation than on the FTP. Although the emission impact of these small-scale variations is difficult to quantify, it is well known that emissions from some vehicles are very sensitive to how they are driven over the FTP. The higher variations of in-use speed indicate that in-use emissions may be higher than on the smoother FTP.

Air Conditioning Operation

Figure 3-5 displays the tailpipe NO_x emissions from the manufacturers' first phase of air conditioning testing, which tested low-mileage, current model-year vehicles in full environmental chambers at 95° F. All but one vehicle had extremely large increases in tailpipe NO_x, with the average increase being over 80 percent. As shown in Figure 3-6, this increase occurred largely in engine-out emissions. Among this sample of vehicles, the Caprice showed no tailpipe emissions increase even though it had about a 70 percent increase in engine-out emissions, indicating that the Caprice had an unexplained increase in NO_x catalyst conversion efficiency. Recent data from the manufacturers' second air conditioning test program, which tested current-technology vehicles with aged catalysts and oxygen sensors, show even higher increases in tailpipe NO_x during air conditioning operation.

Figure 3-7 presents the impact of air conditioning operation at 95° F on fuel economy, based on the test results from the manufacturers' first phase of air conditioning testing. Although every vehicle had a substantial decrease in fuel economy with the air conditioner operating, the decrease was generally in the range of 20 to 25 percent, less than a third of the NO_x increase. This indicates that the additional load imposed by air conditioning operation has a very nonlinear impact on NO_x emissions. The large, disproportionate NO_x increase with air conditioning operation was the biggest surprise of the FTP revision program.

Soak Distributions and Trip Patterns

The in-use data contain a large proportion of intermediate soak periods that are not reflected on the FTP. The FTP contains soak times of 10 minutes and 12 to 36 hours. As shown in Figure 3-8, almost 40 percent of all soak times in Baltimore were between 10 minutes and 2 hours. As catalysts cool off much faster than engines and most are almost completely cold in about 45 to 60 minutes, this is a potential emission concern.

Figure 3-9 illustrates the impact of catalyst cool-down on HC start emissions. Emissions from production vehicles are compared with those from the same vehicles with the catalyst insulated to slow cool-down. Clearly, catalyst cool-down after the 10-minute soak time on the FTP can lead to greatly elevated emissions. Recent data submitted to EPA on LEV prototypes indicate that catalysts on these vehicles warm up much faster than on current production vehicles, minimizing the catalyst cool-down impact on emissions.

Figure 3-5

Impact of Air Conditioning Use on Tailpipe Nitrogen Oxides (NO$_x$) Emissions over the Federal Test Procedure

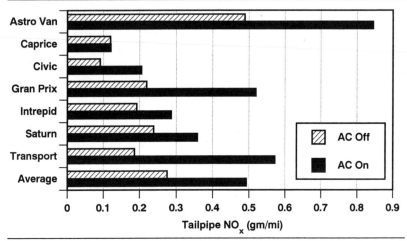

Source: Data from 1995 manufacturer test program.
Note: All tests run in environmental chamber at 95° F.

Figure 3-6

Impact of Air Conditioning Use on Engine-Out Nitrogen Oxides (NO$_x$) Emissions over the Federal Test Procedure

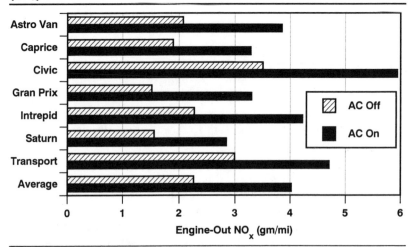

Source: Data from 1995 manufacturer test program.
Note: All tests run in environmental chamber at 95° F.

Figure 3-7

Impact of Air Conditioning on Fuel Economy

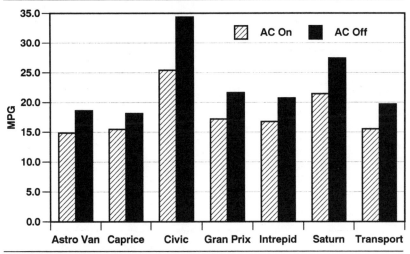

Source: Data from 1995 manufacturer test program.
Note: All Tier I vehicles in environmental cell at 95° F.

Figure 3-8

Soak Time Distributions in 1992 Baltimore Instrumented Vehicle Driving Survey

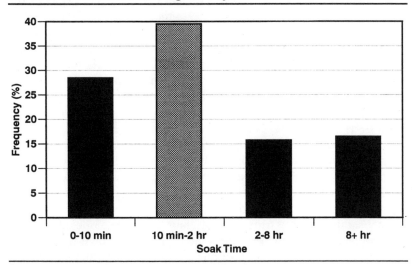

Source: Data from 1992 Baltimore instrumented vehicle driving survey.

Figure 3-9

Impact of Catalyst Insulation on Hydrocarbon Emissions During Start Cycle

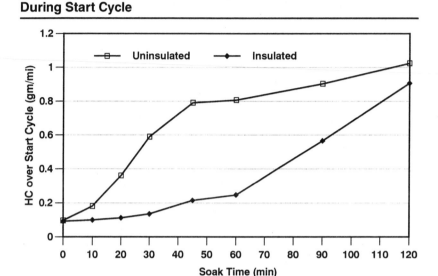

Source: Data from EPA test program on insulated catalysts.
Note: Three-vehicle average during first 1.4 miles of operation after each soak period.

From an emission inventory point of view, the impact of catalyst cool-down is largely offset by the fact that the FTP also overstates the number of cold starts. Analyses indicate that only about 30 percent of all in-use starts occur with catalysts hot enough to be immediately effective; the FTP implicitly assumes that 57 percent of all starts occur with hot catalysts. On the other hand, the FTP implicitly assumes that 43 percent of all starts occur with cold engines, whereas less than 25 percent of in-use starts occur with cold engines.

The primary emission inventory impact is the distribution of trip lengths, as is illustrated in Figure 3-10. In-use trip lengths are heavily skewed toward short trips, with well over 25 percent of all trips less than a mile in length. This appears to be largely due to "trip chaining," with drivers frequently making several stops between their original and final destinations. The result is that the average in-use trip length is 4.9 miles, with a median trip length of only 2.5 miles, and that there are substantially more trips per day than generally modeled. The in-use trip lengths are much shorter than on the FTP, which represents a 7.5-mile trip. One of the implications is that a much higher proportion of overall driving is done within 0.67 mile (or about 2 to 3 minutes) of

Figure 3-10

Distribution of Trip Distance in 1992 Baltimore Instrumented Vehicle Driving Survey

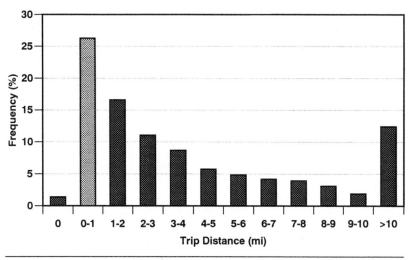

Source: Data from 1992 Baltimore instrumented vehicle driving survey.

vehicle starts (12.0 percent versus 8.9 percent on the FTP), prior to engines and catalysts reaching normal operating temperatures.

The frequency of stops on the FTP is also uncharacteristic of in-use trips; the average distance between stops on the FTP is only 0.41 mile, compared with 0.87 mile in Baltimore. Despite these differences, the FTP and Baltimore trips disagree only slightly in the proportion of time spent in the four operating modes: idle, cruise, acceleration, and deceleration.

Although the FTP has lower speeds and is less aggressive than in-use driving behavior, overall, the reverse occurs for the first few minutes after a vehicle start. The average observed speed during the first 80 seconds of all trips (the initial idle period was not included in this period) was only 14.4 MPH, compared with 23.1 MPH for the first micro-trip on the FTP. The average in-use speed 81 to 240 seconds into the trip was 22.8 MPH, compared with 29.8 MPH for a comparable period on the FTP. The aggressiveness of the FTP was also off substantially, with the first microtrip on the FTP substantially less aggressive than in-use driving and the second FTP microtrip much more aggressive.

Overall Emission Inventory Impacts

To put the impact of emissions from off-cycle operation into context, Figures 3-11, 3-12, and 3-13 present the amount of off-cycle emissions for CO, nonmethane hydrocarbons (NMHC), and NO_x, respectively. The assessment is for the amount of additional emissions compared with the currently modeled emissions for a Tier I vehicle, assuming enhanced inspection and maintenance programs and reformulated gasoline. The baseline NMHC inventory also includes evaporative emissions. The percentage number after each wedge indicates the proportion of the total 2020 inventory from Tier I vehicles due to each type of in-use operation.

As anticipated, commanded enrichment during high-load operation has a large impact on the CO inventory. This impact is illustrated by the set of "in-use driving" wedges in Figure 3-11 and amounts to 32 percent of the expected CO emissions. The impact of off-cycle factors is much less for NMHC, partially due to the large impact of evaporative emissions, but still constitutes 13 percent of the total inventory. The impact of off-cycle factors on NO_x is much larger than anticipated, mainly because of the large impact from air conditioning operation.

The revisions to the FTP that are in process will cut the total off-cycle emissions from future vehicles to roughly half of the proportion shown in Figures 3-11, 3-12, and 3-13. The other half of the off-cycle

Figure 3-11

Potential Impacts on Carbon Monoxide Inventory, 2020

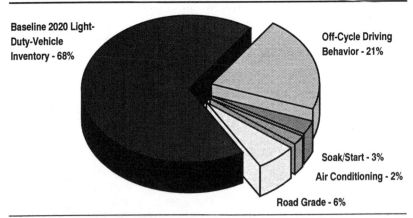

Source: Based on analyses performed in support of EPA 1995.
Note: These emission impacts are preliminary and are based upon Tier I vehicles, reformulated gasoline, and enhanced inspection and maintenance program estimates.

CHAPTER THREE

emissions is not controllable without significant increases in vehicle technology. It is anticipated that this remaining proportion of off-cycle emissions will continue to be reduced in the future in conjunction with more stringent FTP emission standards.

Figure 3-12

Potential Impacts on Nonmethane Hydrocarbons Inventory, 2020

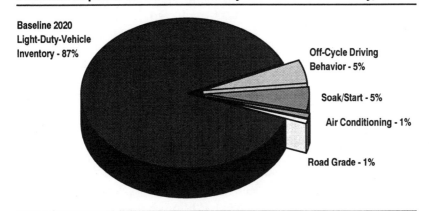

Source: Based on analyses performed in support of EPA 1995.
Note: These emission impacts are preliminary and are based upon Tier I vehicles, reformulated gasoline, and enhanced inspection and maintenance program estimates.

Figure 3-13

Potential Impacts on Nitrogen Oxides (NO$_x$) Inventory, 2020

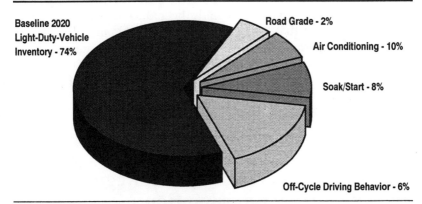

Source: Based on analyses performed in support of EPA 1995.
Note: These emission impacts are preliminary and are based upon Tier I vehicles, reformulated gasoline, and enhanced inspection and maintenance program estimates.

65

Impact on Vehicle Fuel Consumption Modeling

Off-cycle operation can impact fuel consumption in a number of ways. One is the impact of off-cycle operation on modeling of vehicle fuel consumption. Unfortunately, the overall impact on modeling cannot be quantified, as the new cycles developed by EPA reflect typical nonattainment areas, not nationwide driving conditions, and testing on the EPA highway cycle was not conducted. However, there is one area where it is clear that current modeling does not properly reflect in-use driving behavior: air conditioning operation.

It is likely that the additional fuel consumption due to air conditioning operation is higher than is currently modeled. Current estimates implicitly incorporate the air conditioning load factor used for the FTP and the EPA highway cycle. However, as mentioned earlier, the air conditioning load is simulated simply by adding 10 percent to the dynamometer load. This 10 percent additional load increases vehicle fuel consumption by 1.5 to 2.0 percent. However, as noted above, data from the FTP revision test programs indicate that actual air conditioning operation at high ambient temperatures (95° F) increases fuel consumption by 20 to 25 percent. Although an assessment of the amount of average yearly air conditioning operation and load over the entire United States has not been conducted, national vehicle-miles-of-travel (VMT) distributions by temperature range were presented by the U.S. Department of Transportation in a draft 1974 report (DOT 1974). About 30 percent of annual nationwide miles traveled were reported to occur at temperatures above 70° F. Although the fuel consumption impact from air conditioning operation at temperatures closer to 70° F is less than it is at 95° F, this reduction is offset to some degree by the fact that many vehicles engage the air conditioning compressor at temperatures below 70° F for defrost or automatic climate control. Thus, the average annual air conditioning load should be somewhere in the range of 20 to 25 percent of the load at 95° F. This estimate suggests that the actual increase in average, annual fuel consumption due to air conditioning may be in the range of 4 to 6 percent, or two to three times the currently modeled impact.

Impact of Off-Cycle Emission Regulation on Vehicle Fuel Consumption

Improved control of emissions during high-speed and acceleration driving and air conditioning operation will impact fuel consumption of the future vehicle fleet. This includes impacts on both in-use fuel consumption and measured Corporate Average Fuel Economy (CAFE) levels, as discussed below. A subsequent section of this chapter considers indirect impacts of off-cycle regulation on the types of technology that are encouraged and discouraged.

Impact on In-Use Fuel Consumption

The regulations proposed by EPA would eliminate most commanded enrichment. The impact the elimination of commanded enrichment would have on in-use fuel consumption was estimated two ways. One method calculated the theoretical reduction in fuel use associated with a change in air/fuel ratio from 12:1 to 14.6:1 during high-load operation, weighted by the estimated amount of in-use commanded enrichment. The second compared the weighted fuel economy of tests with "no enrichment" calibrations to the same vehicles tested with production calibrations. Both methods yielded very similar results: about a 0.5 percent decrease in fuel consumption was associated with the elimination of commanded enrichment.

Elimination of commanded enrichment also lowers wide-open throttle (WOT) performance by 3 to 5 percent. However, because of the concerns discussed earlier about higher catalyst temperatures at WOT, the regulations currently being promulgated by EPA will likely require elimination of commanded enrichment at WOT only on a relatively small proportion of lower-performance vehicles. Even on these lower-performance vehicles, commanded enrichment would be allowed after a delay of only about four seconds or less. Although the new regulations will largely eliminate commanded enrichment during part-throttle operation, elimination of commanded enrichment is somewhat unique in that the performance loss occurs only at WOT; part-throttle operation is completely unaffected. Since part-throttle operation is not affected, since the WOT effect is relatively small, and since the effect will occur only on a small proportion of the vehicles and then only for a brief period of time, the potential impact of this factor on in-use fuel consumption should be small enough to ignore.

Impact on Measured CAFE Levels

Most of the provisions in EPA's proposed control of off-cycle emissions will not impact the existing test cycles used for CAFE measurements. Instead, new cycles and requirements for high-speed/acceleration and air conditioning operation will be adopted. The exception is a change from the Clayton dynamometer to large-roll electronic dynamometers, which will apply to all testing, including the FTP and the highway cycle. This change will improve the simulation of actual road loads on the vehicle because of the elimination of tire slip on the dynamometer and the ability to match road load at all speeds, not just at 50 MPH.

Testing on a limited number of vehicles indicates that the improved road load simulation may decrease measured fuel consumption by 1 to 2 percent. This measurement change does not have a direct effect on actual in-use fuel consumption, since we are merely doing a better job of reflecting the actual consumption. Nevertheless, there could be an indirect effect on the stringency of the light-duty vehicle CAFE standards (light-duty trucks will not be affected, as the National Highway and Traffic Safety Administration [NHTSA] will incorporate any impacts into future light-duty truck [LDT] CAFE standards). The key issue is whether or not EPA grants CAFE adjustments for this change in road load simulation. If CAFE adjustments are granted, there will be no impact on actual fuel consumption. However, if CAFE adjustments are not granted, manufacturers constrained by the LDV CAFE standards would have to lower their average fuel consumption by 1 to 2 percent. Note that, under this scenario, the "shortfall" of actual fuel economy to measured fuel economy would also decrease by 1 to 2 percent.

Indirect Impact of Off-Cycle Emission Regulation on Future Technology

EPA has determined that regulation of high speed and loads and actual air conditioning operation is needed, in part, because there are nonlinear emission responses from the engine during these conditions. One result is that the technologies and strategies employed by manufacturers to reduce emissions on the FTP may not be the most effective technologies and strategies to meet the new requirements. Thus, some control strategies will be rewarded by the new regulations, and some technologies may face additional hurdles to adoption. Most of the discussion in the following section is summarized from German (1995), to which the reader can refer for a much more extensive discussion of the factors affecting engine-out emissions and catalyst conversion efficiency.

Technology and Strategy Incentives

The higher loads encountered during periods of high acceleration and during air conditioning operation have a nonlinear impact on NO_x emissions. As HC has a much more linear (in particular, a much smaller) response to higher loads, the effect is to greatly increase the emphasis on NO_x control during off-cycle operation. Although some improvements may be possible from better exhaust gas recirculation (EGR) systems, improved NO_x conversion efficiency in the catalyst is likely to be the most cost-effective means of compliance.

NO_x reduction in the catalyst decreases very rapidly in a lean environment (that is, air/fuel ratios greater than stoichiometric, or the ideal air/fuel ratio for complete combustion). HC and CO oxidation drops almost as rapidly in a rich environment (that is, air/fuel ratios less than stoichiometric). Thus, the window within which all three pollutants can be catalyzed at the same time is very narrow.

Manufacturers have made great strides in achieving very high levels of HC, CO, and NO_x conversion simultaneously, thanks in no small part to fuel injection control capability. Many modern vehicles achieve average conversion efficiencies of over 90 percent for all three pollutants once the catalyst has reached normal operating temperatures.

However, NO_x conversion efficiencies vary much more from vehicle to vehicle than HC and CO efficiencies. This appears to be due to an extreme sensitivity to the air/fuel calibration strategy. Figures 3-14 and 3-15 show the second-by-second NO_x conversion efficiency for

Figure 3-14

Impact of Air/Fuel Ratio on Nitrogen Oxides (NO_x) Conversion Efficiency, Grand Am

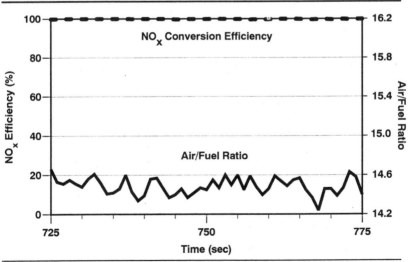

Source: Data from German 1995, 152.

Figure 3-15

Impact of Air/Fuel Ratio on Nitrogen Oxides (NO_x) Conversion Efficiency, Gran Prix

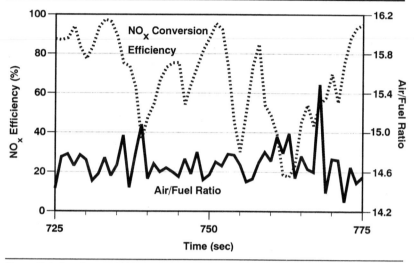

Source: Data from German 1995, 152.

two vehicles during a high-speed cruise from 725 to 775 seconds into the high-speed/acceleration cycle. Figure 3-14 gives data for the Grand Am, which has an average NO_x conversion efficiency of over 98 percent on the high-speed/acceleration cycle. Figure 3-15 gives data for the Gran Prix, which has an average NO_x conversion efficiency of about 76 percent.

The air/fuel ratio of the Grand Am is more tightly controlled, with much smaller excursions. Significantly, it is also biased right at, or slightly rich of, stoichiometry (that is, the air/fuel ratio is generally near, or slightly less than, the stoichiometric ideal for the fuel used in the test program, about 14.55:1). No time is spent with the air/fuel ratio leaner than 14.7:1, with the result that the NO_x conversion efficiency is almost 100 percent for the entire period. By contrast, the much larger air/fuel ratio swings allowed by the Gran Prix and the slightly lean bias of the air/fuel ratio result in significant amounts of time with air/fuel ratios slightly leaner than the stoichiometric ideal. As there is no rich-excursion mechanism similar to lean-excursion oxygen storage, the lean excursions on the Gran Prix trigger immediate reductions in NO_x conversion efficiency. Thus, it appears that, for optimum conversion of HC, CO, and NO_x simultaneously, avoidance of lean excursions is highly desirable.

The need to improve NO_x catalyst conversion efficiency without impacting HC and CO conversion efficiency will be a strong incentive for better air/fuel ratio control. In addition, the new start cycle proposed by EPA for use during air conditioning operation contains more speed variation than found on the existing FTP. This additional speed variation will increase throttle movement during the test, increasing the need for manufacturers to control air/fuel ratios during throttle opening. The net result is that technologies that improve air/fuel ratio control will be encouraged by the off-cycle regulations. Some examples are sequential multipoint fuel injection, more sophisticated computer maps, wide-range oxygen sensors, and drive-by-wire systems (drive-by-wire eliminates the direct linkage between the accelerator petal and the throttle and enables the computer to simultaneously control both throttle and fuel injection in response to an electronic signal from the accelerator).

More efficient air conditioning systems will also be encouraged by regulation of emissions during air conditioning operation. Currently, there is no incentive for manufacturers to reduce air conditioning loads, as the existing air conditioning load on the FTP is a percentage of the dynamometer load and has no connection to the actual load imposed by the air conditioner.

Potential Technology Barriers

Although off-cycle controls will encourage better air/fuel control technologies for vehicles with three-way catalysts, they will also increase NO_x compliance problems for lean-burn technologies, including diesel and two-stroke engines. Until a lean-reduction catalyst is developed, lean-burn technologies must directly control the large increase in engine-out NO_x under high-load conditions. Although this is not impossible, it will likely be more difficult and expensive than improving NO_x conversion in three-way catalysts. For example, recent tests over EPA's proposed high-speed/acceleration cycle on VW and Mercedes diesel engine vehicles yielded NO_x emissions over twice the gasoline average and about six times the level of the proposed stringency.

A major consideration for future low-power, ultra-high-efficiency designs is air conditioning load. The energy distribution chart circulated extensively by the Partnership for a New Generation of Vehicles (PNGV) has a box stating that only 2.2 percent of the energy from combustion is lost to accessories on the FTP, with only 1.5 percent on the highway cycle. These figures are obviously based on the existing air conditioning simulation on the FTP, which has nothing to do with the actual load imposed during air conditioning operation at high temperatures. If high-efficiency designs are to become reality, they must deal with actual air conditioning loads, which currently reach 5 to 10 hp (3.7 to 7.5 kW) at 95° F.

Conclusions

EPA's work on revisions to the Federal Test Procedure has identified a number of areas where in-use driving conditions and emissions are not represented accurately by the current FTP. The current FTP underrepresents high speeds, high acceleration rates, the amount of throttle variation, and the load from air conditioning operation and does not properly characterize soak times and trip length. These factors have potential implications for the modeling of vehicle emissions and fuel efficiency, both for current and future vehicles. In addition, EPA is in the process of revising the FTP to add emission requirements for high-speed and high-acceleration operation, air conditioning operation, and increased throttle variation. These regulations will affect future vehicle emissions and fuel efficiency.

The direct fuel economy impacts both of off-cycle operation and of regulation of off-cycle emissions are likely to be relatively small:

- Elimination of commanded enrichment would decrease in-use fuel consumption by about 0.5 percent.

- A small number of low-performance vehicles may have to eliminate commanded enrichment at WOT for brief periods of time (4 seconds maximum), leading to a small loss in WOT performance (about 3 to 5 percent) during this period.

- The change in dynamometer and road load simulation may impact CAFE results by 1 to 2 percent.

- Current modeling of fuel economy likely understates the increase in fuel consumption caused by air conditioning operation by a factor of two to three.

The impact on emission control technology encouraged or discouraged by regulation of off-cycle emissions is more likely to be significant. Better fuel control, including new technologies such as drive-by-wire and linear oxygen sensors, will be strongly encouraged, with an unquantified reduction in fuel consumption. More efficient air conditioning technology will also be encouraged. On the other hand, off-cycle NO_x standards may significantly increase barriers to lean-burn technologies.

A currently unknown factor is the impact of off-cycle operation and emission control on alternative-fueled vehicles and electric hybrid vehicles. Organizations involved in the development of such vehicles should consider the impact of both off-cycle operation and the proposed off-cycle regulations in their development process.

References

Enns, P., J. German, and J. Markey. 1993. EPA's Survey of In-Use Driving Patterns: Implications for Mobile Source Emission Inventories. Paper presented at the AWMA/CARB Specialty Conference on Emission Inventory: Perception and Reality, Pasadena, Calif., October 19.

German, J. 1995. *Observations Concerning Current Motor Vehicle Emissions*. SAE Technical Paper 950812. Warrendale, Penn.: Society of Automotive Engineers.

Haskew, H., K. Cullen, T.F. Liberty, and W.K. Langhorst. 1994. *The Execution of a Cooperative Industry/Government Exhaust Emission Test Program*. SAE Technical Paper 94C016. Warrendale, Penn.: Society of Automotive Engineers.

U.S. Department of Transportation (DOT). 1974. The Sensitivity of Projected Aggregate Fuel Consumption to the Conditions of Individual Fuel Economy Tests—Part A. Draft.

U.S. Environmental Protection Agency (EPA). 1993. *Federal Test Procedure Review Project: Preliminary Technical Report*. EPA 420-R-93-007. Ann Arbor: National Vehicle and Fuel Emissions Laboratory.

_____. 1995. *Proposed Regulations for Revisions to the Federal Test Procedure for Emissions from Motor Vehicles: Proposed Rule*. 60 FR 7404.

Chapter Four

Combining Vehicle Efficiency and Renewable Biofuels to Reduce Light-Vehicle Oil Use and CO_2 Emissions

JOHN DECICCO AND LEE LYND

For over two decades, the United States has grappled with its dependence on foreign oil. Between 1972 and 1991, oil imports resulted in a 1.2×10^{12} (trillion) transfer of wealth to foreign oil producers, and the total economic costs to the United States were estimated to be $4.1 trillion (Greene & Leiby 1993). Imports have been steadily climbing in both absolute volume and share of consumption, reaching 8 million barrels per day (Mbd), or 46 percent of U.S. oil consumption, in 1994 (EIA 1995b). The direct cost of these imports in 1994 was $45 billion, or 30 percent of the U.S. merchandise trade deficit in that year. The country has been struggling even longer with the air pollution impacts of gasoline consumption. Compounding these concerns is the likely global climate disruption from greenhouse gas (GHG) emissions. Transportation oil use accounts for 32 percent of U.S. GHG emissions (EIA 1995a). These problems are similar throughout the world: in 1990, highway vehicles accounted for about 24 percent of overall fossil carbon emissions in northern industrialized (Organization for Economic Cooperation and Development) nations and for an estimated 16 percent worldwide (OECD 1995).

Three approaches may be taken to reduce the fuel-related impacts of motor vehicles. One is to improve end-use energy efficiency—that is, to improve fuel economy. Another is to shift to alternative fuels, which may be nonpetroleum derived and may have lower GHG emissions per unit of energy consumed. The third is to control the amount of travel, including greater use of more energy-efficient modes of travel than low-occupancy vehicles. In this chapter, we focus on the effects of combining the first two approaches—namely, combining higher vehicle efficiency with alternative, particularly renewable, fuels. For our purposes, the term *renewable* refers to fuels and fuel production processes that, ideally, can be indefinitely replenished *and* result in zero net GHG emissions. Although some fuel cycles can offer GHG emissions that are a small fraction of those from fossil fuels, achieving zero net GHG emissions may be difficult. We treat renewability as an ideal to be approached rather than as a status that is absolutely achieved.

To quantitatively examine the benefits of efficiency improvement and expanded use of renewable fuels, we estimate technically feasible scenarios and judge the outcomes against hypothetical sustainability targets defined for the 1995 Asilomar conference. These targets, interpreted here for light-duty vehicles, are

- Reducing on-road criteria pollutant emissions to California low-emission vehicle (LEV) standards—3.4 g/mi of carbon monoxide, 0.075 g/mi of reactive organic gases (hydrocarbons), and 0.2 g/mi of nitrogen oxides—over the full life of vehicles and to lower levels in severely polluted areas

- Reducing oil use 10 percent by 2005 and further thereafter

- Returning greenhouse gas emissions to their 1990 level by 2015

- Increasing renewable fuels to 15 percent of total fuel use by 2015 and further thereafter

Since our analysis focuses on energy supply and end-use issues, we quantitatively treat only the oil use, GHG emissions, and renewable fuel use targets.

Our analysis specifically examines incremental improvements in conventional-vehicle fuel economy combined with increasing use of renewable ethanol. This fuel can be produced from woody (cellulosic) biomass using emerging production technologies that emit very low net levels of carbon. As production costs drop, ethanol utilization can be readily expanded without major market barriers through low-level blends of gasoline with ethanol or its derivative, ethyl tertiary butyl ether (ETBE), both of which serve as oxygenates. If a nationwide distribution network is established to serve the blends market, then subsequent use of ethanol as a neat or near-neat fuel would face reduced barriers.

Gray and Alson (1989) identified the potential benefits of using methanol in improved internal-combustion-powered vehicles that could have hybrid drivetrains, considering mainly fossil feedstocks for the methanol. Williams et al. (1995) examined the use of biomass-derived methanol or hydrogen in fuel cell vehicles, which offer a long-term promise for very high efficiency. The general point worth high-lighting is that substantial reductions in petroleum consumption can be attained through efficiency improvement and alternative fuel use *in combination*. Unfortunately, with some notable exceptions (for example, the work just mentioned and Bleviss 1989), analyses of alternative motor fuels and analyses of vehicle efficiency have tended to go separate ways.

Additional synergisms of combining higher efficiency with use of renewable fuels include the following:

* *Range and utility enhancement*. Ethanol, like most other alternative fuels, has a lower volumetric energy density than gasoline, so high efficiency alleviates range and on-board vehicle space trade-offs.

* *Consumer cost savings*. In the near term, a transition to renewable fuels will likely involve higher fuel costs, the impacts of which are reduced with more efficient vehicles, easing consumer acceptance.

* *Job creation potential*. Investments in both new biofuels production technologies and efficient vehicle technologies can be made domestically, so dollars directed toward such investments would create net U.S. jobs compared with dollars spent on foreign oil.

* *Lower ecological impacts*. Land use and habitat impacts of biofuels production will be proportional to the scale of use, which decreases with increasing end-use efficiency.

The value of a combined efficiency and renewable-fuels strategy should be well known in principle. As pointed out in *Energy for a Sustainable World*, the contribution of renewable energy supplies, including biomass, can be "quite significant—as long as overall energy demand is not too large" (Goldemberg et al. 1988, 381).

Simple arithmetic can show the combined effects of efficiency improvement and fuel substitution on gasoline displacement. The fraction of gasoline displaced increases linearly with the quantity of alternative fuel supplied on an energy-equivalent (rather than a volumetric) basis. However, the overall displacement depends on vehicle energy intensity (energy use per distance of travel), which is proportional to the inverse of fuel efficiency. For example, given a 50 percent efficiency improvement, which cuts vehicle energy requirements by one-third, a quantity of renewable fuel equivalent to one-third of the original gasoline consumption displaces one-half of the remaining fuel requirements. Thus, the combined strategy will cut the consumption level to one-third of its original value—a two-thirds reduction overall. If energy intensity is cut in half, then half as much renewable fuel is needed to achieve a 100 percent gasoline displacement. This simple relationship does not account for how long it takes for new vehicle and fuel supply technologies to be put into place. Neither does it account for interactions, such as the slight increase in driving due to lower driving costs or efficiency changes (negative or positive) for vehicles using an alternative fuel. Nevertheless, it illustrates the basic power of combining these two approaches to address problems related to transportation petroleum use. The rest of this paper provides more detailed scenarios of how and when such benefits might be achieved.

Background

Cars and light trucks account for the largest share (58 percent) of U.S. transportation energy consumption, and 98 percent of their fuel use is gasoline, including gasohol and other oxygenated blends (Davis 1994). In fact, compounds blended into gasoline now represent the largest portion of alternative (nonpetroleum) fuel use in the United States. On a volumetric basis, ethanol in gasohol accounts for 1.2 percent of delivered motor gasoline; natural gas liquids comprise 3.1 percent of refinery inputs; and other oxygenates, mainly methyl tertiary butyl ether (MTBE), comprise another 1.1 percent (EIA 1994, 1995c). Thus, although it is difficult to allocate shares of various refinery inputs to particular outputs such as gasoline, over 5 percent of U.S. gasoline consumption is already nonpetroleum based. The U.S. Department of Energy (DOE 1995a) estimates that a 10 percent displacement of petroleum in light-duty vehicles is feasible by the year 2000, mainly from greater use of nonpetroleum refinery inputs and without increased sales of alternatively fueled vehicles. Nevertheless, there are limits to how much alternative fuel can be introduced through the conventional gasoline supply system.

Choosing an alternative fuel involves numerous considerations, and the subject has been extensively studied (see DOE 1990 et seq., EIA 1994, and Sperling 1989, among others). DeLuchi (1991) ranked vehicle and fuel choices according to the likely impacts of their full-fuel-cycle GHG emissions relative to those of today's gasoline-powered vehicles. Table 4-1 summarizes results from an updated version of that analysis (Delucchi 1994). The effect of the primary energy resource dominates that of the particular energy carrier (fuel) or drivetrain. Fuels derived from solar energy, even indirectly through biomass, will have substantially lower GHG emissions than those derived from fossil sources, no matter what particular carrier or vehicle design is used.

Predicting the impacts and market acceptance of alternative fuels involves many uncertainties. Issues include the future price of gasoline and gasoline additives; regulations on fuel composition and performance; and also the magnitude, sustained direction, and effectiveness of research and development (R&D). The cellulosic ethanol

Table 4-1

Relative Greenhouse Gas Emissions Ranking of Automotive Fuel Options by Type of Drivetrain, Energy Carrier, and Energy Resource

Vehicle and Fuel Distribution			Primary Energy Resource					
Drivetrain	Energy Carrier	(a)	Solar	Biomass	Nuclear	Natural Gas	Oil	Coal
Battery	Electricity	1	•					
Combustion	Ethanol	2		•				
Fuel cell	Hydrogen	2	•					
Combustion	Hydrogen	6	•					
Battery	Electricity	7			•			
Fuel cell	Hydrides	15			•			
Fuel cell	Methanol	15		•				
Combustion	Methanol	25		•				
Combustion	Methane	29		•				
Combustion	Hydrides	33			•			
Fuel cell	Methanol	56				•		
Battery	Electricity	66				•		
Combustion	LPG	74				•	•	
Combustion	Natural Gas	76				•		
Combustion	Hydrogen	82			•			
Combustion	Diesel	85					•	
Combustion	Methanol	95				•		
Battery	Electricity (marginal mix)	98			•	•	•	•
Combustion	Gasoline	100					•	
Fuel cell	Methanol	102						•
Battery	Electricity	107						•
Combustion	Ethanol (from corn)	112		•				•
Combustion	Methanol	167						•

Source: Adapted from a similar table in *Majority Report* (1995, 34), based on a presentation by Mark Delucchi to the "Car Talk" Committee.
(a) Relative full-fuel-cycle greenhouse gas emissions (gasoline internal combustion = 100).

fuel cycle analyzed by DeLuchi (1991) involves wood feedstocks and current conversion technologies; it would have GHG emissions roughly 2 percent of those of gasoline. Lynd et al. (1995) addressed the question, What are the likely features and cost of a cellulosic ethanol technology at a level of maturity comparable to that of a petroleum refinery? Considering improvements in biological conversion and pretreatment but not other process steps, they projected the selling price for ethanol produced from a dedicated energy crop using mature technology to be $0.50 per gallon (1994$). This ethanol price corresponds to $0.69–$0.76 per gallon of gasoline energy (gge) equivalent, with the higher price for low-ethanol blends and the lower price for dedicated ethanol vehicles, reflecting a 10 percent engine efficiency benefit. Lynd in Chapter 5 of this volume also provides further details on process and feedstock parameters supporting this price estimate.

Relatively little attention has been paid to analyzing energy efficiency in alternatively fueled ICVs. DeLuchi (1991, Table 11) estimated alternatively fueled vehicle efficiencies relative to a baseline gasoline vehicle, drawing mainly on vehicle and component test data and reviewing estimates about the likely evolution of new technologies (batteries, traction motors and controllers, and so forth) for which little commercial experience exists. Aside from relatively minor, fuel-specific refinements (for example, higher compression ratios), little attention was paid to engineering opportunities for improving conventional vehicles. DeLuchi's base case was a conventional car rated at 30 MPG running on reformulated gasoline. This efficiency is only 7 percent higher than the 28 MPG average of today's cars. In contrast, published assessments of potential conventional-vehicle efficiency improvements range up to 55 MPG (the "risk level 2" estimate of EEA 1991), or just about double today's new-car average.

Methodology

Our approach combines scenarios of vehicle efficiency improvement and biofuel supply expansion to project energy use and environmental impacts. Reductions in gasoline use are estimated relative to a baseline scenario that assumes no vehicle efficiency increases over the period examined and little use of alternative fuels, particularly fuels derived from nonfossil sources. Later we suggest the policies needed to realize such scenarios.

We use a stock turnover model to compute changes in efficiency as improved vehicles replace older ones on the road and to project total light-vehicle energy requirements through 2030. We allocate this energy demand among gasoline (derived from petroleum or other nonbiofuel feedstocks), gasohol, and neat or near-neat ethanol fuel. Alternative fuels other than ethanol are not analyzed. At initial stages of biofuel availability, all biofuel is assumed to be used in gasohol or as an oxygenate. Such use expands until 10 percent by volume of the gasoline market is reached (contemporary vehicles can already run on up to 10 percent ethanol). Beyond the 10 percent level, additional ethanol is consumed in dedicated alcohol vehicles. Our model includes efficiency adjustment factors to represent the effects of blending (zero efficiency change) and dedicated alcohol use (10 percent higher efficiency) relative to gasoline combustion.

Projected fuel consumption rates (Btu/mile) and vehicle-miles of travel per year (VMT/yr) are used to compute fuel energy requirements (Btu/yr). GHG emissions are calculated from full-fuel-cycle emissions factors (including effects of methane, nitrous oxide, and other gases as well as carbon dioxide) for gasoline and biofuel, expressed in terms of CO_2 equivalent per unit of energy delivered to the vehicle (for example, g CO_2/Btu). A full modeling of fuel market impacts is beyond the scope of this analysis. The U.S. Department of Energy's "502b" study on petroleum displacement (DOE 1995a) shows how market effects would reduce the savings from pursuing alternative-fuel strategies, since lower oil demand would depress oil prices, stimulating demand in other sectors. Thus, net oil savings and GHG reductions are likely to be lower than the first-order estimates made here.

Technology Assessments

Our scenarios are based largely on reviews of previous assessments of technologies for improving automotive fuel economy and producing ethanol from cellulosic biomass, plus prior studies of fuel-cycle GHG impacts. For a given fuel, GHG emissions are largely proportional to the vehicle fuel consumption rate (inverse fuel economy). The relationship is complicated by upstream emissions and non-CO_2 tailpipe emissions. For example, the emissions rates of tailpipe pollutants (including some GHGs) are highly uncertain. For gasoline, nevertheless, fuel carbon content accounts for 74 percent of the full-fuel-cycle GHG emissions, which amount to 3.3 kg_C/gal (kg of carbon-mass equivalent per gallon) (DeLuchi 1991). Moreover, GHG emissions from upstream processes (petroleum extraction, transportation, refining, and distribution) are largely proportional to the amount of fuel consumed. Cellulosic ethanol offers very substantial GHG emissions reductions over both gasoline and current corn-based ethanol. DeLuchi (1991) estimates full-fuel-cycle GHG emissions for corn ethanol of 3.1 kg_C/gal, but only 0.16 kg_C/gal for cellulosic ethanol. Our scenarios assume that corn ethanol is replaced as soon as cellulosic conversion technology becomes available, since the latter will be more cost-competitive.

Vehicle Efficiency

Recent studies of the near-term (roughly ten-year) potential for vehicle efficiency improvement have identified new-car fleet averages ranging up to 51 MPG (DeCicco & Ross 1993, NRC 1992, OTA 1991). Key assessments include federally sponsored studies based on work by Energy and Environmental Analysis, Inc. (EEA), such as Greene and Duleep (1993). The National Research Council study (NRC 1992) drew mainly on the EEA and industry work. Divergent estimates result from differing assumptions about the benefits, costs, applicability, and marketability of the technologies considered. EEA (1991) estimated higher levels given a longer time horizon but did not provide cost estimates. These EEA estimates for 2010 were given at three "risk" levels: (1) 45 MPG, (2) 55 MPG, and (3) 74 MPG. EEA's level 3 estimate goes beyond conventional technologies, assuming use of either hybrid drivetrains or advanced, turbocharged diesels. Even higher potential fuel economy levels have been identified as research targets (McCarthy 1995, PNGV 1994) through the use of more advanced technologies (see Chapter 7 of this volume) and through radical redesign (Lovins 1995). This chapter draws on DeCicco and Ross (1993), who reanalyzed information considered by the EEA and NRC studies and supplemented it with additional information to provide up-to-date estimates of potential automobile efficiency improvements based only on refinements to conventional gasoline-powered designs.

Incremental improvements in fuel economy can be obtained through more widespread use of technologies already in production plus the introduction of newer refinements of conventional technologies. DeCicco and Ross (1993) projected the potential for fleetwide fuel economy improvement, building on the status of the new-car fleet in a base year (1990) for which average vehicle size and performance are maintained. The analysis was corroborated by engineering modeling and by comparisons to the 1992 Honda Civic VX, which demonstrated a 56 to 85 percent fuel economy improvement over a previous model of the same size and performance.

DeCicco and Ross (1993) developed a range of estimates, reflecting the uncertainties surrounding new applications of technology:

- Level 1 technologies are already in production in at least one mass market vehicle worldwide and face no technical risk in that they are fully demonstrated and available.

- Level 2 technologies are ready for commercialization and face no technical constraints that might inhibit their use in production vehicles but entail some risk because of limited production experience.

- Level 3 technologies are in advanced stages of development but may face some technical constraints (such as emissions control considerations) before widespread application.

Technical risk is interpreted as the risk that a technology cannot be put into widespread use within a given time horizon at acceptably low cost (full-production-scale average cost). For options better characterized by degree of design refinement, such as aerodynamic improvements or weight reduction, the higher levels are successively less conservative regarding the degree of improvement. Table 4-2 summarizes the estimates; details on the technologies, their efficiency benefits, and their costs are given by DeCicco and Ross (1993).

Accurately estimating the cost of improving fuel economy is difficult because of limitations in publicly available data and costing methodologies. Table 4-2 includes estimates of the incremental retail costs of improved, mature technology averaged over its full period

Table 4-2

Average Fuel Economy and Cost Estimates for Potential New-Car Fleet (1995$)

	Technology Certainty		
	Level 1	Level 2	Level 3
Achievable new-car fuel economy (MPG)	39	45	51
Implied new light-truck MPG	30	34	38
Implied overall new-fleet MPG	35	40	45
Improvement over 1990 new fleet (%)	41	60	82
Average added cost per car ($)	560	690	820
Average cost of conserved energy ($/gal)	0.51	0.50	0.50
Marginal cost of conserved energy ($/gal)	1.46	1.48	1.62

Source: DeCicco & Ross (1993), updated to 1995$ using 4% cumulative inflation.
Note: Fuel economy values are the EPA composite 55% city, 45% highway unadjusted test ratings. Cost-effectiveness estimates are based on a 5% real discount rate and 12-year, 10,000 mi/yr vehicle life.

of production. The cost of conserved energy (CCE) is the ratio of incremental technology cost to discounted fuel savings over the life of an improved vehicle. The CCE is an index of cost-effectiveness from the perspective of all consumers (all owners over the car's lifetime rather than only the new-car buyer). A level of technically feasible fuel economy is cost-effective if its marginal CCE is less than the future cost of gasoline expected over the life of the improved vehicles. As summarized in Table 4-2, the estimated cost-effective new-car-fleet averages are 39 MPG, 45 MPG, and 51 MPG (41 percent, 60 percent, and 82 percent higher than the 1990 average), at certainty levels 1, 2, and 3, respectively. The average cost of achieving level 3 is $820 per car. The marginal CCE is $1.62/gal, if fuel savings are discounted at a 5 percent real rate over a 12-year vehicle life. (Cost estimates are presented here in 1995$ unless otherwise noted.)

The DeCicco and Ross (1993) analysis was done only for passenger cars, not for light trucks, which now account for 40 percent of new light-vehicle sales. NRC (1992) also estimated potential light-truck fuel economy increases proportionate to those for cars. Greene and Duleep (1993) estimated potential light-truck fuel economy increases slightly less than proportionate to those for cars. At least 80 percent of light-truck usage is strictly for personal transportation (Bureau of the Census 1990). Light-truck fuel economy has been more leniently regulated than that of cars; the main sources of inefficiency are the same as in cars; and the new light-truck fleet has lower utilization rates for efficient technologies. Therefore, in projecting potential future overall efficiency potential, we assume that light-truck fuel economy can be increased proportionately to that of cars at similar incremental cost. If the above assumptions and the recent overall (car plus light truck) new-fleet average of 25 MPG are used as a base, we obtain potential new-fleet averages of 35 MPG, 40 MPG, and 45 MPG for certainty levels 1, 2, and 3, respectively.

Renewable Ethanol

Although ethanol production from crops such as corn is an established industry in the United States, this product is neither economic at current oil prices nor renewable according to the working definition adopted here. However, a growing literature points to the potential for a competitive industry producing renewable ethanol from cellulosic biomass (DOE 1993, Lynd et al. 1991). Further analysis regarding the potential emergence of such a cellulosic ethanol industry is presented by Lynd in Chapter 5 of this volume and in greater detail by Lynd et al. (1995). In general, the rate at which ethanol might enter the fuels market depends on the relative prices of ethanol and gasoline as well as on the rate at which a biomass ethanol industry could expand given favorable economics.

Relative Price

Primary factors influencing the future cost of cellulosic ethanol are feedstock cost, plant scale, level of technological maturity, and cost of capital. Production volume (annual gallons produced nationwide) is a key determinant of three of these factors:

- *The cost of biomass feedstocks,* because higher-cost feedstocks will be needed at higher production volumes

- *Plant scale,* because larger plants can be expected as the technology matures and as production shifts from wastes to energy crops

- *The cost of capital,* because the technical and business risk will decrease as the ethanol market expands

Production volume depends on time and the prices of ethanol, gasoline, and other competing fuels. A key determinant of future decreases in the cost of producing cellulosic ethanol is the impact of R&D, which in turn depends on its level of effort, the extent of success, and time. Moreover, policy choices as well as market forces affect both R&D and relative fuel prices.

Corn ethanol now sells for about $1.20/gal ($1.80/gge), and current-technology cellulosic production would probably sell for a similar price (DOE 1993). Our analysis assumes that the cost of producing ethanol progressively declines to $0.50/gal, the likely production cost for mature technology estimated by Lynd et al. (1995). ("Production cost" here refers to recovery of operating costs and return on investments; the selling price would be dictated by market conditions.) We represent the pace of progress by two cases summarized in Table 4-3. Case A involves a continuation of the current R&D effort; Case B involves an accelerated effort.

In Case A, the production cost (independent of feedstock and at constant scale) is assumed to decrease by 3 percent per year, so that the ethanol price drops to $0.88/gal by 2005 and reaches the $0.50/gal level by 2025. In Case B, accelerated R&D results in a mature biomass ethanol conversion technology being available for incorporation into production facilities in 2005. The industry-average production cost then decreases over the years 2005–2010 as average plant size increases; new technology displaces older, less efficient plant technology; and the cost of energy crops decreases (also driven by R&D). Thus, in Case B, we assume a very rapid price drop of 6 percent per

Table 4-3

Projected Price and Production Quantity for Cases of Cellulosic Ethanol Industry Expansion (1995$)

Year	Case A (Current R&D)		Case B (Accelerated R&D)	
	Price ($/gal)	Quantity (10^9 gal/yr)	Price ($/gal)	Quantity (10^9 gal/yr)
2005	0.88	0.7	0.65	2.0
2010	0.76	1.3	0.50	4.2
2015	0.65	2.7	0.50	15.0
2020	0.56	7.4	0.50	27.0
2025	0.50	19.0	0.50	40.0
2030	0.50	31.0	0.50	53.0

Note: For price, starting from a current value of $1.20/gal, case A assumes a 3%/yr decline and case B assumes a 6%/yr decline until reaching the $0.50/gal estimate of Lynd et al. (1995). For quantities, projections were made as described in the text.

year, so that the $0.50/gal level is reached by 2010. Case B achieves mature, "advanced technology" production status roughly 15 years sooner than Case A. These prices represent plant sales; the $0.50/gal of ethanol corresponds to $0.76/gge, properly comparable to the wholesale price of gasoline, which averaged $0.60/gal in 1995. Assuming a $0.14/gal distribution cost, similar to that for today's gasoline, brings the pre-tax end-user cost to $0.90/gge (versus $0.74/gal for gasoline in 1995). If used in dedicated (near-neat) ethanol vehicles, the 10 percent efficiency benefit would lower the effective cost to $0.83/gge.

Replacing gasoline with alternative fuels involves transition barriers and costs arising from immature technology, supplier and consumer unfamiliarity, new operational complexities and training needs, higher costs of capital, less realization of economies of scale, lack of available infrastructure, and other factors (see Singh and Mintz in Chapter 6 of this volume). Cellulosic ethanol has a number of attributes implying lower transition costs than most other alternative fuels. Low-cost waste feedstocks may be utilized during early stages of market expansion. The gasohol and oxygenates markets provide a high base of established distribution infrastructure. The costs of expanding this infrastructure would be predictable and relatively low. A transition to ethanol could be less costly than that for most other alternative fuels, but further analysis is needed to estimate such costs in detail.

Expansion Rate

Even with strong economic or regulatory incentives, other factors would still constrain the rate at which cellulosic ethanol production capacity could be expanded. Such constraints include the rate of feedstock development, the availability of capital, the availability of expertise (for example, to design and build plants), and limits in fuel distribution and vehicle infrastructure. This issues present a worthy subject for future analysis.

Approximately 1 billion gallons of corn ethanol capacity were developed between the late 1970s and late 1980s. A higher growth rate should be possible for cellulosic ethanol; such an expansion can build on the foundation provided by an existing fuel ethanol industry, whereas this was not the case for corn ethanol. For 2005, therefore, we use an annual capacity estimate of 2 billion gallons for cellulosic ethanol under Case B (accelerated R&D) and adopt a lower estimate of 0.7 billion gallons for Case A (current R&D).

Accelerated R&D could permit commercial plants to achieve large cost reductions by 2005, resulting in lower ethanol prices and therefore higher production capacity growth. We assume a 22 percent compounded rate of growth from 2 billion gallons to 15 billion gallons of annual ethanol capacity over a 10-year period from 2005 to 2015. This 7.5-fold increase over a decade would correspond to tripling the number of plants together with a 2.5-fold increase in the average capacity of new plants. For capacities above 15 billion gallons, we assume a constant expansion rate of 2.5 billion gallons per year, resulting in 40 billion gallons of annual capacity by 2025 in Case B.

For Case A, we assume a lower-capacity growth rate of 10 percent per year after 2005, consistent with fewer R&D-driven improvements than for Case B. In our policy discussion (see below), we specify R&D expenditures of approximately $800 million over an 8-year period. It would take a considerable amount of time for an R&D effort of this magnitude to be mounted on the basis of the ethanol sales in Case A. The 10 percent growth rate is assumed until 2010; then the growth rate increases by 1 percent per year, up to 22 percent in 2022. As with Case B, annual capacity increases are capped at 2.5 billion gallons. Table 4-3 summarizes the projected availability of ethanol derived from cellulosic conversion technologies for the two cases outlined here.

Although not incorporated into our analysis, combining advanced ethanol production technology with electric power cogeneration promises even greater benefits. For example, combined-cycle gas turbines would utilize biomass feedstock residues to generate process heat and electricity plus excess electricity to sell to the grid. The resulting plant could displace both gasoline and fossil-based electricity, providing even better economics and exceptionally low GHG performance overall.

Technical Compatibility and Criteria Emissions Issues

Achieving more reliable cold-start performance had been considered a technical concern for use of ethanol in conventional vehicles. However, this problem can be solved with adequate engineering; cold-start problems have been resolved for E85 (a mixture of 85 percent ethanol and 15 percent gasoline), but not yet for pure ethanol (Lynd et al. 1991). Neat ethanol has been widely used as a motor fuel in Brazil.

Data on real-world, in-use emissions of regulated pollutants are woefully limited, a knowledge gap that is only recently beginning to be remedied. Standardized emissions tests of ethanol vehicles have produced mixed results. As for oxygenates generally, ethanol is expected to help reduce carbon monoxide emissions. However, gasohol can have increased volatility, aggravating evaporative emissions; such volatility problems do not occur if ethanol is converted to ETBE for use as an oxygenate (EIA 1994). In any case, many of the most important issues in real-world emissions control, such as off-cycle and malfunction emissions, are likely to be similar for any hydrocarbon fuel. Qualitatively speaking, it is unlikely that a given level of emissions control would be more difficult to achieve with ethanol than with gasoline, and in dedicated vehicles, ethanol may facilitate emissions control.

Ethanol could also be used in hybrid vehicles and in fuel cell vehicles, either of which may offer large benefits in pollution control as well as greater energy efficiency. For use in a fuel cell, pure hydrogen offers the highest efficiency and methanol the next highest; ethanol would have a somewhat lower efficiency because it requires a partial oxidation convertor (Williams et al. 1995). However, fuel distribution and storage advantages may counterbalance the efficiency penalty. Thus, expanded use of renewable ethanol is unlikely to be a dead-end strategy, and it could augment the efficiency-driven oil consumption and emissions reductions associated with leap-forward technologies of the future.

Analysis

Our analysis covers the period from 1995 through 2030, with particular attention to results for 2005 and 2015. A baseline projection of light-vehicle fuel use and GHG emissions incorporates assumptions about VMT growth and vehicle efficiency in the absence of policy change or dramatic technology breakthroughs entering the market. Light-duty vehicles are taken to include passenger cars and two-axle, four-tire light trucks as reported in the Federal Highway Administration's *Highway Statistics* (FHWA 1992). We use a stock turnover model to account for vehicle replacement and retirement, assuming that vehicle sales and the size of the stock grow in proportion to VMT (as in DeCicco 1995).

Light-duty VMT was 1.989×10^{12} mi/yr in 1990. We forecast VMT growth using the model of Greene et al. (1995) and an assumed 1 percent/yr real-fuel-price increase between 1995 and 2030, essentially an extension of the EIA (1995a) reference fuel price projection. The result is quite similar to a VMT forecast developed for "Car Talk."[1] Figure 4-1 illustrates this baseline VMT forecast, showing the steady growth in

Figure 4-1

Past and Projected Light-Duty Vehicle-Miles of Travel (VMT) in the United States, 1950–2030

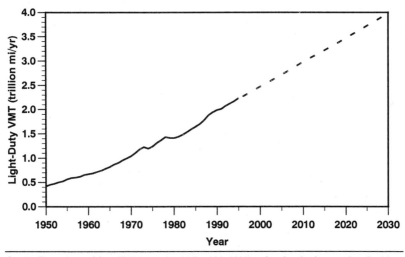

Source: Through 1995: from FHWA (1992, 1995). 1996–2030: authors' projections as described in the text.

[1] "Car Talk" was a colloquial name for the Policy Dialog Advisory Committee to Assist in the Development of Measures to Significantly Reduce Greenhouse Gas Emissions from Personal Motor Vehicles, which met from September 1994 to September 1995; see Resolve (1995) and *Majority Report* (1995).

travel demand that must be offset by improved technology absent drastic increases in the price of driving.

Baseline new light-vehicle fuel economy is assumed to be constant at 25 MPG (EPA unadjusted composite city/highway average for cars and light trucks), which has been the average within ±0.9 MPG from 1982 through 1995. A frozen efficiency assumption is consistent with low gasoline price growth and Corporate Average Fuel Economy (CAFE) standards being currently binding and not raised further. Given market imperfections, this assumption does not contradict the estimates of the potential for cost-effective efficiency improvements given in Table 4-2. Past achievements of policy-driven energy efficiency improvements at relatively low cost refute the notion of a well-functioning market for vehicle efficiency. Such evidence for market failure has been observed in markets for a number of energy-using products (Levine et al. 1994).

The model's 1990 levels are fuel energy consumption of 13 Quads (10^{15} Btu) or 104.4×10^9 gge (billion gallons of gasoline equivalent) and GHG emissions of 343 MT_C (million metric tonnes of carbon equivalent; all energy and volume levels are annual values). The fuel consumption includes 1.1×10^9 gal (0.73×10^9 gge) of ethanol from corn, which is blended with some of the gasoline to provide gasohol, and 103.7×10^9 gal of gasoline from petroleum and other feedstocks. We assume a baseline projection of corn ethanol use constant at 1.1×10^9 gal, the 1992 level reported by EIA (1994, Table 14). Each gallon of ethanol available for blending displaces 0.66 gal of gasoline, based on the ratio of lower heating values. With a 10 percent volumetric blend (typical of gasohol), the volumetric fuel economy of a vehicle is 3.4 percent lower than when operating on pure gasoline.

Although ethanol in principle can be blended up to 15 percent without detracting from gasoline vehicle performance (other than the lower volumetric fuel economy), we hold the blend level to 10 percent in our analysis. Thus, we first apply cellulosic ethanol to back out corn ethanol in blends; once the baseline volume of ethanol for gasohol is reached, remaining ethanol production is used to expand the low-level blend pool, either in the form of gasohol or as ETBE oxygenated gasoline. Finally, once a 10 percent level is reached nationwide, additional capacity is assumed to go to dedicated- or flexible-fuel vehicles.

Our analysis does not explicitly treat alternative or replacement fuels (including oxygenates) other than ethanol. Other analyses (such as DOE 1995a and EIA 1995a) indicate that, although some increases in alternative fuels will occur in the absence of new policies, the expected nationwide effects will be quite small. This simplified baseline suffices for our objective of examining the effects of two particular factors, efficiency improvement and cellulosic ethanol substitution.

The accounting model constructed for this analysis allows us to vary assumptions regarding policy-driven vehicle efficiency improvements and ethanol production capacity expansions. New-fleet (combined car and light truck) fuel economy improvements are assumed to start in 1998 and to continue linearly at various assumed rates up to 6 percent per year. Over a 10-year period, the highest rate implies a 60 percent improvement in new-fleet fuel economy, reaching 40 MPG (level 2 in Table 4-2). Improvements continue up to a maximum of 45 MPG (level 3 in Table 4-2). Thus, efficiency improvements are constrained to those achievable through incremental refinements of conventional-vehicle technology. Renewable-fuels use is analyzed with the two cases given in Table 4-3, for lower and higher (accelerated) rates of capacity expansion for cellulosic ethanol production. Renewable-fuels use is thus constrained by projected fuel production capacity.

We did not estimate the numbers of alcohol vehicles needed, although vehicle numbers could be inferred from the fuel use projections. DOE (1995a) applied vehicle choice modeling to examine how varying assumptions about the availability and costs of alternative fuels and vehicles would affect market equilibrium, leaving aside transition issues. The study found that vehicles fueled by alcohols and liquified petroleum gas (LPG) could sustain significant market shares (15 to 20 percent of the light-duty stock) in 2010, depending on the relative pricing of fuels. Ethanol would have a significant share if its current tax subsidy were retained. As shown below, our projected fuel use shares by 2010 are lower than those estimated by DOE (1995a). Thus, given competitive fuel pricing, vehicle choice considerations would not limit ethanol use at the production capacity–constrained levels examined here.

Results

Our model's baseline forecast is for light-vehicle fuel use rising to 136×10^9 gge by 2005 and 161×10^9 gge by 2015, increases of 30 percent and 54 percent, respectively, over the 1990 level. Baseline GHG emissions show a similar rise, to 444 MT_C by 2005 and 526 MT_C by 2015, compared with a 1990 level of 343 MT_C.

Figure 4-2 shows the results of attempting to control GHG emissions by using efficiency improvement only. The change in light-vehicle GHG emissions from the 1990 level is shown as a function of

---

Figure 4-2

**Projected Change from 1990 Level of Light-Vehicle
Greenhouse Gas (GHG) Emissions in 2005 and 2015 as
Function of Fuel Efficiency Improvement Rate**

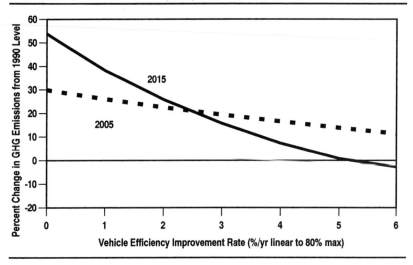

the new-fleet fuel economy improvement rate. Fuel efficiency improvement is modeled linearly, indicated as a percentage of the 1990 average (25 MPG); for example, a 4 percent/yr improvement implies a 1 MPG/yr increase in the new-fleet average, starting in 1998. Fuel economy levels are capped at 45 MPG, which, for example, would be reached in 20 years (by 2018) with a 4 percent/yr improvement rate. Stock turnover limitations constrain the reductions achievable within one decade. At the rates considered here (up to 6 percent/yr), efficiency improvement alone cannot return light-vehicle GHG emissions to the 1990 level by 2005. As shown in Figure 4-2, however, another 10 years makes a big difference, since about 90 percent of the vehicle stock is replaced over the course of a decade. Thus, an efficiency improvement rate of roughly 5 percent/yr will suffice to return light-vehicle GHG emissions to the 1990 level by 2015.

Combining vehicle efficiency improvement with renewable ethanol use increases the gasoline savings and GHG reductions. Table 4-4 summarizes scenarios using three rates of fuel economy improvement (0 percent/yr, 3 percent/yr, and 6 percent/yr) with lower (Case A) and higher (Case B) ethanol production levels. Figure 4-3 plots the resulting changes in year 2015 GHG emissions compared with the 1990 level as a function of efficiency improvement

Table 4-4

Summary Results from Scenarios of Fuel Economy Improvement and Increased Use of Cellulosic Ethanol in U.S. Light-Duty Vehicles

Baseline Projections (years)	1990	2005	2015	2025
Gasoline consumption (10^9 gal/yr)	104	136	161	186
GHG emissions (MTc/yr)	343	444	526	608

Projected Changes in Gasoline Use, Greenhouse Gas (GHG) Emissions, and Renewable Fuel Share:

(A) Lower-Ethanol-Capacity Case (year)	2005	2015	2025
Ethanol production (10^9gal/yr)	0.7	2.7	19
No fuel economy improvement			
Gasoline consumption versus baseline	−0.3%	−1.1%	−6.8%
GHG emissions versus 1990 level	30.0%	52.0%	66.0%
Renewable fuel share	0.3%	1.1%	6.8%
3% (0.75 MPG)) per year improvement			
Gasoline consumption versus baseline	−9.0%	−26.0%	−44.0%
GHG emissions versus 1990 level	19.0%	14.0%	0.0%
Renewable fuel share	0.4%	1.5%	10.7%
6% (1.5 MPG) per year improvement			
Gasoline consumption versus baseline	−15.0%	−38.0%	−48.0%
GHG emissions versus 1990 level	11.0%	−5.0%	−7.0%
Renewable fuel share	0.4%	1.8%	11.4%

(B) Higher-Ethanol-Capacity Case (year)	2005	2015	2025
Ethanol production (10^9gal/yr)	2	15	40
No fuel economy improvement			
Gasoline consumption versus baseline	−1.0%	−6.0%	−15.2%
GHG emissions versus 1990 level	30.0%	45.0%	53.0%
Renewable fuel share	1.0%	6.0%	14.0%
3% (0.75 MPG) per year improvement			
Gasoline consumption versus baseline	−9.0%	−31.0%	−52.0%
GHG emissions versus 1990 level	19.0%	7.0%	−14.0%
Renewable fuel share	1.0%	8.0%	23.0%
6% (1.5 MPG) per year improvement			
Gasoline consumption versus baseline	−15.0%	−43.0%	−57.0%
GHG emissions versus 1990 level	11.0%	−12.0%	−21.0%
Renewable fuel share	1.0%	9.0%	24.0%

Figure 4-3

Projected Change from 1990 Level of Light-Vehicle Greenhouse Gas (GHG) Emissions in 2015 by Ethanol Production Case and Fuel Efficiency Improvement Rate

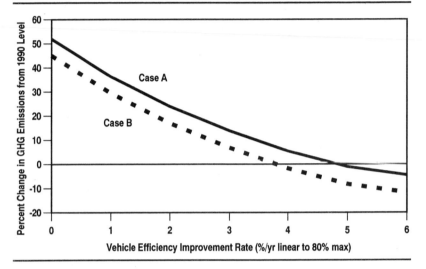

rate. The two curves correspond to the lower and higher biofuels production cases. In 2015, Case A is little different from the efficiency-only case of Figure 4-2, since only 2.7 billion gallons of ethanol (1.1 percent of 2015 baseline fuel consumption on an energy-equivalent basis) are available. With accelerated R&D (Case B), 15 billion gallons of ethanol, or 6 percent of the baseline energy requirement, are provided by 2015, allowing return of emissions to the 1990 level with an efficiency improvement rate of just under 4 percent/yr. In other words, the difference between the lower and higher renewable-ethanol cases shaves roughly 1 percent/yr from the vehicle efficiency improvement rate needed for a 2015 GHG emissions return target.

Table 4-4 shows that projected 2005 gasoline use is 9 percent lower than the baseline for the 0.75 MPG/yr (3 percent/yr) efficiency increase rate for either ethanol production case. Meeting a targeted 10 percent reduction in light-vehicle oil use by 2005 would require a slightly faster efficiency improvement, since even the higher ethanol production case only contributes 1.3×10^9 gge toward the requisite 13.6×10^9 gge reduction. (This analysis ignores other alternative fuels, including nonpetroleum inputs used in gasoline production.) Improving new-fleet fuel economy 6 percent/yr would cut 15 percent from

2005 light-vehicle gasoline use compared with the baseline projection of 136×10^9 gge.

Figure 4-4 shows the share of 2015 light-vehicle fuel consumption that can be met by renewable ethanol for the lower- and higher-production cases. The renewable share increases as a function of the underlying vehicle efficiency improvement. Year 2015 production capacity is small in Case A, amounting to less than 2 percent of light-vehicle energy needs even with a 6 percent/yr efficiency improvement. In Case B, the 15×10^9 gallons (9.6×10^9 gge) of ethanol available by 2015 imply a 6 percent renewable share even without efficiency improvement. With the 6 percent/yr new-fleet efficiency improvement working to reduce the overall fuel energy requirements, Case B provides just over 9 percent of the market—a significant portion, but still shy of a 15 percent renewable share in 2015.

Just as lags in stock turnover make a large difference in what efficiency improvement can accomplish by 2005 versus 2015, constraints in ethanol capacity expansion make a large difference in the impacts of fuel substitution between 2015 and later years. Figure 4-5 shows, for the scenario of lower ethanol production (Case A) and no vehicle efficiency increase, shares of the overall U.S. light-vehicle fuel use for ethanol in blends (gasohol or oxygenate); renewable

---

Figure 4-4

Renewable Share of Light-Vehicle Fuel Consumption in 2015 by Ethanol Production Case and Fuel Efficiency Improvement Rate

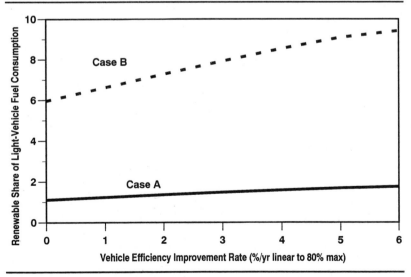

Figure 4-5

Future Shares of Light-Vehicle Fuels Market for Case A Cellulosic Ethanol Production and No Fuel Economy Improvement

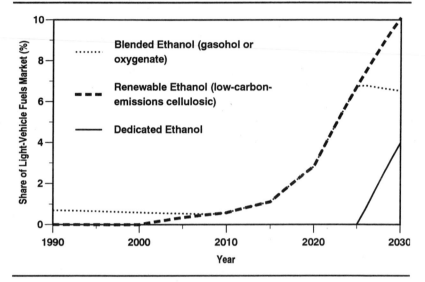

Figure 4-6

Future Shares of Light-Vehicle Fuel Market for Case B Cellulosic Ethanol Production and 6 Percent per Year Fuel Economy Improvement

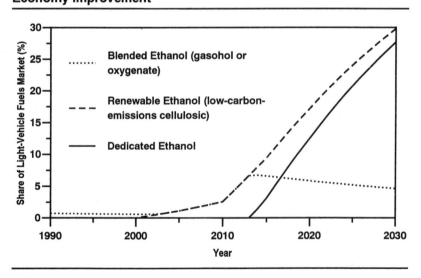

ethanol (low-carbon emissions cellulosic as opposed to corn based); and ethanol use in dedicated vehicles. The same items are shown in Figure 4-6 for the scenario of higher ethanol production (Case B) and a 6 percent/yr vehicle efficiency increase (note that the vertical scale in Figure 4-6 is three times that in Figure 4-5). In Figure 4-5, the renewable energy share is only 1.1 percent by 2015, when cellulosic ethanol capacity expansion is just beginning to take off, and a 10 percent share is not reached until 2030. The fuels market is not saturated with blended ethanol until nearly 2025, after which dedicated vehicles would be needed to utilize the ethanol production capacity. In contrast, Figure 4-6 shows how rapid efficiency improvement coupled with accelerated biofuel production capacity expansion would yield a renewable share of nearly 10 percent by 2015 and a substantial share in later years, nearly 30 percent by 2030. Even in this more ambitious scenario, the renewable share is just starting to rapidly climb in 2010, and widespread use of dedicated vehicles only begins in 2013. The blended-ethanol share falls once dedicated vehicles come into play, since the gasoline fuel market in which blends can be used is then shrinking.

Our principal results are summarized in Figure 4-7, which shows projected baseline light-vehicle GHG emissions plus an ethanol-only scenario (Case B), an efficiency-only scenario (6 percent/yr improvement), and a scenario combining these two approaches. Note that our scenarios do not allow for a progressive decline in gasoline consumption or GHG emissions, since vehicle efficiency improvement is capped at 45 MPG. Ongoing efficiency improvements, most likely requiring advanced technology, would be able to sustain a declining trend, especially if combined with an increasing use of renewable fuel. Results are also, of course, sensitive to VMT growth and the success of efforts to control it.

In any scenario, once the assumed 10 percent volumetric blending limit is reached, use in flexible-fuel or dedicated vehicles would have to rapidly rise in order to keep pace with growth in renewable ethanol production capacity expansion. Although flexible-fuel vehicles are one way to ease the transition, addressing issues associated with greatly expanded use of ethanol in high-level blends is beyond the scope of our work. Our analysis shows that ethanol production capacity is the binding constraint for the next two decades or longer (depending on the degree of vehicle efficiency improvement). Subsequently, expansion could be constrained by vehicle and fuel availability barriers to nongasoline fuel use. However, by that time, an extensive nationwide bulk ethanol distribution network would have been put into place for serving the blended-fuel market. Thus, one major

Figure 4-7

Projected U.S. Light-Vehicle Greenhouse Gas (GHG) Emissions Under Various Scenarios of Efficiency Improvement and Cellulosic Ethanol Use

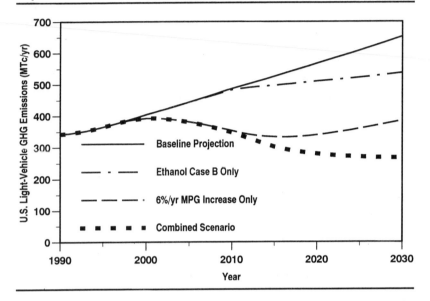

barrier would be greatly reduced, easing the way toward dedicated ethanol fuel use.

A Comment on Costs

Although a full cost-benefit analysis is beyond the scope of this chapter, the technology assessments reviewed above do provide cost estimates for improving fuel economy and supplying cellulosic ethanol. These estimates can be compared with the gasoline price plus its indirect and externality costs associated with energy security and GHG emissions.

For reference, the pre-tax price of gasoline was $0.74/gal in 1995, including roughly $0.14/gal for distribution and marketing costs (EIA 1995b). OTA (1994, 127–128) summarized estimates of the economic and military costs associated with oil imports, which range from $0.26 to $0.63 per gallon (updated to 1995$). OTA's estimates of the GHG emissions externality ranged from $0.03 to $0.32 per gallon. The upper end of this range essentially matches that implied by a carbon tax of $92 per ton (carbon-mass basis). This value falls in the middle of the very wide range of estimates based on carbon sequestration through forest plantings, which Pace University (1990, 165–185) reviewed as ranging from $2/ton for projects in Central America up to $200/ton for forest plantations in North America. Including the midrange value of $0.44/gal for oil import economic and military costs plus $0.32/gal for GHG emissions yields $0.76/gal as an externality for gasoline. Thus, including these social costs essentially doubles the current pre-tax price of gasoline in the United States, bringing the current avoidable cost to $1.50/gal. EIA (1995a) gives a 2010 reference case gasoline price projection of $1.46/gal (1995$) including taxes; deducting the $0.44 of taxes implies an underlying price of $1.02/gal. Including social costs of $0.76/gal brings the estimated 2010 avoidable cost of gasoline to $1.78/gal (1995$), providing a point of comparison for the costs of fuel conservation and renewable fuel supply.

The cost estimates for vehicle efficiency and cellulosic ethanol supply, summarized in Tables 4-2 and 4-3, respectively, provide some of the inputs that would be needed for a cost-benefit analysis. Basic cost comparisons do suggest the likely cost-effectiveness of the scenarios presented here. The estimated marginal cost of energy saved through vehicle efficiency improvements is $1.62/gal. The estimated end-user cost of mature cellulosic ethanol is $0.83–$0.90/gge (including distribution costs). Both of these compare favorably to a projected 2010 gasoline cost of $1.78/gal including energy security and global warming externalities. Note that our renewable ethanol cost is premised on research-driven technology advances; by contrast, our vehicle efficiency cost assumes use of technology that is already largely available. Since efficiency R&D initiatives like PNGV are underway, we expect a drop in the future cost of achieving a given level of efficiency improvement. On the other hand, the current level of R&D commitment to cellulosic ethanol appears low compared with the potential of this technology; timely realization of its benefits would require an expanded development program, such as that premised by Case B.

Policy Needs

Strong institutional and market forces sustain the petroleum-based design of current personal transportation vehicles in the United States and throughout the world. Public policy guidance is necessary to effect changes such as those envisioned here, as for any changes toward a system substantially less resource-consumptive and environmentally damaging.

Whatever approach is taken to addressing transportation energy issues, strong and sustained public and private R&D programs are important. The Partnership for a New Generation of Vehicles, announced in 1993, highlights R&D for advancing fuel economy. PNGV's goal 3 of tripling fuel economy goes beyond the incremental efficiency improvements on which we base our analysis. However, PNGV's goal 1, advancing competitive manufacturing capabilities, and goal 2, developing technologies useful for near-term efficiency and emissions control improvements, support, at least in principle, efficiency improvements of the timing and magnitude illustrated here. On the fuels side, current R&D efforts are less concerted than the PNGV. An expanded R&D effort targeting low-GHG fuels is, therefore, part of a strategy needed to realize scenarios such as those illustrated here. Cellulosic ethanol is a promising option for a low-GHG renewable fuel; other promising options include biomass-derived methanol and hydrogen (particularly suitable for fuel cell vehicles). A new-fuels R&D program should address all promising options.

R&D makes new technology available, but adoption of new technology depends on the market, which currently does not value reductions in either GHG emissions or petroleum use. Policies that cause the market to value such external benefits are likely to be necessary to motivate adoption of new technologies in ways that achieve such benefits. Moreover, the technology pull exerted by a policy-guided market can greatly enhance the success of R&D.

For advancing vehicle efficiency, CAFE standards have demonstrated their effectiveness (including substantial net economic savings), and they are likely to be effective again. Indeed, the CAFE standards drew improved conventional-vehicle technologies—products of private sector R&D—into the market, contributing to the 47 percent improvement in on-road car and light-truck efficiency achieved between 1975 and 1993 (DOE 1995b). The historical experience with standards is most encouraging, for motor vehicles as well as other energy-using products (Geller & Nadel 1994). Ramping standards up to levels identified as being technically feasible and cost-effective would reliably yield vehicle efficiency improvements, gasoline savings, and emissions reductions (DeCicco 1995). The main obstacles are political, given the waxing influence of antiregulatory rhetoric and continuing auto industry objections to stronger standards.

Policies complementary to standards include fees and rebates ("feebates") linked to vehicle efficiency, market creation programs for efficient vehicles, technology R&D, and higher gasoline taxes (which can be designed to offset other taxes). These mechanisms can be structured to motivate both vehicle efficiency and renewable-fuels use. For example, full-fuel-cycle GHG emissions per mile could be used as a basis for vehicle-oriented policies. Higher gasoline taxes could be carbon based. Any of these approaches can be designed for revenue neutrality, so as to avoid a net increase in taxation. Nevertheless, given the limited experience with market mechanisms and the large uncertainties in response to pricing changes, only fuel economy standards, or equivalent approaches such as a regulatory cap on GHG emissions, are likely to provide the certainty needed to reach particular sustainability targets such as those examined here. A set of policies including stronger CAFE standards for both cars and light trucks, extending the gas guzzler tax to a system of largely revenue-neutral fees and rebates, and establishing voluntary market creation programs for efficient vehicles are among the recommendations of the "Car Talk" *Majority Report* (1995), which both authors endorsed.

Higher fuel prices can also help motivate vehicle efficiency improvement as well as reductions in vehicle use. However, the leverage offered by fuel pricing is far too weak to achieve the efficiency levels identified here without a drastic change in fiscal policies (DeCicco & Gordon 1995). Nevertheless, fuel-pricing policies would be valuable for orienting the market and can provide important leverage over fuel choices.

Price is the main barrier to expansion of cellulosic ethanol production capacity. Policy remedies include R&D to decrease the cost of production and providing price incentives to make ethanol competitive with gasoline. The "Car Talk" *Majority Report* (1995) recommended supporting R&D for liquid biofuels, particularly for cellulosic ethanol, by ramping federal biofuels R&D support from the recent level of $25 million per year up to $100 million per year by 1999 and sustaining that level through 2005.

The existing U.S. ethanol subsidy is $0.54/gal, or $0.82/gge. It costs about $650 million per year, about 25 times higher than current federal biofuels R&D spending. Successful R&D would lower the cost of producing ethanol, motivating producers to adopt improved processes and to begin using cellulosic feedstocks (initially from wastes). Nevertheless, if ethanol is valued at its energy content and gasoline prices rise no higher than the EIA (1995a) projections (roughly a 1 percent/yr increase), even our accelerated R&D scenario (Case B in Table 4-3) indicates that a subsidy would be needed through 2018, unless a carbon tax, GHG-based fuel composition standards, or similar measures were instituted. The *Majority Report* (1995) outlined a low-GHG fuels incentive program having the following elements:

- Subsidies proportional to a fuel's full-cycle GHG emissions factor, based on plant-by-plant auditing, available to all liquid and gaseous fuels; the subsidies (which could be either direct payments or tax waivers) would be capped at $180 per metric ton of carbon equivalent reduction compared with gasoline.

- Straight-line phase-out over 2000 through 2010 of the current ethanol subsidy, which would be capped at $650 million per year.

- An overall cap such that the combined expenditures for the fuel GHG reduction subsidy and the current ethanol tax incentive do not exceed $1.1 billion; this subsidy pool would be phased out over 2015 through 2025. Producers could obtain the larger, but not both, of the non-greenhouse-linked ethanol subsidy and the greenhouse-linked subsidy in any given year.

This proposed subsidy is applicable to any fuel, in contrast to the current tax incentive, which subsidizes ethanol no matter how it is produced and irrespective of its embodied fossil fuel use and GHG emissions. Subsidies would need to discriminate fuel deliveries according to their "pedigree" with respect to full-fuel-cycle GHG emissions. Production plant audits according to fossil energy inputs and other emissions could be part of a fuel producer's environmental accounting requirements. Such rating is feasible because of the generally large scale of production; for example, 75 percent of current U.S. ethanol production comes from four plants.

We have not attempted an economic analysis to estimate a market response to the proposed renewable-fuels incentives. For vehicle efficiency, stronger fuel economy standards would, if established, have a very high likelihood of yielding the targeted efficiency levels. In contrast, the impact of incentives is much more difficult to predict. Unlike fuel economy increases that rely mainly on technology already in production, achievement of the ethanol capacity levels requires R&D progress plus commercialization of new production processes, which are inherently difficult to predict. Although we cannot claim a quantitative link, a concerted program of R&D plus low-GHG fuel incentives would plausibly support achievement of the renewable-fuels utilization levels presented here.

This renewable-fuel policy package is designed to help build new fuels industries that, it is hoped, could eventually compete with petroleum refining even if only private market costs are considered. Although incentives such as these are needed to begin moving markets toward renewable fuels, they may not suffice for an ongoing and substantial transition of the U.S. transportation energy system. The long-term establishment of low-carbon, more environmentally benign fuels will probably require additional policy guidance. For example, achieving the substantial oil savings suggested by the combined efficiency and renewable-fuels scenarios identified here would depress the world oil price, particularly if the new technologies also diffused to global markets. Although clearly an economic boon to oil-importing countries like the United States, a lower oil price would make it even more difficult for new technologies to compete.

Such countervailing market forces, as well as general market barriers and imperfections, could be overcome by broad-based interventions, including fuel composition standards and a shift toward environmental taxation. Specifying such policies is beyond the scope of this chapter; however, we can indicate possibilities. Motor fuels have long been subject to composition standards, from privately developed quality standards to environmentally motivated standards such as the phase-out of lead and more recent reformulation standards addressing volatility, oxygenation, and lower sulfur content. This approach can be extended to standards specifying a maximum full-fuel-cycle GHG factor (for example, in grams of carbon-equivalent per joule of energy content), which could be implemented as an average cap on the national motor fuel pool. As in the case of vehicle efficiency, a regulatory approach has the advantage of predictability for achieving environmental goals; it would have the disadvantage of incrementalism, since standard setting is a conservative process in practice. Environmental taxation could entail carbon-based fuels taxes, as well as more general externalities taxes (such as national security costs associated with oil imports). Since even a relatively small transportation fuel tax involves substantial sums on a nationwide basis, environmental taxation is best pursued as part of a broader tax shifting strategy. Further analyses of all such options are needed.

Conclusion

Scenarios that combine vehicle efficiency improvements with increased use of a renewable fuel, specifically cellulosic ethanol, show that likely near- to medium-term national goals for oil displacement and reduction of GHG emissions are achievable without resorting to radical changes in vehicle technology. Although targets of 10 percent oil savings by 2005 and returning light-vehicle sector GHG emissions to their 1990 level by 2015 are in reach, a target of 15 percent renewable share by 2015 was not achieved in any of our scenarios. We did not perform a cost-benefit analysis, but the estimated current costs of fuel economy improvement and projected future costs of cellulosic ethanol appear to compare favorably to the cost of gasoline if environmental and energy import externalities are considered.

Technology-based improvements in vehicle efficiency and increases in renewable-fuels use are complementary strategies. Higher vehicle efficiency can alleviate some of the concerns associated with cellulosic ethanol use by reducing the land area needed for a given gasoline displacement and by reducing pollutant emissions during fuel production, distribution, and use. Both efficiency improvement and renewable-fuels use are constrained by time lags associated with their investment requirements—namely, putting more-efficient vehicle technologies into production and bringing new ethanol production capacity on line. The time periods of their respective constraints are staggered, however. Benefits of both approaches are limited by 2005. Substantial vehicle efficiency improvements can be realized by 2015, but 2015 is just when ethanol capacity expansions would start to have significant impacts. The picture changes dramatically between 2015 and 2025. By 2025, an accelerated ethanol capacity program could provide up to 26×10^9 gge (3.3 Quads) of very-low-GHG fuel; fuel economy increases of 1.5 MPG per year (up to 45 MPG) would cut fuel use by 41 percent (9.5 Quads) relative to the baseline. Combining the two approaches, U.S. light-vehicle gasoline consumption in 2025 would be cut by 57 percent from baseline growth, GHG emissions would be 21 percent below the 1990 level, and the renewable fuels share would be 24 percent.

For moving the United States toward a more sustainable light-duty vehicle transportation system, we identified technology improvements that would suffice to meet near-term goals of reduced petroleum consumption and GHG emissions. However, market forces alone are unlikely to spur sufficient applications of these technology advances—for higher fuel economy and a mature biofuels industry—even if supportive R&D efforts are pursued. A range of public policies, including sustained R&D, particularly for biofuels, plus a set of regulatory and incentive mechanisms for advancing both vehicle efficiency and renewable fuels in the marketplace, are needed to achieve progress as envisioned in our scenarios.

Acknowledgments

The authors thank Barry McNutt and Mark Delucchi for enlightening discussions and critical comments, as well as Martin Bernard and the anonymous reviewers for their comments and suggestions. We are also grateful to members of the "Car Talk" federal advisory committee, which provided a forum for ideas and a milieu that inspired this collaboration. We bear whole responsibility for the analyses, statements, and recommendations presented.

References

Bleviss, D.L. 1989. The Role of Energy Efficiency in Making the Transition to Nonpetroleum Transportation Fuels. In *Alternative Transportation Fuels: An Environmental and Energy Solution*, edited by D. Sperling. New York: Quorum Books.

Bureau of the Census. 1990. *Truck Inventory and Use Survey (TIUS), 1987 Census of Transportation*. Report TC87-T-52. Washington, D.C. August.

Davis, S.C. 1994. *Transportation Energy Data Book*. 14th ed. Report ORNL-6798. Oak Ridge, Tenn.: Oak Ridge National Laboratory. May.

DeCicco, J.M. 1995. Projected Fuel Savings and Emissions Reductions from Light Vehicle Fuel Economy Standards. *Transportation Research* 29A (3): 205–228.

DeCicco, J.M., and D. Gordon. 1995. Steering with Prices: Fuel and Vehicle Taxation as Market Incentives for Higher Fuel Economy. In *Transportation and Energy: Strategies for a Sustainable Transportation System*, edited by D. Sperling and S. Shaheen. Washington, D.C.: American Council for an Energy-Efficient Economy.

DeCicco, J.M., and M. Ross. 1993. *An Updated Assessment of the Near-Term Potential for Improving Automotive Fuel Economy*. Washington, D.C.: American Council for an Energy-Efficient Economy. November.

Delucchi, M.A. 1994. Personal communication.

DeLuchi, M.A. 1991. *Emissions of Greenhouse Gases from the Use of Transportation Fuels and Electricity*. Report ANL/ESD/TM-22. Argonne, Ill.: Argonne National Laboratory, Center for Transportation Research. November.

Energy and Environmental Analysis (EEA). 1991. *An Assessment of Potential Passenger Car Fuel Economy Objectives for 2010*. Report prepared for the U.S. Environmental Protection Agency. Arlington, Va.: Energy and Environmental Analysis, Inc. July.

Energy Information Administration (EIA). 1994. *Alternatives to Traditional Transportation Fuels: An Overview*. Report DOE/EIA-0585/O. Washington, D.C.: U.S. Department of Energy, Energy Information Administration. June.

_____. 1995a. *Annual Energy Outlook 1995, with Projections to 2010*. Report DOE/EIA-0383(95). Washington, D.C.: U.S. Department of Energy, Energy Information Administration. January.

_____. 1995b. *Monthly Energy Review, June 1995.* Washington, D.C.: U.S. Department of Energy, Energy Information Administration.

_____. 1995c. *Petroleum Supply Monthly, November 1995.* Washington, D.C.: U.S. Department of Energy, Energy Information Administration.

Federal Highway Administration (FHWA). 1992. *Highway Statistics 1991.* Report FHWA-PL-92-025. Washington, D.C.: Federal Highway Administration.

Geller, H., and S. Nadel. 1994. *Market Transformation Strategies to Promote End-Use Efficiency.* Washington, D.C.: American Council for an Energy-Efficient Economy. June.

Goldemberg, J., T.B. Johansson, A.K.N. Reddy, and R.H. Williams. 1988. *Energy for a Sustainable World.* New Delhi: Wiley Eastern.

Gray, C.A., and J.L. Alson. 1989. The Case for Methanol. *Scientific American* (Nov.): 108–114.

Greene, D.L., S.M. Chin, and R. Gibson. 1995. *Aggregate Vehicle Travel Forecasting Model.* Report ORNL-6872. Oak Ridge, Tenn.: Oak Ridge National Laboratory, Center for Transportation Analysis. May.

Greene, D.L., and K.G. Duleep. 1993. Costs and Benefits of Automotive Fuel Economy Improvement: A Partial Analysis. *Transportation Research* 27A (3): 217–235.

Greene, D.L., and P.N. Leiby. 1993. *The Social Costs to the U.S. of Monopolization of the World Oil Market, 1972–1991.* Report ORNL-6744. Oak Ridge, Tenn.: Oak Ridge National Laboratory. March.

Levine, M.D., E. Hirst, J.G. Koomey, J.E. McMahon, A.H. Sanstad. 1994. *Energy Efficiency, Market Failures, and Government Policy.* Report LBL-35376. Berkeley: Lawrence Berkeley Laboratory, Energy Analysis Program. March.

Lovins, A. 1995. Hypercars: The Next Industrial Revolution. In *Transportation and Energy: Strategies for a Sustainable Transportation System,* edited by D. Sperling and S.A. Shaheen. Washington, D.C.: American Council for an Energy-Efficient Economy.

Lynd, L.R., J.H. Cushman, R.J. Nichols, and C.E. Wyman. 1991. Fuel Ethanol from Cellulosic Biomass. *Science* 251 (15 March): 1318–1323.

Lynd, L.R., R.T. Elander, and C.E. Wyman. 1995. Likely Features and Costs of Mature Biomass Ethanol Technology. Paper presented at the 17th Symposium on Biotechnology for Fuels and Chemicals. Vail, Colo., May.

Majority Report to the President by the Policy Dialog Advisory Committee to Recommend 1995 Options for Reducing Greenhouse Gas Emissions from Personal Motor Vehicles. 1995. Washington, D.C.: U.S. Environmental Protection Agency, Air Docket. October.

McCarthy, P. 1995. How Government and Industry Can Cooperate to Promote Fuel Conservation: An Industry Perspective. In *Transportation and Energy: Strategies for a Sustainable Transportation System*, edited by D. Sperling and S.A. Shaheen. Washington, D.C.: American Council for an Energy-Efficient Economy.

National Research Council (NRC). 1992. *Automotive Fuel Economy: How Far Should We Go?* Report of the Committee on Fuel Economy of Automobiles and Light Trucks. Washington, D.C.: National Academy Press.

Office of Technology Assessment (OTA). 1991. *Improving Automobile Fuel Economy: New Standards, New Approaches*. Report OTA-E-504. Washington, D.C.: U.S. Congress, Office of Technology Assessment. October.

_____. 1994. *Saving Energy in U.S. Transportation*. Report OTA-ETI-589. Washington, D.C.: U.S. Congress, Office of Technology Assessment. July.

Organization for Economic Cooperation and Development (OECD). 1995. *Motor Vehicle Pollution: Reduction Strategies Beyond 2010*. Paris: Organization for Economic Cooperation and Development.

Pace University. 1990. *Environmental Costs of Electricity*. Report prepared by the Pace University Center for Environmental Legal Studies. New York: Oceana Publications.

Partnership for a New Generation of Vehicles (PNGV). 1994. *Partnership for a New Generation of Vehicles, Program Plan*. Washington, D.C.: U.S. Department of Commerce. July.

Resolve. 1995. *Policy Dialog Advisory Committee to Assist in the Development of Measures to Significantly Reduce Greenhouse Gas Emissions from Personal Motor Vehicles*. Interim Report to the President. Washington, D.C.: Resolve, Inc. March.

Ross, M., R. Goodwin, R. Watkins, M.Q. Wang, and T. Wenzel. 1995. *Real-World Emissions from Model Year 1993, 2000 and 2010 Passenger Cars*. Report for the Energy Foundation. Washington, D.C.: American Council for an Energy-Efficient Economy. November.

Sperling, D., ed. 1989. *Alternative Transportation Fuels: An Environmental and Energy Solution*. New York: Quorum Books.

U.S. Department of Energy (DOE). 1990 et seq. Assessment of Costs and Benefits of Flexible and Alternative Fuel Use in the U.S. Transportation Sector. Series of technical reports. Washington, D.C.: U.S. Department of Energy.

_____. 1993. *Assessment of Costs and Benefits of Flexible and Alternative Fuel Use in the U.S. Transportation Sector. Technical Report Eleven: Evaluation of a Potential Wood-to-Ethanol Process*. DOE/EP-0004. Washington, D.C.: U.S. Department of Energy. January.

_____. 1995a. *Briefing on EPACT 502b Study*. Washington, D.C.: U.S. Department of Energy, Office of Policy.

_____. 1995b. *Energy Conservation Trends*. Report DOE/PO-0034. Washington, D.C.: U.S. Department of Energy, Office of Policy. April.

Williams, R.H., E.D. Larson, R.E. Katofsky, and J. Chen. 1995. Methanol and Hydrogen from Biomass for Transportation. *Energy for Sustainable Development* 1 (5): 18–34.

Cellulose Ethanol: Technology in Relation to Environmental Goals and Policy Formulation

LEE R. LYND

Enhanced energy independence, reduced emissions of priority air pollutants, and the desirability of options that are sustainable with respect to greenhouse gas emissions as well as other criteria have motivated researchers, planners, and policymakers to consider a variety of alternative transportation fuels.

Lynd et al. (1991) and Wyman and Goodman (1993), among others, have pointed to cellulose ethanol as a leading option for a sustainable transportation fuel. Others see a more limited role for this alternative (Pimentel et al. 1994), and Sperling (1995) excludes it from the category of fuels that can lead to a sustainable transportation sector.

This chapter addresses cellulose ethanol production technology largely in terms of its inputs and outputs. In particular, the cost of cellulose ethanol production is examined, as well as environmental impacts and benefits for large-scale ethanol production with respect to greenhouse gas emissions, priority pollutant emissions, waste utilization, land use, and land availability. Findings are then discussed in relation to policy formulation and evaluation in terms of sustainable transportation goals.

Cost of Production

The term *cost of production* is used here to denote a calculated selling price based on operating costs plus an allowance for recovery of capital investment. The actual selling price would be dictated by market factors. Most analyses of the cost of cellulose ethanol have focused on near-term projects, with technology that incorporates few research-driven improvements. For example, the U.S. Department of Energy (Hinman et al. 1993, 639) projects production costs comparable to those for corn—on the order of $1.20/gallon (Ladisch & Schwandt 1992, II-4). However, a modern, full-scale cellulose ethanol plant has never been built, and thus projections of the cost and performance of such a facility are inherently uncertain. It is a mistake to assume that cellulose ethanol technology is technologically mature just because commercial opportunities for its application exist today (Wyman & Goodman 1993). Failure to use a consistent basis in terms of technological maturity is a key reason for the disparity in the conclusions of comparative studies.

In the evaluation of technological evolution, a technology is considered mature when further improvements are expected to offer only incremental cost reductions. Lynd, Elander, & Wyman (1996) examined the question, What are the likely features and cost of a facility producing ethanol from cellulosic biomass at a level of maturity comparable to a modern petroleum refinery? The methodology and results of this analysis are summarized below.

In forecasting mature biomass ethanol technology, Lynd, Elander, & Wyman (1996) examined cost reductions relative to current designs arising from three factors: increased scale, decreased feedstock cost, and improved conversion technology. Projecting cost impacts from future research and development (R&D) is, of course, challenging. Lynd and his colleagues considered two approaches. The first takes best values for individual process parameters from the literature and then assumes that through future R&D these can be realized simultaneously. The second approach uses results reported in the literature in conjunction with judgment to establish a set of process parameters that are less than or equal to the best values used in the first approach. The first, best-parameter approach indicates the potential for R&D-driven cost reductions. The second, advanced-technology approach indicates the author's best estimate of the most likely features of mature technology.

Scale

A scale of 2.7 million dry tons (dry basis) per day of a short-rotation poplar feedstock is assumed, corresponding to the roughly 330-million-gallon annual capacity of today's largest corn ethanol plants. This capacity requires that 10 percent of the area within a 50-mile radius be devoted to biomass energy crops (neglecting any contribution from wastes) at a productivity of 5 tons/acre/year, with lower fractional areas at higher productivities.

Feedstock

For a mature biomass ethanol facility, it is reasonable to assume that technology for feedstock production will be similarly advanced. A cost of $38.60 per delivered dry ton is used for the advanced-technology scenario. This value corresponds to the average future cost value projected by Perlack and Wright (1995) based on projections in the 2020 time frame and assuming a threefold to fourfold increase in R&D expenditures. For the best-parameter scenario, a value of $34 per delivered dry ton is assumed, corresponding to the national average productivity goal of the Biofuels Feedstock Development Program (Cushman 1995). Lynd, Elander, & Wyman (1996) offer further justification for these feedstock cost values, observing that the notion of "mature" technology may be more applicable to conversion technology than to feedstock production.

Conversion Technology

Improvements in conversion technology very likely offer the largest cost reductions. This situation arises because the most expensive steps in biomass ethanol production—biological conversion, pretreatment, and the power cycle—also have the greatest potential for improvement through R&D. On the other hand, improvements in conversion technology are perhaps the most difficult to predict. Lynd, Elander, & Wyman (1996) consider improvements in biological conversion and pretreatment only, not improvements in other steps such as distillation, the power cycle, wastewater treatment, and tankage. Nevertheless, the potential exists for further technical improvements and cost reductions in the power cycle. All scenarios considered by Lynd and his colleagues incorporate a conventional Rankine cycle with 25.8 percent power generation efficiency, whereas much higher efficiencies are associated with power generation using biomass gasification and combined-cycle gas turbines (BGCCGT), or fuel cells. The power cycle is responsible for over 50 percent of total plant capital cost in the advanced scenario of Lynd, Elander, & Wyman (1996). An economic analysis of incorporating BGCCGT into an advanced biomass ethanol plant is beyond the scope of this chapter. However, a thermodynamic analysis is more straightforward and permits calculation of impacts on process efficiency and greenhouse gas emissions. A reasonable first-order estimate of the increased electricity export using a BGCCGT power cycle can be made by multiplying the gross electric power output of the advanced process using a Rankine cycle by the ratio of efficiencies of the BGCCGT and Rankine power cycles, and then subtracting the process power requirements (which are the same for both cases).

Table 5-1

Summary of Process Parameters for Cellulose Ethanol Technology Scenarios at Various Levels of Technological Maturity

Scenario/Power Cycle	Current, Rankine	Advanced, Rankine	Advanced, BGCCGT[a]	Best-Parameter, Rankine
Capacity (10^6 gal)	60.1	295.0	295.0	350.0
Cost of feedstock (1994$/ton)[b]	42.0	38.6	38.6	34.0
Ethanol yield (gal/ton)	91.3	107.5	107.5	127.7
Electricity yield (kWh/gal)	2.24	3.06	5.13	3.16
First-law efficiency (% HHV)[c]	50.3	61.2	65.8	69.3
Total cost (1994$/gal)[d]	117.8	50.3	—	34.3

Source: Lynd, Elander, & Wyman (1996).

[a]BGCCGT = biomass gasification and combined-cycle gas turbines. The electricity yield and thermodynamic efficiency for the advanced, BGCCGT scenario are calculated via the approach described in the text using a 40 percent efficiency for the BGCCGT power cycle (Marrison & Larson 1995) and a 25.8 percent efficiency for the Rankine cycle (Lynd et al. 1995).

[b]Delivered, dry.

[c]Calculated from the energy content of exported ethanol and electricity/energy content of the feedstock.

[d]Total cost is calculated from a 0.2 capital recovery factor that converts the plant capital cost into an annualized operating cost. For the construction lead times and start-up periods anticipated for advanced technology, this factor corresponds to a 14.2 percent internal rate of return.

Table 5-1 presents a summary of results for four scenarios: the current-technology, advanced-technology, and best-parameter scenarios with Rankine power cycles as reported by Lynd et al. (1991), plus an advanced-technology case with a BGCCGT power cycle. Biomass feedstocks typically contain substantial quantities of unfermentable lignin, which is available as a process residue that can be burned as a high-energy, low-sulfur boiler fuel. Therefore, all process scenarios presented here result in the net export of electricity after satisfying all process steam and power demands. Electricity is expected to be an increasingly significant co-product of ethanol manufacture from woody materials as the technology matures. As an illustration, the energy exported as electricity in the advanced/BGCCGT turbine scenario is roughly 20 percent of that exported as ethanol. Since the country uses over twice as much transportation fuel as electricity, every 1 percent of current transportation sector energy demand displaced by ethanol would displace over 0.4 percent of electricity demand (in terms of electricity at 3,412 Btu/kWh) in the advanced/BGCCGT scenario. Relative to the current-technology scenario, yields of both ethanol and electricity increase for all other scenarios because of more efficient processing, while the selling price of ethanol decreases markedly.

The cost of biological conversion, currently the most expensive step, is reduced almost tenfold in the advanced scenario. More efficient biological processing is the major factor behind higher electricity export in the advanced case and is significant in reducing the cost of raw materials and increasing process yields. These improvements in biological processing result primarily from consolidated processing, whereby the biologically mediated events involved in ethanol production (production of hydrolytic enzymes, cellulose hydrolysis, hexose fermentation, and pentose fermentation) are accomplished in a single step using a single system of anaerobic microorganisms. By contrast, the current scenario entails biological conversion achieved in three separate steps with separate organisms, some of which are grown aerobically.

There are no apparent bioenergetic or metabolic barriers to co-producing ethanol and hydrolytic enzymes under anaerobic conditions as required for consolidated bioprocessing. Moreover, it is not necessary to develop a better cellulase enzyme system or a more ethanol-tolerant microorganism than has been documented to date in order to realize the benefits of consolidated bioprocessing. Rather, such realization requires that the properties of separate existing microorganisms be combined into a single organism (or system of organisms). Since such combination of properties is the salient feature of genetic engineering, the author believes that creating organisms compatible with consolidated processing would be achievable given sufficient R&D effort.

In the advanced scenarios, costs are also reduced for feedstock production because of lower delivered cost and higher process yields. Pretreatment costs are reduced by about twofold, primarily because of R&D-driven improvements. The cost of "other" raw materials (exclusive of feedstock) decreases by almost tenfold, consistent with the eliminated requirements for acid and limestone as well as reduced requirements for microbial nutrients because no cells are grown aerobically. Although distillation technology is not changed, distillation cost markedly decreases because energy is supplied by pretreatment flash vapor. Exported electricity revenues roughly double for advanced technology as compared with current technology, with costs for the power cycle and "other" items decreasing on a per-gallon basis because of increased ethanol yields.

Environmental Impacts and Benefits

Environmental impacts and benefits of cellulose ethanol are associated with greenhouse gas emissions, as well as priority pollutant emissions, and considerations pertaining to land use and availability.

Greenhouse Gas Emissions

In the "Car Talk" meetings (see NEC 1996) and other fora, cellulosic ethanol has been recognized as a leading alternative for lowering emissions of greenhouse gases. Table 5-2 presents estimated greenhouse gas (GHG) emissions for the four cellulose ethanol technology scenarios defined above and the percent reductions relative to a reformulated gasoline (RFG) base case.

The methodology used for these estimates involves treating electricity as a co-product that is evaluated on the basis of GHG emissions reductions avoided by the displaced electricity. Since cellulose ethanol production per se involves very low net GHG emissions, inclusion of the electricity credit results in negative emission values for the advanced and best-parameter scenarios.

Priority Pollutant Emissions

Emissions accompanying fuel ethanol use in various forms have been reviewed elsewhere (Lynd 1996). Available information suggests that using ethanol will not make it more difficult to achieve low-emission vehicle (LEV) standards. Ethanol's emissions performance depends on the form in which it is used, as indicated in Table 5-3.

Table 5-2

Greenhouse Gas (GHG) Emissions Reductions for Cellulose Ethanol Technology Scenarios

Scenario/Cycle	GHG Emissions (g/mile)[a]	Change from RFG Base Case[b] (%)
Current, Rankine	−0.9	−0.2
Advanced, Rankine	−32.9	−8.1
Advanced, BGCCGT	−105.4	−25.8
Best-parameter	−38.4	−9.4

[a]G/mile values are differences in full-fuel-cycle CO_2-equivalent emissions, without considering vehicle manufacture, between ethanol and gasoline, as calculated by Delucchi (1995), based on process inputs supplied by the author and as given in Table 5-1.
[b]Changes are relative to a base case involving internal combustion engine vehicles operated on reformulated gasoline (RFG).

Table 5-3

Potential for Priority Pollutant Benefits in Relation to Ethanol Utilization Mode

Utilization Mode	Potential for Priority Pollutant Benefits[a]
ICE[b]/Low-level	Generally small, can be zero or negative in some ethanol blends for some seasons and locations
ICE/ETBE[c] blends	Small, but generally positive
ICE/E85[d]	Moderate
ICE/E100[e]	Moderate to large
Hybrid vehicle	Moderate to large
Fuel cell	Large

[a]Includes criteria pollutants and toxics. Ratings developed by the author in consultation with Barry Wallerstein (South Coast Air Quality Management District).
[b]ICE = internal combustion engine.
[c]ETBE = ethyl tertiary butyl ether.
[d]E85 = 85 percent ethanol, 15 percent gasoline blends.
[e]E100 = 100 percent ethanol.

One relevant comparison, although by no means the only one, involves the relative emissions for high-level ethanol blends and RFG (Phase II) in internal combustion engines. Data relevant to this comparison are sparse, as are all ethanol emissions data, and stem largely from a study of 21 vehicles undertaken by NREL (Kelly et al., in press) and a study of 3 vehicles undertaken as part of the Auto/Oil (1995) study. As presented by Lynd (1996), both studies indicate higher aldehyde emissions and lower benzene and butadiene emissions for E85 (a mixture of 85 percent ethanol and 15 percent gasoline) relative to RFG. When these emissions are weighted by their toxicity potency factors (CARB/OEHHA 1994), toxicity-weighted air toxics emissions are 65 percent lower for E85 according to the NREL study and 38 percent lower according to the Auto/Oil study. There is much less agreement between the two studies with respect to exhaust emissions. Whereas the NREL study found reductions of non-methane hydrocarbons, nitrogen oxides (NO_x), carbon monoxide (CO), and ozone of 24, 27, 18, and 27 percent, respectively, for E85 relative to RFG, the Auto/Oil study found organic material hydrocarbon equivalent emissions for E85 to be 25 percent higher for E85, NO_x emissions to be 37 percent lower, CO to be 56 percent higher, and ozone formation to be 19 percent higher. Reconciliation of the significant discrepancy between these studies awaits further work.

Data for E85 evaporative emissions are particularly sparse. It is reasonable to expect E85 to have lower evaporative emissions than

RFG because of its lower vapor pressure, and this expectation is supported by comparative data for E85 and indolene (Baudino, Voelz, and Marek 1993). Blending ethanol with gasoline at ratios greater than 85:15 can be expected to lower both exhaust and evaporative emissions and may have little if any penalty in terms of performance and vehicle compatibility at ethanol contents up to 95 percent.

Waste Biomass

The first materials used for biomass ethanol production will almost certainly not be energy crops, but rather wastes (Wyman & Goodman 1993). Waste feedstocks generally cost less than dedicated energy crops. Conversion of waste materials into ethanol generally presents fewer environmental dilemmas than does conversion of dedicated feedstocks because no crop land is required, land may even be saved by decreasing material flows to landfills, and little or no resource investment is needed save for collection. Depending on the wastes, collection may be either more easily accomplished relative to energy crops (as in the case of a waste produced at a centralized processing facility such as a paper mill) or less easily accomplished (as in the case of agricultural residues that would not otherwise be collected). Collecting some wastes would displace their use in helping to maintain soil fertility. Conversely, some agricultural residues already present environmentally damaging disposal problems—for example, open-field burning of straw or sugar cane leaves.

Tyson (1994) recently completed a detailed waste inventory, presented in Table 5-4. This study is distinguished from most earlier efforts in that it presents prices for waste materials in addition to estimates for available tonnages. Tyson's estimates total 187 million tons of wastes costing not more than $56 per delivered dry ton, and about 143 dry tons at not more than $45 per delivered dry ton (linearly interpolating for the high-cost agricultural waste). If we assume an advanced production process (see Table 5-1), the corresponding ethanol yields are 20 billion gallons (1.5 Quads) and 15 billion gallons (1.2 Quads) for material available at prices up to $56 and $45 per delivered dry ton, respectively. Because of scale considerations, only a fraction of the lower-cost material is likely to be utilized in plants processing wastes only. However, most of this material could probably be utilized once a fuel ethanol industry were established and co-utilization of wastes and dedicated feedstocks became possible. Wastes costing more than $45 per dry ton may never be used for ethanol production because energy crops are expected to be available at lower cost. It may be noted that Tyson projects smaller (on the order of threefold)

116

Table 5-4

Availability and Cost of Cellulosic Wastes

Waste	Availability (million dry tons)	Cost (1994$/delivered dry ton)
Mixed paper	26.0	0–19.0
Packaging	14.0	0–5.2
Urban wood	3.5	12.9–25.9
Yard waste	11.0	0–12.9
Agricultural residues	120.0	12.9–56.0
Low-cost	4.0	12.9
Medium-cost	36.0	38.8
High-cost	50.0	47.4
Forest residues—logging	9.0	12.9–43.1
Low-cost	3.0	12.9
Medium-cost	3.0	25.9
High-cost	3.0	43.1
Forest residues—mill	3.0	17.2

Source: Modified from values developed by Tyson (1994). Tyson considered the contiguous 48 states, with values based on the year 2000. For consistency with other values in this report, Tyson's values are multiplied by 0.862 (consistent with a compounded annual consumer price index increase of 2.5 percent to convert from 2000$ to 1994$.

amounts of material available than most previous estimates (reviewed in Lynd et al. 1991). One reason may be that many previous studies were done before the early 1980s, often based on data that were yet older, when accounting of forest industry wastes and paper recycling were much less established.

If we use Tyson's numbers with a $45/ton cutoff, the potential contribution of wastes (about 1.3 Quads) is still significant. Moreover, a fuel cycle based on wastes is quite different from a fuel cycle based on dedicated energy crops. In general, evaluating greenhouse gas emissions for ethanol production from cellulosic wastes has received much less attention than have emissions for production from energy crops.

Land Use and Availability

Notwithstanding the variation in estimates of waste availability, large-scale displacement of conventional transportation fuels with cellulose ethanol will require significant production from dedicated energy crops. Examples are short-rotation woody crops (for example,

Table 5-5

Comparison of Agricultural Intensity Metrics for Energy Crops and Conventional Crops

Metric	Reduction Relative to Corn-Wheat-Soybean Average	
	Woody Short Rotation	Herbaceous Perennial
Erosion	12.5-fold	125.0-fold
Fertilizer	2.1-fold	1.1-fold
Herbicide	4.4-fold	6.8-fold
Insecticide	19.0-fold	9.4-fold
Fungicide	39.0-fold	3.9-fold

Source: Data from Ranney & Mann (1994).

poplar and willow) and perennial herbaceous crops (for example, switchgrass). Perhaps the greatest reservations with respect to large-scale deployment of cellulose ethanol are associated with the prospect of devoting significant quantities of land to this enterprise.

Most land use–related impacts depend on the form of land use replaced by energy crops. Increasingly, analyses of energy crop production focus on cropland. Most metrics of environmental quality improve when short-rotation woody crops or herbaceous perennial crops replace conventional row crops (Christianson et al. 1994; Ranney & Mann 1994). Table 5-5 compiles some of the more quantifiable land use impacts associated with production of energy crops. Compared with row crop production, energy crops involve far less erosion, slightly less fertilizer application, and much reduced pesticide application. These trends are consistent with the possibility of very positive water quality benefits resulting from energy crop planting (Perlack & Wright 1995). Ranney and Mann (1994) also project improved soil organic carbon levels when energy crops are grown on cropland, resulting in slower leaching of nutrients, more efficient use of nutrients by energy crops, and reduced nitrogen oxide emissions.

Most analyses stress the incomplete understanding of the environmental impacts of energy crop production. A common observation is that good management practices can help protect the environment, whereas poor management represents a significant potential liability (Beyea & Keeler 1991). These themes are especially relevant to biodiversity concerns. Christianson et al. (1994) indicate that bird and mammal abundance and diversity are generally as high or higher on energy crop plantations as on row crop or small-grain croplands. Similarly, Ranney and Mann (1994) project slightly improved wildlife habitat when energy crops are planted on croplands. However, conversion of wildlands to energy crop production would negatively affect biodiversity (Christianson et al. 1994). Although caution and further research are certainly needed regarding biodiversity as well as other land use–related impacts, well-managed energy crop production need not negatively affect biodiversity.

The United States has had a surplus of cropland for most of this century. Moreover, recent trends indicate that productivity increases are outstripping increased demand, with the result that cropland surplus is expected to increase in the future (Graham 1994). Federal programs have idled an average of 60 million acres over the last ten years (USDA 1994). The Conservation Reserve Program (CRP) removes about 36 million acres from production, primarily to control erosion. Most CRP land is planted in perennial grasses that could be harvested as energy crops while still meeting the goal of erosion prevention, were this not prohibited. Acreage reduction programs designed to support farm prices remove about 25 million acres, although this amount is highly variable from year to year. The amount of land that could be used to grow energy crops without significant displacement of food crops is probably less than the amount idled by federal programs. A reasonable estimate is roughly 35 million acres (Walsh 1995) since not all idled land is suitable for energy crop production.

Figure 5-1 presents a perspective on land availability and requirements for cellulose ethanol production while also stressing the reduction in land area requirements available from increased vehicle efficiency. For this exercise, 15 Quads of fuel use (approximately the current level of U.S. gasoline use, or 130 billion gallons) are assumed. Wastes are assumed to provide 15 billion gallons of ethanol, or 1.2 Quads (see discussion above) with no land requirements. An energy crop productivity of 8.4 dry tons/acre/year is assumed, corresponding to the average research goal productivities presented by Perlack and Wright (1995). The ethanol yield is taken to be 107.7 gal/ton, consistent with the advanced technology scenario outlined earlier in this paper. From these assumptions, the amount of land required to displace a given quantity of conventional fuel can be calculated readily. In Figure 5-1, such calculations are presented in relation to a vehicle efficiency multiplier, which reflects the multiple of current vehicle efficiency. Three cases are developed on the basis of how electricity is considered: (1) ethanol only; (2) ethanol plus electricity (valued based on energy content) with electricity yields as for the advanced/Rankine scenario (see Table 5-1); and (3) ethanol plus electricity with yields as for the advanced/BGCCGT scenario. Note that the land area requirements correspond to a constant level of travel, with land requirements

Figure 5-1

Land Area Requirements for Cellulose Ethanol (EtOH) Production in Relation to Transportation Efficiency (Vehicle-Miles of Travel = 3.6 Trillion)

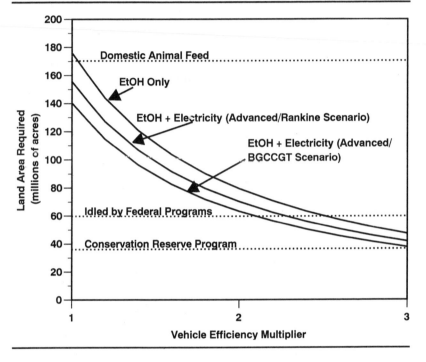

decreasing as vehicle efficiency increases. In addition, that portion of priority pollutant emissions associated with the scale of fuel use would also decline analogously to the curves presented in Figure 5-1.

Land area benchmarks presented as horizontal lines in Figure 5-1 include the acreage idled by the CRP program, the average total amount of land idled by federal programs over the last decade, and the total amount of land devoted to production of animal feed for domestic consumption (USDA 1995). At an efficiency multiplier of 1, which is probably conservative in light of the potential to increase vehicle efficiency, an amount of land equal to the CRP program represents on the order of one-quarter of the land required to provide fuel for a current level of mobility, depending on the accounting and subject to the assumptions of this analysis. At an efficiency multiplier of 3, which some project for leap-forward types of vehicles, this same acreage would provide most or all of this land requirement. The acreage devoted to production of animal feeds, much of which would be available were the country to shift to a diet emphasizing vegetable protein, is roughly commensurate with the land required at an efficiency multiplier of 1, and far exceeds the land required at an efficiency multiplier of 3. Consideration of land devoted to feed production emphasizes the point that society has options for making land available for energy production, and not all of these options involve reducing the number of people that we feed from cropland.

Overall Evaluation

Table 5-6 presents the author's summary evaluation of cellulose ethanol in matrix form, using a qualitative 0 to 3 scale of increasing advantage relative to other motor fuels.

The 3 rating for sustainability is based on (1) the outstanding greenhouse gas reduction potential of cellulose ethanol; (2) the potential for cellulosic energy crop production to be compatible with long-term soil fertility; and (3) the fact that few, if any, exotic elements from depletable sources are involved in the cellulose ethanol fuel cycle.

The 2 rating for potential supply is based on the capacity to produce this fuel being ultimately limited by land availability and the modest foreseeable efficiency of photosynthesis. High-efficiency solar electricity converted to hydrogen would require less land area per unit

Table 5-6

Summary Evaluation of Cellulose Ethanol

Feature	Key Determinant	Rating
Sustainability	feedstock	3
Potential supply	feedstock	2
Cost of production	feedstock[a]	3
Priority pollutants	fuel	0–3
Enhanced strategic security	feedstock	3
Transition barriers	fuel	3
Fuel performance	fuel	3
Compatibility with high-efficiency vehicles	fuel	2

Key:
3 = A strength relative to other fuels.
2 = Similar to most other alternatives but less favorable than the best.
1 = Demonstrable benefits, but smaller than most other alternatives.
0 = No change relative to status quo.
[a]Supported by the very high proportion of costs attributable to feedstocks for mature process designs.

energy output and could use land unsuited for many other purposes. Comparison of life-cycle ecological impacts per unit land area for energy crops and other energy-harvesting strategies (for example, photovoltaics) is relevant in this context but has received little systematic study to date.

The 3 rating for cost of production is based on the expectation of very low production costs for cellulose ethanol, as discussed elsewhere in this paper. The 0 to 3 rating for priority pollutant reduction reflects the differing impacts associated with different modes of ethanol utilization. Cellulose ethanol would rate as strongly as any other domestically produced fuel in terms of enhanced strategic security.

The 3 rating for transition barriers reflects the fact that ethanol production could be expanded to about 15 billion gallons with the existing vehicle fleet and retail delivery infrastructure, using ethanol either in direct low-level blends or as ethyl tertiary butyl ether (ETBE). Further expansion would still entail relatively small vehicular transition barriers because of the low cost of flexibly fueled gasoline/alcohol vehicles. Although some transition barriers exist with respect to ethanol distribution, these appear less than or equal to distributional issues associated with any other alternative fuel. Overall, ethanol appears to have fewer transition barriers than other alternative motor fuels. Although many transition issues are similar for ethanol and methanol, methanol cannot be used directly in low-level blends because of volatility concerns, whereas ethanol can. Also, ethanol is superior to methanol for flexible-fuel vehicles because evaporative emissions for gasoline fill-ups following use of high-level alcohol blends are unacceptably high for methanol, whereas this issue is much smaller for ethanol. Methanol is considerably more poisonous than gasoline, requiring greater care in handling, whereas ethanol is much less poisonous. Finally, ethanol has a less reduced vehicle range than does methanol. Because a decision to promote cellulose ethanol use does not require a massive infrastructure investment, it does not compete for financial resources required to make such investments for other alternative fuels.

It is widely accepted that ethanol is a high-performance fuel (Black 1991; Sinor & Bailey 1993), implying the 3 rating in this category.

The 2 rating for compatibility with high-efficiency vehicles reflects the differing interactions of ethanol with various high-efficiency-vehicle technologies as well as uncertainty over which technology such vehicles will employ. Ethanol would be entirely compatible with hybrid vehicles; is compatible with fuel-cell-powered vehicles, but not as readily as hydrogen-based systems (Wyman et al. 1993); and is inapplicable to battery-powered electric vehicles. Recent work by Mitchell et al. (1995) indicates that low-cost and high-efficiency partial oxidation reforming of ethanol for fuel cell use may be more feasible than previously thought. The choice among high-efficiency alternatives is usually viewed solely in terms of the vehicle technologies involved. However, the author feels that the cost and availability of compatible energy sources could be a key factor influencing choices among these technologies.

Policy Needs

As considered by DeCicco and Lynd in Chapter 4 of this volume, the primary policy needs for accelerating the deployment of cellulose ethanol are R&D and some form of incentive to overcome the difference in price between ethanol and gasoline. Before considering these options in more detail, let us first examine how such policies might be justified. One rationale is to make fuel prices reflect societal values (for example, greenhouse gas reductions and energy independence) that are not currently valued by the market. In addition, it is desirable to address the considerably shorter time-horizon of market-based decision making than that for developing new energy supply industries (such as cellulose ethanol). The public thus has a legitimate interest in anticipating the need for such industries before it becomes acute.

The author recommends that most R&D support be devoted to developing lower-cost conversion processes. Smaller but still important components should target lower-cost feedstock production as well as assessment and minimization of feedstock-related environmental impacts. Although modest relative to other energy R&D programs, the United States has the largest and arguably best R&D efforts in the world in the areas of production of cellulosic feedstocks and cellulose ethanol conversion technology. Both are threatened to the point of elimination by legislative initiatives under discussion at the time of the 1995 Asilomar meeting. In consultation with others, the author has estimated that a $100 million/year R&D effort, representing roughly a fourfold increase over current expenditures, would suffice to rapidly approach mature biomass ethanol technology with production costs (for similar scale of production and cost of feedstock) corresponding to the advanced technology case presented herein.

If ethanol is valued at its energy content and gasoline prices between flat and a 1 percent per year increase are assumed, an ethanol subsidy/incentive would likely be required at least through 2010 even with a high degree of R&D success. An example of an incentive policy is that developed by the Alternative Fuel Ad Hoc Working Group of the "Car Talk" committee (see chapter appendix). In brief, this policy entails:

- a greenhouse emission–proportional subsidy available to all liquid and gaseous fuels capped at $180/million metric tons carbon equivalent

- an overall cap such that the combined expenditures for this policy and the current ethanol tax incentive do not exceed $1.2 billion per year

- benefits to be realized by fuel producers for both the greenhouse gas–proportional subsidy and the current ethanol tax incentive

- a straight-line phase-out of the current ethanol tax incentive over the period 2000–2010

- a straight-line phase-out of the greenhouse fuel subsidy over the period 2015–2025

Projected values for cumulative cost per cumulative metric ton of CO_2-equivalent saved relative to gasoline use are $180, $30, and $11 for the years 2005, 2015, and 2025, respectively. Cellulosic ethanol market penetration estimates developed in conjunction with this policy are 2, 15, and 40 billion gallons of ethanol in 2005, 2015, and 2025, respectively. Expansion at this rate assumes the availability of advanced technology in the post-2005 time frame, which is likely to be possible only with an accelerated R&D effort.

Continuation of the current ethanol tax incentive in combination with an R&D policy such as that described above might well result in similar or even greater market penetration as compared with the "Car Talk" policy. However, the cost of the current incentive would greatly exceed the cost of the "Car Talk" policy at high production levels because the former is based on a flat per-gallon amount, whereas the latter is constrained by an overall cap with decreasing unit subsidies at higher production volume. Furthermore, the current incentive does not target reduced greenhouse gas emissions and would thus not promote the transition of corn-based plants to cellulose-based plants. The fastest way to jump-start a cellulose ethanol industry may well be to give the corn ethanol industry an incentive to make a transition to cellulosic feedstocks. Those critical of the corn ethanol industry and the incentive that it currently receives should note that this scenario involves, and depends upon the continued existence of, the current fuel ethanol industry. Eliminating the current subsidy would end the current corn ethanol industry, making it more difficult to launch a cellulose ethanol industry. This author suggests that policy with respect to the current fuel ethanol industry should be viewed less in terms of what it is and more in terms of what it could become.

In addition to R&D and price supports, additional policies responsive to the needs of a nascent cellulosic ethanol industry include encouraging production of cellulosic energy crops (on both CRP and other land), ensuring the availability of ethanol/gasoline flexible-fuel vehicles, and making low-cost capital available for constructing first-of-a-kind plants.

Conclusion

Cellulosic ethanol offers particular benefits in terms of sustainability, low-cost production, enhanced strategic security, relatively few transition barriers, and excellent fuel performance, while also having a significant strength with respect to large-scale supply. Information reviewed by the author to date suggests potential priority pollutant emission reductions through ethanol utilization in internal combustion engines. It is ironic that perhaps the least clear-cut benefit of ethanol—the reduction of priority pollutant emissions—is so often offered to justify this fuel alternative. Policies to accelerate deployment of cellulose ethanol entail costs ($100 million/year in R&D through 2005, up to $400 million per year in fuel subsidies over and above the current ethanol tax incentive) that are small by many measures. During the 1995 Asilomar conference, this chapter was presented within a session entitled "Alternative Fuels: Small Benefits, Small Costs?" but the author offers that "Large Benefits, Small Costs" is a defensible characterization of cellulose ethanol. As this characterization is not yet widely accepted, it is hoped that this chapter will stimulate more active discussion and consideration of the associated issues. In particular, it is hoped that those involved in evaluating environmentally motivated technology can lessen the currently disparate evaluations of cellulose ethanol.

The 1995 Asilomar conference was motivated by the question, Is technology enough? Considered generally, no amount of technology is likely to adequately meet the challenges posed by indefinitely continued population growth. With respect to sustainable transportation, technology does not appear to be enough in the absence of supportive policies. But with supportive policies, technology can probably take us a long way toward achieving sustainability goals such as those formulated for the conference.

Finally, the "is technology enough?" question can also be considered in terms of lessons from the example of cellulose ethanol production. Co-production of ethanol and electricity, production of ethanol from waste materials, improving soil and water quality while producing well-managed biomass energy crops, and providing farm economy employment and revenue through energy crop production: all of these features indicate the potential for achieving multiple goals simultaneously. Increasing vehicle efficiency in conjunction with cellulose ethanol deployment suggests the powerful synergies that often-separately considered technologies can have with respect to goals such as gasoline displacement, reduced greenhouse and priority emissions, and minimizing the land area needed for biomass-based fuel production. The example of reducing animal protein consumption points to the powerful potential of changed behavior to lower technological and environmental hurdles, as in the case of land allocation for energy crops. The animal protein example also points out that not all behavioral changes impacting sustainability goals, such as those of the conference, involve transportation.

Acknowledgments

The author gratefully acknowledges the following colleagues for significant and generous contributions to the development of ideas and analyses presented in this chapter. Conversion technology: Rick Elander, Chris Jones, Eric Larson, Kevin Stone, and Charles Wyman. Analysis of greenhouse gas emissions: Mark Delucchi and Barry McNutt. Priority pollutant emissions: Barry McNutt and Barry Wallerstein. Waste availability and price: Paul Bergeron and Shane Tyson. Cost and land use implications of energy crop production: Janet Cushman, Marie Walsh, and Lynn Wright. Policy formulation and analysis: John DeCicco, Robert Harris, Dan Lashof, Jerry Levine, Barry McNutt, and members of the "Car Talk" federal advisory group.

Appendix: Liquid Biofuels Policy Developed by Members of the "Car Talk" Committee

Author's Note: "Car Talk" was a colloquial name for the Policy Dialog Advisory Committee to Assist in the Development of Measures to Significantly Reduce Greenhouse Gas Emissions from Personal Motor Vehicles, which met from September 1994 to September 1995. This policy statement was the working version at the time the committee declared its inability to reach consensus and was disbanded in September 1995 (see *Majority Report* 1995; NEC 1996). Although this was one of the committee's more thoroughly reviewed policies and widespread support for the policy was apparent among committee members, neither this nor any other policy was finalized by the committee.

Description of Policy

This policy involves increasing R&D funding and providing price support to encourage production of low-greenhouse-gas-emitting alternative fuels. The R&D program would target reducing the cost of cellulosic ethanol via improved biochemical conversion technology as well as improved cellulosic energy crops and procedures for their cultivation. The program could be broadened to include biomass-derived methanol if new information were to suggest that R&D-driven improvements could result in production costs and greenhouse gas savings on the order of those projected here for ethanol. R&D funding would increase from about $25 million per year currently, to $50 million in FY 1997, $75 million in FY 1998, and $100 million per year for FY 1999 to 2005. Price support would be achieved by establishing an annual pool of $1.1 billion that would be available to producers of alternative fuels in proportion to full-cycle greenhouse gas emissions (based on a facility-by-facility audit), with the pool phased out over the period 2015 to 2025. The pool would also include the current ethanol tax incentive, which would be capped at its current value of about $650 million and would be phased out linearly over the period 2000 to 2010. Currently, the ethanol tax incentive is authorized through 2000. An amount of funds corresponding to the difference between the $1.2 billion and the amount of the current ethanol tax incentive in that year would be allocated to alternative-fuel producers on a basis proportional to reduced greenhouse gas emissions. Corn ethanol would qualify either for the remainder of the current ethanol tax incentive or the greenhouse-based price support, whichever is greater, but not both. Price support to producers would be through tax waivers and/or direct payment, with the total amount capped at $180 per metric ton of carbon-equivalent emissions reduction (or about 54 cents/gal based on the greenhouse gas savings in Delucchi's [1995] wood/ethanol scenario).

This policy fosters development of low-greenhouse-gas-emitting fuels while also attaching a market value to reduced greenhouse gas emissions. An R&D program devoted to liquid biofuels is consistent with their greenhouse gas benefits. Both the possibility of including methanol as well as ethanol and the availability of price supports to all fuels are intended to provide flexibility in pursuing the goal of reduced emissions. The price support component is designed to give a large cost advantage to low-greenhouse-gas-emitting fuels at low levels of production when the technology is least mature, with subsidies per gallon of fuel and per ton of carbon decreasing as volume increases. Thus, the impact on the treasury is capped, and expanded production of alternative fuels will only proceed as the fuels become more cost-competitive. The cost of the policy is independent of actual ethanol and gasoline prices, both of which are uncertain. The magnitude of the price support is chosen so as to eliminate the cost differential between ethanol and gasoline, assuming successful R&D to reduce costs and a gasoline price in between the flat and rising-price scenarios. If the actual ethanol-gasoline price differential were larger than assumed, rates of ethanol market penetration would be slowed and/or profits for ethanol producers would be smaller, with the opposite result if the actual price differential were smaller than assumed. The fastest way to get a cellulose ethanol industry established, and to begin to realize greenhouse gas benefits therefrom, is by a transition from corn to cellulosic feedstocks in existing facilities. The timing of the phase-out of the current tax incentive is chosen in order to give the current ethanol industry and the farmers it supports time to make such a transition.

Estimated Impact on Emissions

Reduced greenhouse gas emissions resulting from this policy are driven by the assumed amount of ethanol produced. On the basis of work by committee member Lee Lynd, ethanol production is estimated to be 2 billion gallons in 2005, 15 billion gallons in 2015, and 40 billion gallons in 2025. Ethanol is assumed to be blended with gasoline either directly or as ETBE at levels rising to 17 percent ethanol by volume. Around 2015, projected ethanol production will exceed the level at which it can be blended into gasoline without vehicle modifications, and ethanol will begin to be used as a near-neat fuel (at least 85 percent ethanol by volume). The transition from low-level blends to neat fuels is expected to be market driven with little if any federal intervention. The policy is scored assuming that R&D results in lower ethanol production costs (50 to 70 cents per gallon ethanol), consistent with analyses of R&D-driven improvements by Lynd, Elander, & Wyman (1996). Some other analyses have projected higher prices; however, these estimates were generally based on a lower R&D intensity or more near-term application than considered by the committee. The greenhouse gas impact was derived from the ethanol production volume assumption and Delucchi's estimates of greenhouse gas emission savings (97 percent reduction compared to reformulated gasoline). As an illustration, Table 5A-1 presents projected values used in scoring this policy for a flat oil-price scenario and R&D success as projected by Lynd,

Elander, & Wyman (1996). Cumulative GHG reduction is about 930 million metric tons carbon equivalent. Figure 5A-1 presents a graph of base-case carbon emissions and the impact of this policy on projected emissions in the transportation sector. All emissions are evaluated on a

Table 5A-1

Summary of Production, Price Support, and Emissions Reduction

	2005	2015	2025
Ethanol production (billions of gallons)	2	15	40
Ethanol price support (cents/gal)	54	7.3	0
Greenhouse gas emissions reduction (million metric tons carbon equivalent)	5.1	38	100

Source: Data from *Majority Report* (1995).

Figure 5A-1

Contribution of Alternative Fuels to Greenhouse Gas (GHG) Reduction Targets

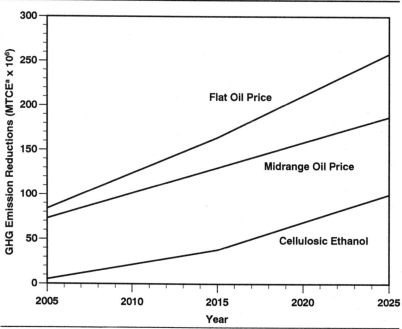

Source: NEC 1996.
[a]MTCE = Million metric tons carbon equivalent.

Table 5A-2

Summary of Cost and Cost-Effectiveness

	2005	2015	2025
Cost ($billion)	$0.55	$0.45	$0
Cumulative cost ($billion)	$2.3	$6.8	$10.2
$/metric ton carbon equivalent	$110	$12	$0
Cumulative $/cumulative metric ton	$180	$30	$11

Source: Data from *Majority Report* (1995).

full-fuel-cycle basis. The two target prices, developed by the committee, are based on a flat oil price through 2025 and the DOE midrange prediction of an average 1 percent/year price increase over the same period.

Cost and Cost-Effectiveness

For the purposes of scoring this policy, it is assumed that $25 million per year is in the base case in terms of ethanol and R&D costs and that $650 million per year is in the base case for ethanol subsidy. Cellulosic ethanol production begins in 1997 and exponentially grows to 2 billion gallons in 2005, so the subsidy cap of $450 million is not reached until 2004. Between the years of 2004 and 2021, the full subsidy of $450 million is assumed to be used. The subsidy amount falls below $450 million between years 2021 and 2025, as the subsidy is phased out. Total additional R&D spending is $600 million, and total additional tax subsidy is $9.6 billion. Cost and cost-effectiveness are summarized in Table 5A-2. The cost per metric ton emission reduction declines over time as the volume of ethanol production increases.

References

Auto/Oil Research Program. 1995. *Exhaust Emissions of E85 Ethanol Fuel and Gasoline in Flexible/Variable Fuel Vehicles.* Technical Bulletin 16. Detroit, Mich.: Auto/Oil Air Quality Improvement Research Program. July.

Baudino, J.H., F.L. Voelz, and N.J. Marek. 1993. Emissions Testing of Three Illinois E85 Demonstration Fleet Vehicles. In *Proceedings, Tenth International Symposium on Alcohol Fuels,* vol. 1. Colorado Springs, Colo.

Beyea, J., and H. Keeler. 1991. Biotechnological Advances in Biomass

Energy and Chemical Production: Impacts on Wildlife and Habitat. *CRC Critical Review of Biotechnology* 10 (4): 305.

Black, F. 1991. *An Overview of the Technical Implications of Methanol and Ethanol as Highway Motor Vehicle Fuels*. SAE Technical Paper 912413. Warrendale, Pa.: Society of Automotive Engineers.

California Air Resources Board and the Office of Environmental Health Hazard Assessment (CARB/OEHHA). 1994. Benzo[a]pyrene as a Toxic Air Contaminant. Sacramento, Calif.: California Air Resources Board, Office of Environmental Health Hazard Assessment.

Christianson, D.P., G.J. Niemi, J.M. Hanowski, and P. Collins. 1994. Perspectives on Biomass Energy Tree Plantations and Changes in Habitat for Biological Organisms. *Biomass Bioenergy* 6 (1/2): 31.

Cushman, Janet. 1995. Oak Ridge National Laboratory. Personal communication.

Delucchi, Mark. 1995. U.C. Davis. Personal communication.

Graham, R.L. 1994. Analysis of the Potential Land Base for Energy Crops in the Continuous United States. *Biomass Bioenergy* 6 (3): 175–198.

Hinman, N.D., D.J. Schell, C.J. Riley, P.W. Bergeron, and P.J. Walter. 1993. *Applied Biochemistry & Biotechnology* 34/35: 639–649.

Kelly, K.J., B.K. Bailey, T. Coburn, W. Clark, and P. Lissiuk. In press. Federal Test Procedure Emissions Test Results from Ethanol Variable-Fuel Vehicle Chevrolet Lumina. SAE Technical Paper. Warrendale, Pa.: Society of Automotive Engineers.

Ladisch, M., and R. Schwandt. 1992. Report of the Starch Conversion Work Group. In *Proceedings, Technology for Expanding the Biofuels Industry*. Washington, D.C.: Department of Energy, Biofuels Program.

Lynd, L.R. 1996. Overview and Evaluation of Fuel Ethanol from Cellulosic Biomass: Technology, Economics, Environment, and Policy. In *Annual Review of Energy and Environment*, vol. 21, edited by R.H. Socolow, D. Anderson, and J. Harte, 403–465.

Lynd, L.R., J.H. Cushman, R.J. Nichols, and C.E. Wyman. 1991. Fuel Ethanol from Cellulosic Biomass. *Science* 251: 1318–1323.

Lynd, L.R., R.T. Elander, and C.E. Wyman. 1996. Likely Features and Cost of Mature Biomass Ethanol Technology. *Applied Biochemistry & Biotechnology* 57/58: 741–761.

Majority Report to the President by the Policy Dialog Advisory Committee to Recommend Options for Reducing Greenhouse Gas Emissions from Personal Motor Vehicles. 1995. Washington, D.C.: U.S. Environmental Protection Agency, Air Docket. October.

Marrison, C.I., and E.D. Larson. 1995. Cost Versus Scale for Advanced Plantation-Based Biomass Energy Systems in the U.S.A. and

Brazil. Paper presented at the Second Biomass Conference of the Americas, Portland, Ore., August.

Mitchell, W.L., J.H.J. Thijssen, J.M. Bentley, and N.J. Marek. 1995. *Development of a Catalytic Partial Oxidation Ethanol Reformer for Fuel Cell Applications.* SAE Paper 952761. Warrendale, Pa.: Society of Automotive Engineers.

National Economic Council (NEC). 1996. *Policy Dialog Advisory Committee to Assist in the Development of Measures to Significantly Reduce Greenhouse Gas Emissions from Personal Motor Vehicles.* Report to the President by the Interagency Steering Committee on the Outcome of the Deliberations. Washington, D.C.: National Economic Council. February.

Perlack, R.D., and L.L. Wright. 1995. Technical and Economic Status of Wood Energy Feedstock Production. *Energy* 20 (4): 279.

Pimentel, D., G. Rodrigues, T. Wang, R. Abrams, K. Goldberg, H. Staecker, E. Ma, L. Brueckner, L. Trovato, C. Chow, U. Govindarajulu, and S. Boerke. 1994. Renewable Energy: Economic and Environmental Issues. *BioScience* 44 (8): 536–547.

Ranney, J.W., and L.K. Mann. 1994. Environmental Considerations in Energy Crop Production. *Biomass Bioenergy* 6 (3): 211.

Sinor, J., and B.K. Bailey. 1993. *Current and Potential Future Performance of Ethanol Fuels.* SAE Technical Paper 930376. Warrendale, Pa.: Society of Automotive Engineers.

Sperling, D. 1995. *Future Drive: Electric Vehicles and Sustainable Transportation.* Washington, D.C.: Island Press.

Tyson, S. 1994. Unpublished memo prepared for the National Renewable Energy Laboratory, provided by Paul Bergeron.

U.S. Department of Agriculture (USDA). 1994. *1994 Agricultural Resources and Environmental Indicators.* U.S. Department of Agriculture, Economic Research Service, Natural Resources and Environmental Division. Agricultural Handbook No. 705. Washington, D.C. December.

_____. 1995. *1995 Agricultural Outlook.* USDA Economic Research Service AO-217. Washington, D.C. April.

U.S. Department of Energy (DOE). 1993. *Assessment of Costs and Benefits of Flexible and Alternative Fuel Use in the U.S. Transportation Sector. Technical Report Eleven: Evaluation of a Wood-to-Ethanol Process.* DOE/EP-0004. Washington, D.C.: U.S. Department of Energy.

Walsh, Marie. 1995. Oak Ridge National Laboratory. Personal communication.

Wyman, C.E., and B.J. Goodman. 1993. Near-Term Applications of Biotechnology for Fuel Ethanol Production from Cellulosic Biomass. In *Opportunities for Innovation: Biotechnology,* edited by R.M.

Busche, 151–190. Gaithersburg, Md.: U.S. Department of Commerce, National Institute of Standards and Technology.

Wyman, C.E., N.D. Hinman, R.L. Bain, and D.J. Stevens. 1992. Ethanol and Methanol from Cellulosic Biomass. In *Fuels and Electricity from Renewable Resources*, edited by R.H. Williams, T.B. Johansson, H. Kelly, and A.K.N. Reddy, 865–924. Washington, D.C.: Island Press.

Alternative Fuels and Vehicles: Transition Issues and Costs

MARGARET K. SINGH AND MARIANNE MINTZ

The transition from a personal transportation system dominated by petroleum to one fueled by a mixture of energy sources is unlikely to be seamless for any of the key players. Vehicle purchasers will be faced with systems having different operating characteristics and maintenance requirements. Their vehicles will be more costly and have uncertain resale values. Refueling and servicing will be less convenient, at least initially, and may require specialized and potentially time-consuming procedures. Vehicle manufacturers will be confronted with additional complexity in producing, certifying, and servicing alternative-fuel vehicles (AFVs); in training their assembly, sales, and service personnel; and in marketing vehicles with unproven track records, uncertain resale value, and unknown customer loyalty. Fuel suppliers will encounter similar marketing and production challenges, as well as more complex distribution requirements and formidable investment risk. The vehicle service industry (including aftermarket converters, parts suppliers, independent garages, and insurance companies) will need to establish a supply pipeline of replacement parts, certify parts and conversion procedures, train technicians, and develop operating procedures appropriate to AFVs. State and local governments will be faced with reviewing and perhaps revising emergency plans and procedures; amending local codes for fuel storage and handling, equipment installation, and facility inspection; and revising ordinances governing vehicle operation and servicing.

For each of the players, out-of-pocket costs for AFVs and alternative fuels are likely to be greater during the transition than these same costs will be when large-scale production and distribution of AFVs and their fuels are achieved. Perceived costs could be greater still. It is well known that new technologies tend initially to be more costly than the technologies they are attempting to displace. As demand, production volumes, and experience grow, however, marginal costs decline. Depending on the magnitude of the transition costs and the success of policies to reduce them, the transition costs could undermine the market success of AFVs.

This chapter was prepared as part of a U.S. Department of Energy (DOE) analysis of the market benefits of alternative motor vehicle fuel use. The DOE analysis was conducted in response to the requirements of Section 502b of the Energy Policy Act of 1992 (EPACT), which require DOE to determine the feasibility of producing sufficient fuels to replace 10 percent of light-duty-vehicle (LDV) motor fuel use by the year 2000, and 30 percent by 2010. The published results of the DOE analysis are referred to in this chapter as the "502b study."

This chapter summarizes key issues and barriers that need to be overcome for successful AFV penetration and presents a methodology for developing initial estimates of the costs of these barriers. The total costs developed with this methodology represent a first-cut estimate of the magnitude of the hurdle that must be overcome to achieve market success.

Transition Issues and Barriers

Each of the key players in the transition from conventional to alternative fuels must overcome a set of market and institutional barriers that hinder significant AFV market penetration.

Market Barriers

As discussed above, marginal costs for AFVs and alternative fuels are likely to be higher in the short run than in the long run. Although some of these costs may fall and yield net benefits over time, their distribution may also present barriers. Quite likely, some players will bear a disproportionate share of costs, whereas others will reap a disproportionate share of benefits. Those who take on risks early (for example, AFV producers and purchasers and alternative-fuel suppliers) are more likely to incur higher marginal costs, whereas those who are initially more cautious may benefit from the risk taker's experience. This is especially true on the supply side, where players are faced with making long-term commitments of corporate resources. Original equipment manufacturers (OEMs), fuel producers, and other suppliers have a strong incentive to "look and listen"; to maintain an active research program; and to enter into cooperative agreements with firms that are strong in complementary areas. However, little incentive exists for suppliers to unilaterally launch new technologies or to develop new markets for those technologies.

Vehicle Purchasers

As with all new products, the features that set AFVs apart from conventional gasoline- or diesel-fueled vehicles (CVs) may attract some purchasers but repel others. Some buyers seek out new and untried products (such as the General Motors IMPACT electric car) and sign up to purchase one long before the first unit rolls off the assembly line. Other buyers have a low tolerance for unfamiliar procedures and would never consider purchasing a newly redesigned model, let alone one with a new type of fuel or propulsion system. Without government mandates or other incentives, conventional wisdom suggests that the most likely early adopters of AFVs will be individual "car buffs," public agencies, and businesses either involved in the AFV industry or with a reputation for innovation or public service. A recent survey of electric vehicle (EV) owners in California tends to support this assumption (Kurani, Turrentine, & Sperling 1994). Nearly half of the current EV owners surveyed were either EV enthusiasts or had an entrepreneurial interest in the EV market. Beyond these groups, the limitations of immature technologies or a skeletal transition infrastructure suggest that early adopters will also include motorists with relatively short daily driving ranges, a relatively low perceived value of time, greater flexibility in their daily routines, or a pioneer spirit in which they view such limitations as only minor inconveniences.

In addition to the risk associated with purchasing a new technology that may not succeed in the marketplace, consumers face the additional gamble of choosing the "wrong" technology from the menu of alternative fuels and vehicles offered. Buyers must bet not only that AFVs will become a permanent feature of the automotive market, but also that a particular vehicle/fuel combination will be available 5, 10, or even 15 years in the future. Pity the poor consumer who purchased an eight-track tape deck, a Beta-format videocassette recorder (VCR), or a transitional AFV when popular tapes (or transition fuels) become unavailable or replacement parts are needed. Both the VCR and the personal computer market appear unable to support two competing formats—VHS has become the norm for VCRs, and the personal computer market is shifting to the hybrid DOS-Windows/Power-PC configuration. Although fuel diversity marked the early days of the automotive market and may mark a transition to nonpetroleum fuels, it is not obvious that diversity can be sustained over the long term.

Recognizing that many buyers are unlikely to consider AFVs, both manufacturers and regulatory agencies responding to requirements in the 1990 Clean Air Act Amendments and EPACT are seeking to identify niche markets in which AFVs are more likely to achieve initial market success. To date, most of these efforts have focused on government and business fleets with centralized refueling capabilities.

Vehicle Manufacturers

Like buyers, some vehicle manufacturers seem more averse to risk than others. Both corporate culture and the preferences of existing customers combine to make one manufacturer's strategy seem particularly conservative while another's appears more risky. For manufacturers, "getting out in front of the customer" can be dangerous. Many can recall the rush to produce small, fuel-efficient cars in the wake of the 1973–74 and 1979 oil crises, only to have demand evaporate when oil prices plummeted in 1986. Although demand for lower-emission vehicles consuming domestically produced fuels may be more long-lived, the incremental cost of these vehicles may provoke "sticker shock" among buyers who have long considered themselves environmentalists or advocates of a "buy American" philosophy. Will these buyers spend an extra two, three, or more thousand dollars (or even $500) for an AFV? Limited survey data suggest that they will not (Fairbank, Maullin, & Associates 1993). Of course, manufacturers initially may not price AFVs to recover costs.

Thus, when it comes to commercializing AFVs and the technologies they embody, vehicle manufacturers face a high level of risk. Quite possibly, one or more of today's front-running alternative fuels will falter and go down in history as a transitional technology. To guard against this possibility, manufacturers can diversify their AFV portfolio, pursuing several complementary technologies, or they can ignore the riskiest AFV technologies.

Even if we assume an assured market supported by mandates, price incentives, and other policies, current manufacturers will encounter a costly transition to AFVs. Since AFVs are likely to be produced alongside CVs, product lines will become more complex. A host of new expenses will result from smaller-batch material purchases; retooling; training of assembly, sales, and service personnel; vehicle certification; and product distribution. Unless manufacturers are unusually nimble, AFVs are likely to cause overall unit costs to rise and profits to drop. Alternatively, it is possible that AFVs will be produced by nontraditional manufacturers. Certain states (for example, California) have policies that encourage new manufacturers.

Fuel Suppliers

Fuel suppliers are faced with many of the same issues as vehicle manufacturers. They too run the risk that one or more of today's promising alternative fuels might falter and be only a transitional fuel. Further, unless some existing products are dropped (which seems unlikely), product slates must be expanded to make room for one or more alternative motor fuels. The resulting increase in complexity is costly and cascades downstream from production to storage, distribution, and retailing. Production, storage, and distribution capacity must be added; existing facilities must be modified; specialized equipment to handle new products with different properties must be acquired; workers must be retrained to safely produce, transport, or dispense these new products; and separate distribution and dispensing facilities may have to be developed. Again, alternative fuels may increase overall unit costs and decrease the profits of existing fuel suppliers.

The cost of expanding the existing infrastructure or of developing a completely new infrastructure can be substantial. To develop a methanol or natural gas infrastructure sufficient in capacity to displace 1 million barrels/day of gasoline could cost $5 to $8 billion (DOE 1990). It has been suggested that fuel suppliers use rate basing (spreading the cost over their rate base) to raise the necessary funds. Although simple in concept, the issue of rate basing raises difficult operational and distributional questions (that is, who pays versus who benefits) and is unlikely to be implemented on a large scale until legal challenges have been resolved.

Institutional Barriers

In addition to the legal questions surrounding rate basing (which may render the option unfeasible), institutional barriers include tax inequities, insurability, and the availability of adequate service and support.

Tax Inequities

At the federal level, gasoline and diesel fuels are taxed at $0.184/gal and $0.244/gal, respectively. Federal tax rates on alternative fuels are somewhat lower. However, since all alternative fuels have a lower energy content than gasoline, the rates translate into higher taxes on an energy-equivalent basis (except for electricity, which currently does not pay a highway tax). At the state level, some states tax alternative fuels at a rate lower than gasoline, but most apply the same rate per gallon regardless of energy content. For example, Arizona's flat $0.18/gal tax varies from $0.066/gal for compressed natural gas (CNG) to $0.59/gal for methanol on an energy-adjusted basis (Gushee & Lazzari 1993).

Insurability

The ability to obtain affordable insurance could become another significant barrier. Insurers typically require extensive data on operating experience and claims reporting to assess risk and set rates for different vehicles, often by make, model, engine displacement, and body style. In the absence of detailed databases, insurers may be extremely conservative in rate setting. Combined with relatively higher replacement costs (a function of the incremental costs of AFVs relative to CVs), the cost of insuring an AFV could be substantially higher than that of a CV during the transition period. Moreover, owners of home refueling equipment could be saddled with higher property insurance rates. To date, most AFVs are operated by utilities, public agencies, and large private fleets, many of which are self-insured. As AFVs begin to enter smaller-fleet and household markets, the issue of insurance availability and cost could become important.

Vehicle Service and Support

The service and support sector includes vehicle converters and retrofitters, aftermarket parts manufacturers, maintenance and repair shops, and vocational training programs. Today, most of the firms within this sector that actively participate in the AFV industry are aftermarket converters. The OEMs are currently producing over a dozen models with factory-installed alternative-fuel capability, but converters are likely to remain major suppliers of AFVs in the near future.

Because AFVs are new and different, purchasers expect to require aftermarket support. Historically, the conversion industry has been fluid, growing and shrinking with economic conditions and market demand. Thus, some firms may not be in business two, three, or more years in the future to provide the service and support that AFV purchasers will need. Moreover, since OEMs typically restrict warranty coverage on modified vehicles, aftermarket customers may have access to little or no warranty service even for apparently unrelated problems. Ford Motor Company has begun to address the barrier posed by uncertain aftermarket support. As of 1994, Ford began offering vehicles with special "prep engines" that, when converted or retrofitted by firms certified under the Qualified Vehicle Modifier Program, carry full Ford warranty coverage. A Ford dealer administers the warranty of the alternative-fuel components, but the responsible party is actually the equipment supplier.

With a limited supply of certified technicians, dealer service assistance is another important feature of the Ford program. Currently, few vocational programs offer specialized training in the installation, service, modification, and repair of alternative-fuel engines, fuel systems, compression devices, and fueling equipment. Oklahoma and California, states with major programs to promote alternative fuels and vehicles, are becoming actively involved in training issues (CEC 1994; Tulsa World 1994). As mandated by Section 411 of EPACT, the federal government is also becoming increasingly involved in training.

Another important barrier to converters, as well as to end-users concerned about lost on-board diagnostic (OBD) capability, is access to OBD data. Possible solutions include improved OEM-converter interfaces, through Qualified Vehicle Modifiers or other programs, and regulations governing access under upcoming OBD II requirements.

State and Local Regulations

For the most part, state and local codes are intended to protect public safety. In practice, however, they do much more. Regulations include limits on the location, hours, and method of operation of vehicles and refueling facilities; restrictions on the types of refueling and recharging devices; and requirements for fuel handling.

Restrictions on Vehicle Use

Although numerous examples may be found throughout the 50 states, the most striking and best known is the former ban against vehicles transporting natural gas through the tunnels and bridges of New York City. The restrictions were lifted only after a risk assessment in 1990 showed that the overall risk from a CNG-fueled vehicle in a tunnel is comparable to or less than that from a gasoline vehicle (Cannon 1993). Today, a growing number of municipalities permit CNG-fueled vehicles to traverse local bridges and tunnels. However, it is unclear whether the risk level is also comparable for vehicles using liquefied natural gas (LNG), hydrogen, or certain of the advanced, high-temperature batteries currently under development.

Restrictions against on-board fuel storage anywhere except under a vehicle represent another set of local regulations that may effectively ban CNG and LNG vehicles. Efforts are underway to educate local officials about the relative safety of rooftop storage of natural gas and to overturn these restrictions (Cannon 1993).

Restrictions on Refueling/Recharging

In most cases, refueling and recharging facilities for AFVs are not covered under specific codes. Thus, officials often must research and apply related codes to regulate the installation of these new facilities. In applying related codes, officials will tend to err on the conservative side. For example, local ordinances governing storage, dispensing, and maintenance facilities that use hazardous materials may be applied to the installation of alternative-fuel facilities. Then, only "approved" or "listed" equipment (that is, equipment listed by a recognized testing agency such as Underwriters Laboratory) may be installed, and the installation must be inspected and tested under conditions exceeding normal operation before a certificate of occupancy can be obtained. Equipment certification by state or regional agencies may also be required.

Although the steps are straightforward, several difficulties may arise in practice. For example, safety criteria for dispensing fuel into vehicles may not be covered by state or local ordinances and codes. Appropriate test procedures may not be covered under National Fire Protection Association standards. Finally, because of the expense and lead time involved in preparing standards, specialized and relatively new equipment assemblies may not yet be approved. Thus, local authorities may have to develop alternate methods of determining adequate performance before allowing a facility to go into service (Buys 1994).

Home refueling and recharging is generally not specifically covered under existing codes. The major barrier is cost, ranging from $800 to $1,000 (CEC 1994) to retrofit a home for EV charging to $3,500 for a home gas compressor (Webb 1992). However, if CNG is defined as a hazardous material, local codes could bar indoor installation of gas compressors.

Emergency Response

Each alternative fuel has its own hazards and safety solutions. None is inherently more hazardous than another, or than gasoline and many other materials routinely used in our everyday lives. However, when alternative fuels are used in volume, accidents will occur, and thus emergency preparedness must be incorporated into the transition strategy. Emergency personnel must be trained in understanding the unique hazards, the most effective firefighting and mitigation procedures, and appropriate methods of handling each fuel. Preparedness must include development of standard mechanisms to quickly and effectively identify the type of power system and fuel used in a vehicle so that appropriate procedures can be followed (CEC 1994).

Conclusions

In sum, a wide variety of issues and barriers to the use of alternative fuels and AFVs exist. Several barriers are both crucial and obvious:

- consumer uncertainty with respect to the permanence and performance of AFVs

- vehicle manufacturer and fuel supplier uncertainty regarding consumer response to AFVs in general and to specific technologies in particular

- the increased complexity and initial costs faced by vehicle manufacturers and fuel suppliers in bringing AFVs and alternative fuels to market

Transition Costs and Benefits

In the following analysis of the general magnitude of the costs of the transition to AFVs, we see the chief issues to be (1) the extent to which the magnitude of these costs may undermine or delay the market success of AFVs and (2) the relationship between transition costs and the long-run benefits of AFVs.

We include in our analysis only those barriers that are relatively discrete and quantifiable, and only those whose costs will be higher in the transition than "at equilibrium." By "at equilibrium" we mean that the large-scale production of alternative vehicles and fuels is in place and that vehicle support and fuel distribution systems are well established. Thus, our transition cost model includes the following variables: fuel production cost, retail fuel markup, vehicle production cost, vehicle servicing cost, and the cost of time to travel to refueling facilities. The costs estimated for each variable are costs incremental to the equilibrium costs of these variables.

Many cases were analyzed in the 502b study (DOE 1996), but all ignore transition issues. The 502b study assumes that a well-developed infrastructure exists to produce and provide alternative fuels and vehicles and focuses on estimating the costs and benefits of AFVs at equilibrium. In the transition analysis presented in this chapter, we estimate transition costs (and benefits) for one AFV market penetration case modeled in the 502b study, namely the "unconstrained equal tax case." This case assumes the reference oil prices estimated in the Energy Information Administration's 1994 *Annual Energy Outlook* (AEO) (EIA 1994). The case is termed "unconstrained" because AFV market penetration is not constrained by major policy initiatives designed to reduce greenhouse gases or oil imports. It is an "equal tax" case because all the alternative fuels and gasoline are taxed equally, on a Btu-equivalent basis. In this unconstrained case, AFVs were projected to number over 90 million and to be responsible for over 30 percent of light-vehicle fuel use in 2010. This case also provides the greatest economic benefit of all the 502b study cases.

AFV Stock and Fuel Use Estimates

The 502b study presents total AFV stock and fuel use in 2010. In our transition analysis, estimates are developed for vehicle sales and stock and alternative-fuel use in the years leading up to 2010. The vehicle stock model used is based on the Alternative Motor Fuel Use Model (Greene & Rathi 1990).

Key assumptions include the following:

- An AFV sales increase by 5 percent per year, from 5 percent of light-duty-vehicle sales in 1995 to 80 percent in 2010. (These increases are not to be interpreted as a projection; other percent increases could have been used.)

- The distribution of AFVs by fuel system and type (for example, dedicated alcohol versus flex-fuel alcohol versus natural gas) projected for 2010 in the 502b study applies to AFV sales and stock for all years.

- Utilization for AFVs (that is, annual miles per vehicle) is equivalent to CV utilization. Over time, this utilization level causes a drop in total fuel use per average AFV as the average age of AFVs on the road rises and fuel economy improves slightly.

- For dedicated alcohol vehicles, the mix of fuels is constant for all years. For flex- or dual-fuel vehicles, alternative-fuel use increases over time to the level estimated for 2010. The build-up in alternative-fuel use follows the same pattern as the build-up in AFV sales.

- Electric vehicles penetrate the market only by mandate. Thus, EV stock and fuel use do not follow the same pattern as other AFVs, and they are not included in the transition cost analysis.

Table 6-1 presents the non-EV AFV sales, stock, and alternative-fuel use estimates for selected transition years and 2010 with comparisons

Table 6-1

Alternative-Fuel Vehicle Sales, Stock, and Fuel Use Estimates for Selected Years of Transition Scenario (Nonelectric Vehicles)

	Total AFV Sales (millions)	Percentage of Total AEO[a] Sales (%)	Total AFV Stock (millions)	Percentage of Total AEO Stock (%)	Total Alternative-Fuel Use (billions GEG)[b]	Percentage of Total AEO Fuel Use (%)
1995	0.7	5.0	0.7	0.4	0.3	0.3
2000	4.6	30.1	15.8	7.5	6.3	5.5
2005	9.0	55.2	49.2	22.1	19.9	16.6
2010	13.6	80.3	95.8	40.9	40.1	32.0

[a]*Annual Energy Outlook* (EIA 1994).
[b]GEG = gasoline-equivalent gallons.

Table 6-2

Fuel Use by Alternative-Fuel Vehicles (AFVs) as Calculated for Transition Scenario

Year	Fuel Use by AFVs (GEG[a] in millions)						AFV Sales (millions)	AFV Stock (millions)
	M85[b]	E85[c]	CNG[d]	LPG[e]	Gasoline	Total		
1995	123	3	39	122	204	491	0.7	0.7
2000	2,626	56	770	2,812	3,367	9,631	4.6	15.8
2005	8,206	173	2,237	9,326	7,886	27,828	9.0	49.2
2010	16,234	337	4,138	19,363	11,114	51,187	13.6	95.8

Source: Year 2010 estimates (except sales) from DOE 1996.
Note: These rows may not add to total because of rounding.
[a]GEG = gasoline-equivalent gallons.
[b]M85 = 85% methanol, 15% gasoline.
[c]E85 = 85% ethanol, 15% gasoline.
[d]CNG = compressed natural gas.
[e]LPG = liquefied petroleum gas.

to the AEO estimates of total (AFV and non-AFV) vehicle sales, stock, and fuel use. Table 6-2 presents total fuel use by AFVs by type of fuel for the same years. In both tables, the 2010 estimates are those of the unconstrained case.

Fuel-Related Costs

In this transition analysis, the retail price of alternative fuels is assumed to reflect the full cost of production and distribution. In other words, no subsidies exist for any fuels.

Fuel Production Costs

The Alternative Fuels Trade Model (AFTM) used in the 502b study estimates plant gate fuel prices in 2010 (Leiby 1993). However, during the transition period, these fuel prices may be either higher or lower. In calculating the net benefits from alternative-fuel use, the interim price paths of these fuels need to be taken into account.

The transition analysis assumes the following:

- The price of CNG and liquefied petroleum gas (LPG) will rise between now and 2010. This assumption is based on AEO projections (EIA 1994).

- The price of methanol will decline between now and 2010. The 2010 prices are determined by the AFTM, assuming the price is market determined and thus a function of the cost of production. The estimate of the 2010 methanol price is based on the assumption that methanol will be produced in plants with a capacity of 10,000 tons per day. However, it seems likely that during the early part of the transition, methanol will continue to be produced in smaller, 2,500 ton/day plants. The production cost of smaller plants exceeds that of larger plants by $0.14 per GEG (DOE 1989). This analysis assumes that smaller plants are used exclusively until the market for methanol reaches approximately 5 billion gal/yr; then a mix of small and large plants are used until methanol demand is approximately 10 billion gal/yr. At that volume, methanol is assumed to be produced entirely in large plants.

- The price of ethanol will decline between now and 2010. Ethanol is assumed to be produced from cellulosic feedstocks. (In the early years, some ethanol will be corn based, but this is not accounted for.) Production is assumed initially to be in small plants (1,920 tons per day of dry wood feed) at a cost that is $0.36/gal higher than the cost in large plants. The large plants use 9,600 tons per day (DOE 1993). All production is assumed to be in the large plants when the market reaches equilibrium.

Table 6-3 presents the cost or benefit achieved with the use of each gallon of alternative fuel in selected transition years, both relative to its final equilibrium price in 2010 and relative to the lower price of gasoline in the transition years. The AEO projects that gasoline prices will increase gradually between now and 2010 because of increases in crude oil prices. Since gasoline prices are projected to be lower during the transition period than in 2010, relative gains from alternative-fuel use in the transition are also lower.

146

Table 6-3

Incremental Cost of Using Fuels in the Transition Relative to the Cost of Using These Fuels in 2010 at Equilibrium (1990$)

Year	M85[a] ($/GEG[e])	E85[b] ($/GEG)	CNG[c] ($/GEG)	LPG[d] ($/GEG)	Gasoline ($/GEG)
1995	0.41	0.63	(0.37)	(0.11)	(0.27)
2000	0.33	0.43	0.02	(0.08)	(0.19)
2005	0.10	0.22	0.03	(0.05)	(0.10)
2010	0	0	0	0	0

Note: Parentheses indicate lower costs in transition.
[a]M85 = 85% methanol, 15% gasoline.
[b]E85 = 85% ethanol, 15% gasoline.
[c]CNG = compressed natural gas.
[d]LPG = liquefied petroleum gas.
[e]GEG = gasoline-equivalent gallons.

Fuel Distribution Infrastructure Costs

At least two components of the fuel distribution infrastructure may have transition costs. Stations providing alternative fuels will be constructed over time, but these alternative-fuel stations are likely to be underutilized initially. As a result, the alternative fuels sold at these stations would experience a higher markup to recoup capital costs than at equilibrium. Additionally, because the stations will be phased in, AFV users will likely spend more time traveling to and from alternative-fuel facilities (refueling trip time) during the transition than at equilibrium.

Markup. To estimate these markup costs, we develop estimates of the annual stock of alternative-fuel stations (by type of fuel) and annual average station utilization rates. Key assumptions include the following:

- Each station will be capable of dispensing sufficient alternative fuel to replace 50,000 gallons of gasoline per month.

- The station utilization rate will be 50 percent (25,000 GEG/month) until all the alternative-fuel stations that will ever be needed are constructed. The total number of stations needed is determined by the total fuel use in 2010 (as estimated in the 502b study).

- Once all the stations needed for a given fuel are constructed, average station utilization rates will increase annually as total alternative-fuel use increases annually.

The retail markups for each fuel when sold in stations with a 50 percent station utilization rate and a 100 percent rate are presented in Table 6-4. Linear interpolation is used to estimate the markups for

Table 6-4

Average Station Fuel Markup (1990$)

Fuel	Station Utilization Rates 50% ($/GEG[a])	100% ($/GEG)
M85[b]	0.15	0.12
E85[c]	0.15	0.12
CNG[d]	0.61	0.40
LPG[e]	0.17	0.13
Gasoline	—	0.08

Source: EEA 1994.
[a]GEG = gasoline-equivalent gallons.
[b]M85 = 85% methanol, 15% gasoline.
[c]E85 = 85% ethanol, 15% gasoline.
[d]CNG = compressed natural gas.
[e]LPG = = liquefied petroleum gas.

station utilization between 25,000 and 50,000 gal/month. The markup rates thus derived are then combined with the average station utilization rates estimated above and total alternative-fuel volumes sold to develop total annual estimates of the station markup costs.

Refueling trip time. The following assumptions are used to develop the refueling trip time costs for each individual alternative fuel:

• Only dedicated AFVs will spend incremental time traveling to stations with alternative fuels. For flex-fuel or dual-fuel vehicles, having the option to use gasoline eliminates the need to make longer trips to obtain alternative fuel.

• A refueling location (for any fuel) can be a stand-alone station or a cluster of stations. Of the approximately 120,000 public service stations nationwide, 50 percent are independently located and 50 percent are in clusters of approximately three stations. Thus, there are 80,000 refueling locations nationally.

• No incremental refueling trip time will be required (that is, equilibrium will be achieved) when one-fifth of all refueling locations provide the alternative fuel being evaluated. (The stations will also provide gasoline.) This means that approximately 16,000 stations will provide the alternative fuel.

• When one-tenth (8,000) of all refueling locations provide the alternative fuel, the total incremental refueling trip time will be 10 minutes (5 minutes to find the station and 5 minutes to return to normal activity).

148

• In 1995, with approximately 200 alternative-fuel stations in existence, refueling trip time is 30 minutes.

This approach to develop refueling trip time costs works well with LPG and the alcohols. Sufficient volumes of these fuels are tentatively projected in the unconstrained case in 2010 to indicate that well over 16,000 stations will be needed, and refueling trip time equilibrium will be achieved. The two alcohols are combined for the refueling trip time analysis since the alcohol-fueled AFVs are assumed to be capable of using either fuel.

However, the CNG fuel volume in the unconstrained case—and thus its service station total—is not sufficient to reach refueling trip time equilibrium in 2010 using the above approach. An alternative approach is necessary because the 502b study results are equilibrium results; the transition analysis is constrained to achieve equilibrium by 2010 or earlier. It is thus assumed that, in the unconstrained case, CNG is a special-purpose fuel used only in a few concentrated markets. Fewer total stations would be required to provide the CNG: the assumption in this analysis is 4,000 stations by 2010. They represent the equilibrium point for CNG, and no incremental refueling trip time is required in that year. For earlier years, the maximum refueling trip time is 30 minutes, but it is reduced as the number of stations increases with increasing CNG use.

In addition to these assumptions, two other estimates are necessary to complete the analysis of refueling trip time. First, for each AFV type, an estimate of the amount of alternative fuel dispensed per refill is needed to estimate the number of refills per year. Refill volumes per dedicated AFV are estimated to be as follows: 6.7 GEG for methanol; 9.3 GEG for ethanol; 7.4 GEG for CNG; and 12.9 GEG for LPG (EA-ES&T 1993). The variation in refill volumes across AFVs is based on a number of assumptions, including one that all dedicated AFVs will refuel when their driving range (as determined by the amount of fuel left in the "tank") drops to 90 miles. Second, the cost of refill time is assumed to be $10/hour (Tuthill 1994).

Vehicle-Related Costs

Vehicle-related costs include the cost of producing an AFV and servicing it.

Vehicle Production and Related Costs

Several components of total vehicle cost should be higher during the transition than at equilibrium: the cost of producing the vehicle, warranty cost, and promotion or advertising cost. The transitional incremental costs used in this transition analysis are based on the following assumptions:

- AFVs will cost more to produce at equilibrium than CVs: $100 for alcohol-fuel vehicles and $600 for gaseous-fuel vehicles. These cost increments will be achieved when an AFV type (for example, alcohol) penetrates in ten car and light-truck markets at a penetration rate of 50,000 vehicle sales/year/market.

- The initial (1995) incremental cost of producing AFVs rather than CVs will be $200 for the alcohol-fuel vehicles and $2,400 for the gaseous-fuel vehicles.

- The difference (or delta) between the initial and equilibrium incremental cost of AFV production will decline by 50 percent in the first 5 years of AFV production, no matter what the level of AFV production. If at least one model of each AFV type is produced beginning in 1995, the delta will have been halved by the year 2000. The delta could drop to $0 by the year 2000, or earlier if the first assumption above is met.

The incremental cost for warranties and advertising in the transition will be $500/vehicle. The phasing of this increment is assumed to be the same as that of the cost of producing the vehicle.

Vehicle Servicing Costs

Higher maintenance and repair costs are estimated to add $0.006/mile to the cost of AFV operation until the year 2000, when this increment will disappear. This estimate is based on the following assumptions:

- An incremental cost of $6 every 3,000 miles for maintenance (for example, high-cost oil).

- A $200 increment for repairs (for example, injectors) over the first 50,000 miles. These costs may be borne by the manufacturer (warranties) or consumers.

The stock model used in this analysis contains vehicle-miles-of-travel (VMT) estimates to which this cost estimate was applied.

Total Benefit

The total benefit associated with the availability and use of alternative fuels and AFVs is estimated in the 502b study to be $13 billion in 2010 for the unconstrained case and is comprised of several components.

Supply benefits total $6 billion and result largely from reduced fuel import and fuel conversion (for example, crude oil refining) costs. Demand-related benefits are $4 billion and account for increased consumer satisfaction due to the availability of new classes of vehicles and less expensive fuels, dampened to some degree by the higher cost of AFVs.

Combining supply and demand benefits, the economic benefit of the availability and use of AFVs in the unconstrained case is $10 billion. Environmental benefits (from a potential reduction in criteria pollutants due to the use of AFVs) add another $3 billion, so the total benefits of AFV use in the unconstrained case is $13 billion. For further information on the various components of the total benefit, the reader should refer to the 502b study (DOE 1996).

In our transition analysis, we use the estimates of total benefits described above to estimate the benefits of the availability and use of AFVs in the transition years. The average total benefit per AFV in 2010 in the unconstrained case is $136 (total benefits divided by total AFV stock). For each transition year, we apply the $136/AFV benefit to the total AFV stock estimated for that year to estimate a total benefit (including supply, demand, and environmental components) from AFVs for that year. The per-vehicle benefits (and thus total benefits) may actually be lower in the earlier years when fewer vehicle classes exist, less alternative fuel is used by each vehicle, and fuel prices are higher than at equilibrium, but we do not account for this potential reduction in benefits.

Adjustment to Total Costs and Benefits to Account for Base Case Use of AFVs

The benefits described above for the unconstrained case in the 502b study exclude the benefits derived from a base case of alternative-fuel use. As a result of several federal and state AFV sales mandates, AFVs will be purchased by a variety of fleets. The 502b study estimates that approximately 3 million AFVs will be in operation in 2010 as a result of these mandates. (This estimate does not include the EVs required by EV-specific mandates, such as California's ZEV mandate.) The benefits and costs that the 502b study estimates for the unconstrained case are over and above the benefits and costs that would occur from the operation of these 3 million AFVs in the base case.

For the sake of consistency, we also exclude the benefits and costs associated with the base case in our transition analysis. We estimate a vehicle sales and stock transition path leading to 3 million total AFVs in 2010. We assume that the average costs and benefits estimated for all AFVs in each year of the transition also apply to these base case

Table 6-5

Transition Costs and Benefits of Alternative-Fuel Vehicles (1990$)

Benefit (or Cost) Element [a]	1995 (millions of $)				2000 (millions of $)				2005 (millions of $)				2010 (millions of $)			
	Alcohol	CNG[b]	LPG[c]	Total	Alcohol	CNG	LPG	Total	Alcohol	CNG	LPG	Total	Alcohol	CNG	LPG	Total
Vehicle production	−191	−238	−617	−1,045	0	−742	0	−742	0	−234	0	−234	0	0	0	0
Vehicle servicing	−25	−8	−22	−55	0	0	0	0	0	0	0	0	0	0	0	0
Station markup	−3	−4	−5	−13	−84	−118	−122	−324	−266	−335	−412	−1,014	0	0	0	0
Search time	−88	−22	−45	−154	−586	−325	−472	−1,383	0	0	0	0	0	0	0	0
Fuel price	−39	7	12	−19	−783	−11	213	−582	−756	−53	448	−361	0	0	0	0
Benefits of AFV[d] use	42	13	36	91	965	316	813	2,094	3,037	1,004	2,549	6,590	5,995	2,002	5,001	13,008
Net benefits	−303	−251	−641	−1,195	−488	−880	431	−937	2,015	382	2,585	4,982	5,995	2,002	5,001	13,008

Note: These rows and columns may not add to totals because of rounding.
[a] Costs are negative; benefits are positive.
[b] CNG = compressed natural gas.
[c] LPG = liquefied petroleum gas.
[d] AFV = Alternative-fuel vehicle.

vehicles, and we exclude their total costs and benefits from our estimates of transition costs and benefits.

Results

Table 6-5 presents the total transition costs and benefits of AFVs for selected years. Figure 6-1 presents these data for 1995 through 2010. Figure 6-2 disaggregates the costs by component. As can be seen, total transition costs are higher than benefits in the early years of the AFV transition. The crossover to net benefits occurs in the year 2002. The time of the crossover varies by fuel type. Cumulative costs are $35 billion, with about half related to fuel distribution costs. Cumulative benefits are more than double the costs: $80 billion. The total benefit in 2010 is $13 billion as estimated by the 502b study for the unconstrained case. A net present value analysis of these results, assuming a 10 percent discount rate, indicates that the crossover year for net benefits is 2008 and that the cumulative benefit in 2010 is $7 billion.

Analysis

As indicated previously, the above results are meant to be initial, first-cut, order-of-magnitude estimates. Many assumptions are made and thus the results entail substantial uncertainties. Specific criticisms can be leveled at this analysis, including the following:

- Refueling facilities may not be constructed as rapidly as assumed, and thus transition station markup to account for overcapacity may not be as great as estimated here.

Figure 6-1

Transition Costs and Benefits of Alternative-Fuel Vehicles, 1995–2010 (1990$)

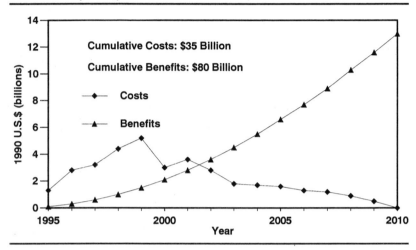

Figure 6-2

Transition Costs of Alternative-Fuel Vehicles by Component, 1995–2010 (1990$)

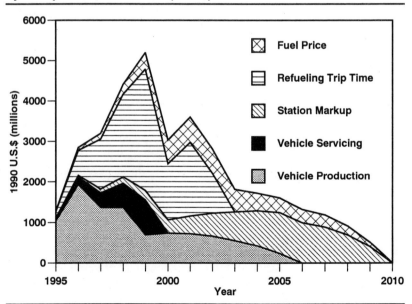

- Alternatively, station markup for the gaseous fuels may be slightly higher than estimated because the transition costs of the construction of fuel distribution systems (not service stations) are not accounted for.

- Individually, each assumption made in the analysis may be reasonable, but alternative, equally reasonable assumptions could lead to higher costs.

- The total benefits could be higher, both at equilibrium and during the transition, because the current estimates do not account for the economic benefits of reducing the impacts of future oil crises.

- Alternatively, the transition benefits could be lower in the early years because the consumer benefit derived from the availability of new classes of vehicles and less expensive fuels should not be as great as at equilibrium.

Additionally, the total transition costs estimated here indicate the costs of just one of many scenarios analyzed in the 502b study. Analysis of other scenarios or other cases with different market penetration rates would lead to different total costs and benefits.

In spite of these criticisms, our transition cost analysis demonstrates that

- transition costs can be substantial relative to the benefits of AFV use over the next 15 years.

- in the early years of a transition to AFV use, transition costs will be greater than the near-term benefits of AFV use.

Conclusion

This chapter has attempted to elucidate the issues and barriers that must be addressed and overcome before significant market penetration of AFVs can occur. Key players in the AFV market must deal with a number of discrete issues, but uncertainty is a major issue that applies to all of them. Will AFVs become a permanent part of the vehicle market, and will the efforts of these players to overcome barriers be rewarded?

This chapter has also taken a first cut at estimating the cost of these transition barriers. Although many caveats can be attached to the specific analysis presented, an overall conclusion is that transition costs are likely to be significant in the early years and higher than the benefits of AFV use. Although long-term benefits outweigh the transition costs, the magnitude of these costs itself presents a substantial barrier to be overcome.

Finally, the transition cost analysis presented here also supports the need for additional work in this area. A more detailed analysis is required so that the effectiveness of various policies designed to eliminate transition barriers and reduce transition costs can be evaluated. The Department of Energy is developing a dynamic transition model with which such an analysis can be conducted.

References

Buys, R. 1994. A Fire Marshal's Experience with Alternative Fuels. Paper presented at the International Alternative Fuels and Clean Cities Conference, Milwaukee, June 30.

California Energy Commission (CEC). 1994. CALFUELS Plan. Draft Report 500-94-002. June.

Cannon, J.S. 1993. *Paving the Way to Natural Gas Vehicles.* New York: Inform, Inc.

EA-Engineering Science and Technology (EA-ES&T). 1993. *Light-Duty Vehicle Queuing Analysis for Alternative Fuel/Gasoline and Conventional Gasoline Refueling Stations.* Silver Spring, Md.

Energy and Environmental Analysis, Inc. (EEA). 1994. Memorandum to DOE on Alternative Fuel Retail Markups. Arlington, Va., March 25.

Energy Information Administration (EIA). 1994. *Annual Energy Outlook 1994.* DOE/EIA-0383(94). Washington, D.C.

Fairbank, Maullin & Associates. 1993. As cited in *Automotive News,* Nov. 22.

Greene, D., and A. Rathi. 1990. *Alternative Motor Fuel Use Model: Model Theory and Design and User's Guide.* ORNL/TM-11448. Oak Ridge, Tenn.: Oak Ridge National Laboratory.

Gushee, D.E., and S. Lazzari. 1993. *Disparate Impacts of Federal and State Highway Taxes on Alternative Motor Fuels.* Congressional Research Service Report for Congress. 93-330 E. Washington, D.C.

Kurani, K.S., T. Turrentine, and D. Sperling. 1994. *Electric Vehicle Owners: Tests of Assumptions and Lessons on Future Behavior from 100 Electric Vehicle Owners in California.* Washington, D.C.: Transportation Research Board.

Leiby, P.N. 1993. *A Methodology for Assessing the Market Benefits of Alternative Motor Fuels.* ORNL-6771. Oak Ridge, Tenn.: Oak Ridge National Laboratory.

Tulsa World. 1994. As reported in *Alternative Energy Network Online Today,* Environmental Information Networks, Inc. July 15.

Tuthill, B. (EEA, Inc.). 1994. Personal communication to authors.

U.S. Department of Energy (DOE). 1989. Assessment of Costs and

Benefits of Alternative Fuel Use in the U.S. Transportation Sector, Technical Report 3. *Methanol Production and Transportation Costs*. DOE/PE-0093. Washington, D.C.

_____. 1990. Assessment of Costs and Benefits of Alternative Fuel Use in the U.S. Transportation Sector, Technical Report 4. *Vehicle and Fuel Distribution Requirements*. DOE/PE-0095P. Washington, D.C.

_____. 1993. Assessment of Costs and Benefits of Alternative Fuel Use in the U.S. Transportation Sector, Technical Report 11. *Evaluation of a Potential Wood-to-Ethanol Process*. DOE/EP-0004. Washington, D.C.

_____. 1996. Assessment of Costs and Benefits of Alternative Fuel Use in the U.S. Transportation Sector, Technical Report 14. *Market Potential and Impacts of Alternative Fuel Use in Light-Duty Vehicles: A 2000/2010 Analysis*. DOE/PO-0042. Washington, D.C.

Webb, R.F., Corp. 1992. *Investigation Regarding Federal Policy Actions for Encouraging Use of CNG as a Motor Vehicle Fuel*. Washington, D.C.: R.F. Webb, Inc.

Evolutionary and Revolutionary Technologies for Improving Automotive Fuel Economy

K. G. DULEEP

The Partnership for a New Generation of Vehicles (PNGV) and the California zero-emissions-vehicle mandate have emphasized advanced automotive technologies that purportedly leapfrog existing automotive technology, leading to very high public expectations for the performance of these technologies. Since much of the information on leapfrog technologies comes from technology developers, the Office of Technology Assessment (OTA 1995), with technical assistance from Energy and Environmental Analysis, Inc. (EEA 1995a), undertook a critical evaluation of these technologies for the U.S. Congress. This chapter presents only the results of the technical evaluation conducted by EEA and does not necessarily represent the views of OTA. Our analysis focuses on fuel economy benefits and costs while also providing a limited examination of emissions implications.

Auto manufacturers can obviously choose a wide variety of technologies for adoption into their vehicles, and the number of combinatorial possibilities is great. The purpose of our analysis, however, is not to explore issues regarding which particular combination is most cost-effective or optimal from the market viewpoint, but to develop estimates for vehicles adopting all of the technologies that can be combined into a single high-technology vehicle. Hence, the scenarios constructed here can be considered, in some sense, as maximum-technology scenarios that are useful for exploring the limits of fuel efficiency. We do not cover fuel-cell-powered vehicles since our analysis for OTA (EEA 1995a) suggests that such vehicles may not be much more efficient than hybrid vehicles, but their incremental price may range from \$8,000 to \$54,000, depending on the type of technology breakthroughs achieved (OTA 1995). However, the cost and performance of fuel cells in 2015 is far more uncertain than the cost and performance of the other technologies discussed here.

An important issue is that manufacturers have the flexibility to vary the size, comfort, safety, and performance features of any vehicle within fairly wide ranges. Even within a size class specification, manufacturers have the option of varying body rigidity, interior volume (within limits), safety and luxury options, and acceleration performance. In the last decade, all of these amenities have increased significantly for almost every market class of car and light truck. For this analysis, we have chosen the median 1995 characteristics of a midsize vehicle as a reference and have held these characteristics constant in scenarios for the future.

We have set performance requirements as follows: *Continuous power demand* (that is, power output that must be sustained indefinitely) is set to a level that allows the vehicle to climb a 6 percent grade at 60 MPH with a modest payload, implying a power-to-mass ratio of 30 kW/ton. Of course, such a long grade is encountered rarely, but this requirement also covers a number of other situations demanding high power—for example, when the vehicle is fully loaded with five passengers and luggage and cruising at 55 MPH up a 3 or 4 percent grade. *Peak power demand* is based on a 0 to 60 MPH acceleration time under 11 seconds with a nominal load, which requires about 60 kW/ton. We have required that peak power be sustained for over one minute, to cover situations in which two highway merge cycles are required back-to-back, or in which there is the need to climb a steep highway entrance ramp (for an elevated highway) and then have enough power to merge into 70 MPH traffic. Hence, the peak 60 kW/ton and sustained 30 kW/ton power requirements are to cover a wide variety of traffic conditions under full load, not just the example cases cited above. Most gasoline-engine-powered vehicles meet these performance levels. Note that, because of the shape of its torque curve, an electric motor can provide equivalent performance at a lower peak output of 50 kW/ton.

The choice of 1995 median vehicle attributes reflects an "accepted" market outcome today. However, it is debatable if these characteristics should be reproduced by nonconventional vehicle types, such as electric or fuel-cell-powered vehicles. In fact, as our analysis shows, these requirements pose significant difficulties for nonconventional vehicle design. Reduction of vehicle capabilities, especially acceleration performance, may make more sense economically. Yet, we utilize these reference attributes precisely because they allow definition of such tradeoffs very explicitly. Without a reference set of attributes, it is not clear how much they can be reduced and what the implications of these reductions are for vehicle marketability. Studies conducted in California have found that consumers may be willing to accept low performance in an EV (Bunch 1992). However, it would be appropriate to include a hedonic cost for reduced performance.

Another important issue is the definition of the term *cost*. There are many types of costs, such as fixed cost, variable cost, and cost to the consumer. Much of the literature on advanced-technology vehicles is not explicit in defining costs. Our analysis uses retail price equivalent (RPE), which has a very specific meaning. Incremental RPE refers to the average change in retail list price associated with technology improvements and is an indication of average consumer price impact, all else being constant. Actual retail prices may vary considerably among models, but this variation represents cross-subsidies among products and is not of specific concern to this analysis. Finally, it should be noted that all results pertain only to new vehicle prices and not to life-cycle costs, which involve a range of issues, such as fuel prices, maintenance requirements, scrappage, or recycle value, that are beyond the scope of this analysis.

Advanced Conventional Vehicles

Previous projections of fuel economy by EEA for the Department of Energy (DOE) (e.g., EEA 1994) suggest that considerable technological improvement could occur in all cars even in the absence of any policy intervention in the market. However, attaining the maximum potential of conventional technology by 2005 and 2015 would require some form of intervention in the market to become a reality. We created two scenarios for each date, one using the mean or manufacturers' average estimate of technology benefit and the second using the most optimistic benefit estimates obtained from the auto manufacturers (virtually all of the data on conventional technologies were obtained from auto manufacturers). EEA has several reports (e.g., EEA 1994) in the public domain that describe the range of conventional technologies available to improve fuel economy over the next 20 years, and their descriptions are not repeated here. Our analysis serves primarily as a refinement or validation of earlier EEA estimates based on auto manufacturer inputs. In this context, auto manufacturers' inputs were surprisingly consistent, and we believe that the technology cases constructed below are both feasible and relatively accurate. Body technologies include lightweight materials, low-drag body shapes, improvements to vehicle packaging, and low-rolling-resistance tires. Engine and drivetrain improvements include low-friction components, improvements to peak thermal efficiency, reduced pumping loss, and lean-burn engine technologies, as well as advanced transmissions.

Many of these technologies are relatively cost-effective. Reduction of factors such as aerodynamic drag, tire rolling resistance, engine friction, and transmission loss are expected to be adopted even in a business-as-usual scenario, although the reductions are not as large as those postulated in our optimistic scenario. Other technologies, such as four valves/cylinder, variable valve timing, advanced fuel injection, and variable-tuned intake manifolds, are likely to be adopted for reasons of performance, drivability, and low-emissions potential, although the market penetrations of these technologies are expected to grow slowly over the next two decades. In the optimistic scenarios, we have examined the fuel economy potential of a hypothetical best-in class car if all technologies that are fully developed and available for commercialization are adopted in such a way as to maximize fuel economy while keeping size and performance constant at 1995 levels.

The most popular car in the intermediate class, the Ford Taurus, served as the 1995 benchmark, or reference, vehicle in our analysis. The current vehicle has an interior volume of 100 cu ft and a trunk volume of 18 cu ft. It is powered by an overhead valve (OHV) two-valve V-6 engine that produces 140 hp and has a peak torque of 165 ft lb at 3,250 RPM. It uses a four-speed automatic transmission with lock-up torque converter, an axle ratio of 3.37, and a relatively steep overdrive ratio of 0.67. The Taurus's curb weight is 3,130 lb; it is tested at 3,500 lb inertia weight; and its engine provides 60 kW/ton. Its composite fuel economy is 28.0 MPG, which is 1.5 to 2 MPG higher than for many other competitors in its class. Its performance is characterized by a 0 to 60 MPH acceleration time of less than 11 seconds (based on car enthusiast magazine tests). The Taurus has a remarkably high ratio of highway to city fuel economy of about 1.69, probably as a result of its low numerical overdrive ratio. This number is usually closer to 1.5 in most cars.

Table 7-1 traces the hypothetical evolution for 2005 and 2015 of a midsize car equivalent to the Taurus under each of the two scenarios. The largest difference between the baseline and the optimistic scenarios is in material substitution and the resultant weight. In other respects, the 2005 scenario projections are relatively mundane. In 2005, the 3.0-liter V-6 is forecast to be replaced by a 2.3-liter four-valve four-cylinder engine with variable valve timing (VVT). Low-speed performance is kept constant by controlling the variable: torque × axle ratio/weight to the baseline level, based on torque at 2,000 RPM, an

Table 7-1

Hypothetical Midsize Car with Advanced Technology

Year	1995[a]	2005 Median[b]	Optimistic[c]	Median[b]	2015 Median[b]	Optimistic[c]
Weight (lb)	3130	2840	2675	2290	2045	1960
Engine						
Size	3.0 l	2.3 l	2.2 l	2.0 l	2.4 l	1.7 l
Type	OHV[d] V-6	OHC[e] I-4[f]	OHC[d] I-4[f]	DISC[g] I-4	OHC[e]/Diesel	DISC I-4[f]
Features	—	4V[h]/VVT[i]	4V[h]/VVT[i]	4V[h]/VVT[i]	4V[h]/Turbo	4V[h]/VVT[i]
HP	140	168	158	144	132	122
Peak torque (ft lb)	165	160	154	140	140	111
Torque @ 2000 RPM	155	150	143	129	130	109
Transmission	L-4[i]	L-5[i]	L-5[i]	CVT[k]	CVT[k]	CVT[k]
Axle ratio	3.37	3.20	3.18	3.09	3.09	3.18
Drag coefficient	0.32	0.28	0.26	0.25	0.25	0.22
Rolling resistance coeff.	0.0105	0.0085	0.0080	0.0070	0.0070	0.0065
0–60 time (sec.)	10.4	9.1	9.1	9.2	10.0	9.2
Fuel economy (MPG)	28.0	38.8	41.7	53.2	59.0	63.5
Incremental price ($) over 1995 base	Base	920	2,100	2,550	2,870	6,250

[a]The Ford Taurus was used as the 1995 reference vehicle.
[b]Median of technology estimates.
[c]Optimistic technology estimate.
[d]OHV = overhead valve.
[e]OHC = overhead cam.
[f]I-4 = in-line, 4-cylinder.
[g]DISC = direct-injection stratified charge gasoline engines.
[h]4V = four valves per cylinder.
[i]VVT = variable valve timing.
[j]L-4/L-5 = automatic lock-up transmission with 4/5 gears.
[k]CVT = continuously variable transmission.

engine speed typical of 30 MPH in second gear or 45 MPH in third gear. This leads to an axle ratio of 3.18, which would normally be very low for a four-valve engine. However, in this case, the VVT is optimized for low-speed torque, making the low axle ratio possible. A five-speed automatic transmission is forecast under this scenario. There are no differences in the assumptions concerning the types of drivetrain technologies for 2005 between the mean and optimistic scenarios, but the benefit for each technology is different, leading to different fuel economy estimates. In many respects, the 2005 maximum-technology hypothetical vehicle is not technologically very different from what can be expected in a business-as-usual 2015 vehicle. This

2015 vehicle, however, is expected by EEA to utilize a 2.5-liter V-6 engine and to offer better acceleration performance and comfort relative to the 2005 maximum-technology hypothetical vehicle.

For 2015, the mean scenario includes the weight projections discussed above and the use of a direct-injection stratified charge (DISC) engine with variable valve timing. The scenario assumes that the lean-NO_x catalyst technology is perfected to meet a NO_x standard of 0.2 g/mile. The reduced weight results in a small-displacement DISC engine, and the resultant fuel economy estimate is 53.2 MPG, with an incremental retail price of $2,550 relative to the baseline 1995 vehicle. It is also possible that the direct-injection diesel can meet this stringent emissions standard by 2015, and we have estimated its fuel economy at 59.0 MPG on diesel fuel. The high efficiency of the DISC engine essentially narrows the difference between gasoline and diesel versions to almost identical levels on an energy content basis since diesel fuel has about 12 percent more energy per gallon than gasoline. The optimistic 2015 scenario forecasts a hypothetical vehicle with a carbon fiber body and a small-displacement DISC engine, with a fuel economy of 63.5 MPG, but the retail price increment is estimated at $6,250, chiefly because of the expensive carbon fiber construction.

All of the above scenarios are for a 2015 emission standard equivalent to the California low-emissions-vehicle (LEV) levels. Current technologies have been shown to be capable of meeting LEV and even ultra-low-emissions-vehicle (ULEV) standards without a significant fuel economy penalty. However, lean-burn engines such as the DISC or diesel would need a lean-NO_x catalyst to meet such standards. Auto manufacturers are quite optimistic that such catalysts will be developed for gasoline engines and be commercially available within 10 years, but their success with a diesel engine is still speculative. It should be noted that even the introduction of oxidation catalysts for diesels lagged the introduction of such catalysts in gasoline vehicles by 18 years. The diesel may also be adversely affected by proposed changes to the test procedure to include a high-speed, high-acceleration phase in the driving cycle, and the prospects for the diesel may be quite poor in the future unless the existing waivers to emission standards are continued or compression ignition engines using methanol are developed.

Electric Vehicles

Electric vehicles (EVs) are now the subject of much technological speculation, given how California's zero-emissions-vehicle initiatives have spurred technology development. The range of public claims about EV prices and capabilities suggests considerable technological and economic uncertainty around these forecasts. However, we found that much of the variability came from the fact that no set of EV attributes regarding size, range, acceleration performance, or comfort features was referenced, and EV prices were often for vehicles with widely differing attributes. Second, many analysts confusingly use the word *cost* to denote price in some instances and manufacturer's variable costs in others. Regarding technology, however, a fair degree of consensus on the status and performance of battery and motor technologies exists among experts at national laboratories and at auto manufacturers in the United States, Japan, and Germany.

Many of this chapter's statements on battery technology are at odds with public claims made by some battery manufacturers. Some advanced battery developers have boldly asserted that their designs will be commercialized by 2000. Given that auto manufacturers were, in late 1995, in the preliminary stages of designing the 2001 model-year cars, such claims cannot be taken seriously for any type of high-sales-volume product. In addition, established battery manufacturers have stated categorically that nearly a decade of testing and research would be required before a single-cell battery concept could be developed into a manufacturable and reliable product capable of powering an EV.

The energy efficiency of an electric vehicle can be estimated largely from knowledge of potential battery characteristics. The following factors enhance EV energy efficiency relative to the efficiency of conventional vehicles:

- elimination of braking and idle fuel consumption

- potential to recover braking energy loss

- reduced accessory-drive-related parasitic power loss

- increased efficiency in converting stored energy to shaft power

If EV accessory power consumption is only 25 percent of the power consumed by accessories in conventional vehicles, it can be shown that an EV uses approximately 14 percent of the energy used by a similar current conventional vehicle if the weights of both vehicles are identical. If electricity generation efficiency, transmission loss, charger efficiency, battery storage efficiency, and battery internal self-discharge are taken into account, the picture is quite different, and the EV of the same weight consumes 60 percent or more of the energy consumed by a current conventional gasoline vehicle of equal weight. In order to obtain sufficient range and performance, however, EVs can be much heavier than similarly sized conventional vehicles. Therefore, an EV can be less efficient on a primary energy basis than even a conventional vehicle of equal size and acceleration performance.

One such primary energy comparison, between a BMW E1 and VW Polo diesel (Scheurer 1992) of 1992 vintage and comparable in size, is shown in Figure 7-1. In this comparison, the overall BMW E1 motor efficiency is low—66 percent rather than 75 to 80 percent. If, however, the motor's efficiency were increased to 80 percent, the EV

Figure 7-1

Losses Within the Overall Energy Chain in Diesel and Electric Cars

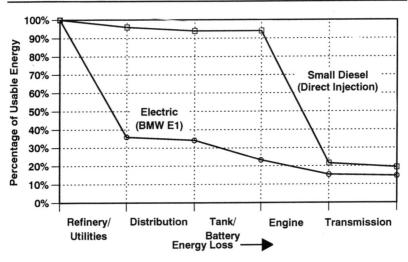

Efficiency	Diesel Car	Electric Car[a]
Refinery or power station	96%	36%
Distribution	98%	95%
Tank/battery	100%	68% (charge cycle and heating loss during standstill)
Engine (depending on driving cycle)	23%	66%
Transmission	90%	95%
Final result (overall efficiency)	19%	15%

Source: Scheurer 1992.
Note: Losses are calculated without energy losses from the oil well to the refinery or from the energy resource to the power station.
[a]Figures for the electric car are for a daily mileage of 30 km (18.6 mi).

would have the same primary energy efficiency as the diesel car. Discharge losses are also high because of the type of battery used (sodium-sulfur) since some electric power is used for battery heating when the vehicle is not in use. The BMW comparison also shows some real-world effects of energy loss due to battery heating and includes accessory losses. Internal self-discharge or battery heating losses reduce efficiency in inverse proportion to miles driven per day. Accessories such as power steering and power brakes typically consume a few hundred watts of power, but the air conditioner, heater, and window defrosters are a major drain on power. Some EVs, such as the GM Impact, have replaced the conventional air conditioner or heater with a heat pump, resulting in an accessory load of 3 kW (GM 1994). Ambient temperature also impacts battery storage capacity, so that the range and efficiency reductions due to accessory power loss are only one part of the picture.

The effect of overall vehicle weight on the range and performance tradeoffs is especially important for an electric vehicle. The battery energy storage capacity and the peak power capacity affect the range and performance capability, and the more batteries used, the greater the capacity. However, as battery weight increases, structural weights must also increase to carry the loads, and a larger motor is required to maintain performance. The weight spiral effects lead to a situation in which benefits decline rapidly with each additional battery weight increment.

To derive EV characteristics, we used a so-called lumped parameter model. A key variable is specific traction energy, defined as the battery output energy per distance traveled, normalized by vehicle curb weight. The energy consumption of several recent EVs indicates that specific traction energy is similar across most cars, ranging between 0.09 and 0.15 kWh/ton-km. Vehicles at the high end of the spectrum had either low regenerative braking efficiency, a less efficient motor, or less efficient electronics. However, the body characteristics or total weight did not have a significant impact on the specific traction energy. For example, by this measure, the GM Impact is less efficient than the Cocconi CRX. The Cocconi CRX stands out with a specific traction energy value of 0.084 kWh/ton-km, but it has no accessories, not even power steering. These energy consumption figures are based on Federal City cycle driving and are often not the ones quoted in the press.

In order to develop the characteristics of a midsize EV, we needed to make certain assumptions regarding the market. In each case, in order to establish economies of scale, we assumed that each EV make or model could be manufactured on a conversion assembly line to produce 2,000 units per month (24,000 units per year), implying a total EV sales of at least several hundred thousand vehicles. The assumption that EVs will be based on "gliders" (conventional vehicles stripped of their drivetrain and modified as necessary) was necessary to establish that the vehicle body technology will be similar to the technology described for conventional vehicles in each scenario. It should be noted that the scenarios imply that the glider uses lightweight materials and has very low aerodynamic drag and rolling resistance. Although GM and BMW have displayed purpose-designed EVs, it is not clear how design and engineering costs can ever be amortized at low sales volumes, and GM officials have publicly stated that the $250 million invested in the Impact to date will never be recouped (*Business Week* 1995, 47). We estimated total investment in assembly line equipment, tooling, development, and launch for a glider conversion facility at $60 million (EEA 1995b), amortized over a four-year cycle. However, it should be noted that total costs are dominated by battery costs so that EV cost is not greatly affected by modest errors in the $60 million estimate.

We performed calculations by setting the EV range to 100 or 200 miles when the energy in the battery is used completely under city cycle efficiency. This figure implies that the real-world highway range will likely be 110 or 220 miles, whereas the city range will likely be 80 or 160 miles. However, since lead-acid batteries should be discharged only 80 percent, these ranges should be discounted by an additional 20 percent for EVs using such batteries. In each case, we controlled performance to average levels of 50 kW/ton based on electric motor output, with weight based on curb weight plus nominal payload.

In 2005, an EV powered by an advanced semi-bipolar lead-acid battery with an 80-mile range and gasoline-car-equivalent acceleration performance appears to be a technically viable prospect. We base the costs of this battery on one manufacturer's input, and we note that lower-specific-energy batteries are available for a lower price. We estimate the incremental price for the intermediate-size car at about $11,000, an estimate consistent with the results of estimates produced by Sierra Research (1994) under contract to the American Automobile Manufacturers Association, although the assumptions embodied in their calculations are not provided. Auto manufacturers, however, estimate incremental RPE levels twice as high ($20,000 to $25,000); their claims have also not been documented, but the prices may be associated with low sales volumes. Even so, an intermediate car's weight increases from less than 1,300 kg (2,860 lb) to over 2,030 kg (4,400 lb). Very significant weight reductions would occur if the battery used were a nickel–metal hydride design and if the range were restricted to about 100 miles. We estimate incremental prices at almost twice that of a lead-acid battery, even though we have estimated that the battery will be almost three times as expensive (at $400/kWh) as a lead-acid battery per unit of stored energy. However, if the nickel–metal hydride battery can be manufactured for $200/kWh, it will be lower in cost than the lead-acid battery (at $150/kWh) because of the weight-compounding effects, and the incremental vehicle price would be only $8,800.

An example of the components of the incremental RPE calculation is shown in Table 7-2. We derived battery and motor/controller costs from motor manufacturer data, whereas we derived incremental costs of electric power steering and heat pump over conventional systems from supplier quotes (AC-Delco 1995). Those "costs" are the costs to an auto manufacturer buying the components at a sales volume of 20,000 to 25,000 per year for this model, but there is an implicit assumption that total battery and motor sales across all models is over 100,000 units/year. We based costs of the internal combustion engine,

Table 7-2

Incremental Costs and Retail Price Equivalent for 2005 Midsize Electric Vehicle

Gasoline Vehicle Equivalent, 80-Mile Range in the City

Component	Size	Cost Basis[a]	Cost ($)
Battery (lead-acid)	34.9 kWh	$150 kWh	5,240
Motor-controller	105.9 kW	$(300 + 30 \times kW)$	3,480
Total electric drivetrain	—	—	8,720
Engine	125 kW	$(400 + 18 \times kW)$	2,650
Transmission	5-speed automatic	$(300 + 2 \times kW)$	550
Emission controls	evaporation + exhaust	$300	300
Net savings	—	—	3,500
Electric power steering	—	$65 (increment)	65
Heat pump A/C	—	$300 (increment)	300
Total variable cost (V)	—	—	5,585
Unit fixed investment (F)	—	4-yr amortization	900
IRPE[b](1995$)	—	$(1.4 V + F) \times 1.25$	10,900

[a]The costs are much lower than current costs and include the learning curve effects for batteries, motors, and controllers. Battery charger cost not included in IRPE, which is relative to the 2005 (median) scenario vehicle defined in Table 7-1.
[b]IRPE = incremental retail price equivalent.

Table 7-3

Characteristics of 2015 Midsize Electric Vehicle

Acceleration Performance Similar to Gasoline Vehicle

Battery	Lead-Acid	Nickel–Metal Hydride	Nickel–Metal Hydride	Sodium-Sulfur	Lithium-Polymer
Scenario	(m)	(m)	(o)	(o)	(o)
Range (miles)	80	100	200	200	300
Battery wt (kg)	515	216	525	245	195
Vehicle wt (kg)	1,430	947	1,366	922	1,333
Energy efficiency (kWh/km)	0.167	0.103	0.140	0.093	0.150
IRPE[a] (1995$)	2,620	8,830 (2,750)[b]	23,900	18,600	10,400

Source: EEA 1995a.
Note: Vehicle parameters other than the drivetrain are identical to those of the 2015 (median) vehicle described in Table 7-1. Scenarios are (m) for manufacturers' median expectations and (o) for optimistic expectations.
[a]IRPE = incremental retail price equivalent relative to 2015 (median) vehicle described in Table 7-1.
[b]If nickel–metal hydride battery is available at $180/kWh instead of $360/kWh.

transmission, and emission control systems on EEA (1994), adjusted for inflation. Our analysis of fixed costs is based on formulae derived from a net present value analysis described in EEA (1994). Note that such issues as the learning curve effects are included in the costing of batteries and motors, since there is no learning curve effect for EV assembly.

Table 7-3 provides the EV projections for 2015 with a variety of batteries. We expect battery costs to decrease by 10 to 15 percent relative to the 2005 values if EVs are successful in the market. As body weight is reduced with new materials technology, and with the modest battery improvements to increase specific energy that are expected to occur by 2015, weight-compounding effects should provide more reasonable prices by 2015. We estimate the incremental price for a lead-acid-powered EV with a range of 80 miles and with reasonable performance at roughly $2,600 over a similar conventional car in an advanced-technology scenario, whereas a nickel–metal hydride battery–powered version with a range of 100 miles could retail for $8,800 more at a battery cost of $360/kWh, or for as little as $2,750 more if battery costs reach $180/kWh. In a more optimistic scenario, even a 200-mile range is possible with nickel–metal hydride batteries at incremental prices of about $24,000, whereas sodium-sulfur batteries can provide this range at a cost of about $17,600. However, if the lithium-polymer batteries succeed in meeting expectations, an EV with a 300-mile range could become available at an incremental price of $10,400 for a midsize car, even after accounting for the fact that these batteries are likely power limited and that ultracapacitors would be needed to provide the peak power requirements for acceleration. These price and range estimates make it clear why there is interest in the lithium-polymer battery.

All of these estimates are based on assumed performance levels and assumptions regarding battery costs and component efficiency. As a sensitivity analysis, we estimated the effects of battery cost reductions, performance reductions, range reductions, and component efficiency changes on the 2005 lead-acid-battery-powered intermediate-size EV. Range reductions have a very large effect on cost and battery requirements. Reducing the range to 50 miles reduces the EV incremental price to $3,170, and battery size is less than 40 percent the size for a range of 80 miles. Reducing performance levels (with a range of 50 miles) provides only modest reductions in battery weight, largely because the lead-acid battery is energy storage limited, not power limited, but reduced motor controller costs reduce the incremental price to $2,130. If battery costs fall from $150/kWh to $100/kWh, the vehicle incremental price is reduced to $960; including the maximum level of component efficiency of motor/controllers and drivetrain reduces the vehicle incremental price to $410. Hence, it is theoretically possible to build a reduced-range EV for a very low incremental price if the most optimistic assumptions are used in all facets of the analysis. In fact, Renault and Peugeot-Citroen have chosen to market limited-range low-performance vehicles in France at a low price (Bureau 1994). Even if range were kept at 80 miles, the incremental price would be $4,125 if very different assumptions regarding performance, component efficiency, and battery cost were used. However, our base assumptions are likely to provide the most realistic forecast of actual EV cost for an equal-performance comparison.

Hybrid Electric Vehicles

The range limitations of the electric vehicle and its potential cost have driven many analysts to suggest a hybrid electric vehicle (HEV) combining an internal combustion engine with an electric motor system as a more optimal and more viable prospect. Indeed, several papers claim that hybrids are capable of fuel economy values of over 80 MPG (e.g., Burke 1995); one has even suggested that several hundred MPG should be possible (Lovins 1995). Our reviews of these papers suggest that a number of factors regarding the capability of the HEV, such as hill climb capability or performance repeatability, were not considered and that the vehicle specifications utilized in some such studies would not meet the goals set for our study. In some studies, the electrical power storage medium had assumed efficiencies and specific power ratings far in excess of anything available now even in prototype form.

A hybrid vehicle is defined here as one that features both an internal combustion engine and an electric drivetrain, but other analysts have used alternative definitions—for example, fuel cell/battery combinations. The term *hybrid* is applied to a wide variety of designs with different conceptual strategies on the use and size of the two drivetrain systems. Classifications of hybrid vehicles have delineated two basic types: series and parallel. In a series hybrid, the power generated by the combustion engine is always converted to electricity and either stored or used to drive an electric motor connected to the vehicle's wheels. In a parallel hybrid, the combustion engine or the electric motor drives the wheels directly. It is noteworthy that most of the manufacturers who have displayed prototype hybrid vehicles have selected the series design. The exception is VW: their engineers believe that series designs are being displayed largely because they are very easy to develop but that they are inefficient for reasons explained below. Another method classifies hybrids according to whether the vehicles require externally supplied electrical power (like an EV) or can operate solely by using on-board fuel; these categories are labeled as nonautonomous and autonomous hybrids, respectively.

For either the series or parallel type of hybrid, the combustion engine and the electrical system can be of widely different sizes. In both hybrid types, at one end of the spectrum, the engine would act as a range extender by charging the battery (or other energy storage device) and the electric drivetrain would be quite similar to that of the EV. Hence, if the engine maximum output were sized close to average power demand during a 70 MPH cruise on the highway (for example, 15 to 20 kW/ton of vehicle weight), the range of the vehicle would be similar to that of a conventional car, and the electrical storage device's state of charge could be maintained at a near-constant level except under an abnormally long hill climb. Typically, such vehicles are designed to be nonautonomous, and the storage devices are charged from the electric mains. At the other end of the spectrum, the engine would be large in size and the battery or power storage device relatively small so that the engine could be employed to provide peak power for acceleration and battery recharging capability. Obviously, an infinite array of combinations exists in between the two extremes. The amount of energy stored in the battery or storage device, as well as its peak power capability, determines the control algorithm of how the engine and battery/storage device supply power to the drivetrain under any arbitrary driving cycle. Autonomous hybrids of either the parallel or series type usually utilize larger engines than nonautonomous ones. We have not considered the nonautonomous hybrid in our analysis since its characteristics are similar to those for an EV and it is not efficient or powerful enough to be driven normally if the batteries are depleted. It is of interest to note that the winner of last year's DOE HEV challenge was a nonautonomous hybrid from the University of California at Davis with a limited performance capability beyond the driving range when the batteries were depleted (Chattot 1995).

Series Hybrids

In this type of hybrid, the engine is used only to drive a generator, and the wheels are powered exclusively by an electric motor. A battery (or flywheel/ultracapacitor) is used to store energy, obtaining some energy input from regenerative braking and most of the input from the engine/generator. The motor can be powered either by the engine/generator, the battery, or both (at high power). Strategy considerations about when to use the battery or the engine/generator lead to decisions about the relative power output of each unit, as well as the energy storage capacity requirement for the battery.

Since the battery is capable of providing peak power in short bursts only, the critical engine size is limited by the maximum continuous demand under the most severe design conditions. Consistent with the analysis for EVs, we imposed the requirement that a series HEV must have a continuous power capability of 30 kW/ton of vehicle and payload weight. This assumption sets a lower limit on engine size. The peak power requirement is 50 kW/ton of vehicle and payload to permit a 0 to 60 MPH acceleration time of less than 12 seconds so that the batteries must supply the additional 20 kW/ton (above the engine output) for peak accelerations. Calculations show that operating the engine at its single best-efficiency point at all times is not optimal because the engine size becomes quite large, with attendant weight and cold-start fuel consumption penalties under this strategy.

A better strategy would allow the engine to operate at much higher peak power if the control logic determines that the load is not a transient one. For example, if high peak loads persist for over 20 or 30 seconds, the control logic can allow the combustion engine to rapidly provide more power (albeit with much lower efficiency) so that the batteries are not taxed too heavily. In addition, the engine can provide a range of horsepower if efficiency is allowed to decline to within 10 percent of the maximum. Such an operating strategy does not require as much power and energy to be available from the storage device with potential charge/discharge losses. In the case of battery storage, for example, the 10 percent efficiency loss in the engine is compensated by a 20 percent gain in avoiding the charge/discharge loss. These requirements could be achieved by a smaller engine that is capable of providing the peak power requirement at its maximum RPM while meeting continuous power requirements at or near its most efficient operating point.

Solving for vehicle weight using the 1995 Taurus baseline example, we find the total weight of this type of series hybrid system to be very similar to that of the current intermediate-size car. On the urban cycle, the engine would be on 28 percent of the time and shut off for the rest of the cycle. On the highway cycle, the engine would be on for 62 percent of the time and would operate continuously at speeds above 70 MPH on level ground. This situation is favorable for fuel economy since the engine would be operating at or near its optimal efficiency point, and energy can flow directly from generator to motor without going through the battery. This example calculation (using the 1995 midsize car body and prototype battery and engine/generator, whose efficiencies may equal the 2005 production component efficiencies) shows that urban fuel economy for the HEV "Taurus" is 33 MPG, highway fuel economy is 41 MPG, and composite fuel economy is 36 MPG—about 30 percent better than the current Taurus. However, most of the improvement is in the urban cycle, with only a small (8.4 percent) improvement on the highway cycle.

The 30 percent figure is an optimistic number for current technology, since each of the components has been selected to be at the potential 2005 expected efficiency, which is higher than the currently observed range. It also assumes the availability of a semi-bipolar battery that can produce high peak power for acceleration. It is easy to see that in the absence of such high-peak-power capability, fuel economy drops precipitously. If a current lead-acid battery with a peak-power capability of 125 W/kg is used, composite fuel economy is only 24.5 MPG, which is almost 12 percent lower than that of the conventional Taurus. These findings are in good agreement with the observed fuel efficiency of some HEVs with conventional lead-acid batteries. Both Nissan and BMW reported lower fuel economy for their series hybrid vehicles, which used nickel-cadmium batteries with specific peak power of 125 to 150 W/kg.

Table 7-4 shows energy storage projections for a 2015 HEV vehicle using three different types of energy storage. The use of a lightweight

Table 7-4

Attributes and Estimated Fuel Economy of 2015 Series Hybrid Vehicles

Electric Energy Storage	Bipolar Lead-Acid	Ultra-capacitor	Flywheel
Vehicle weight (kg)	907	865	852
Electric storage wt. (kg)	82.5	59.5	52.2
Engine size (L)	0.7	0.7	0.7
Engine peak HP	42	40	40
Motor peak kW	55.3	53.2	52.6
Fuel economy (MPG)			
Urban	59.2	65.9	67.7
Highway	74.6	78.9	80.1
Combined	65.3	71.2	72.8
Range as EV (miles)	26	5.4	11.2
Time at maximum power (minutes)	5.5	1.2	2.6
IRPE[a] (1995$)	3,170	8,300	6,100

Source: Adapted from EEA 1995.
Note: Vehicle non-drivetrain characteristics identical to 2015 (median) scenario level in Table 7-1.
IRPE is relative to 2015 (median) car in Table 7-1.
[a]IRPE = incremental retail price equivalent.

aluminum body with low drag and low-rolling-resistance tires per the 2015 (median) scenario in Table 7-1, along with a high-efficiency engine, permits the HEV with a bipolar battery to be 280 lb lighter than the conventional drivetrain, although the engine must be a 0.7-liter two-cylinder engine with potential noise and vibration problems. Only 82 kg of battery is required if it is of the advanced bipolar type rated at 500 W/kg of specific power. Even so, the fuel efficiency at 65 MPG is only 23 percent better than that of the equivalent 2015 advanced vehicle with a conventional drivetrain.

The flywheel- and ultracapacitor-equipped vehicles are estimated to be even lighter and more fuel efficient at 71 to 73 MPG, but again the problems of energy storage persist. Assuming that the ultracapacitor meets the DOE long-term goal of a specific energy storage capacity of 15 Wh/kg, it can still provide peak power for only about 25 seconds starting from a fully charged condition if sized for peak power. A flywheel sized for peak power can provide this peak power for only 65 seconds. Such low values make it impossible for a vehicle to have repeatable acceleration characteristics—for example, if subjected to two or three hard accelerations over a few minutes. Doubling or tripling the flywheel or ultracapacitor size is a solution and is assumed in Table 7-4, although it has cost and weight penalties. The main point of this discussion is that a high-peak-power lead-acid battery is a potentially better solution than the ultracapacitor or flywheel with respect to an HEV, especially if local EV operation is desirable.

There are also significant issues with respect to emissions. Popular opinion is that the series HEV facilitates constant speed or load operation of the combustion engine, so that low emissions should be an automatic outcome. This assumption ignores the fact that 75 percent of all emissions in a conventional car occur in the first two minutes after cold start. This phase also occurs in HEVs, but the use of electrically heated catalysts becomes easier if the storage device has adequate energy reserves. However, Honda is already close to certifying a conventional car to ULEV levels so that the advantages of HEVs in emission terms appear minimal. In addition, since the HEV's engine is on for a small fraction of the time (around 27 percent) during the urban cycle, cold-start emissions will be a much larger fraction of total emissions, up to 90 percent. Due to high load operation, cold-start NO_x could be a problem at LEV standards. In this context, limited energy storage capacity would result in frequent restarts of the engine. Hot-restart emissions could be reduced in the future but may involve some cost penalty.

Parallel Hybrids

The parallel hybrid differs from the series hybrid in that the engine and the motor drive the wheels in the parallel design. The close coupling between engine and motor duty cycles makes the parallel hybrid difficult to analyze without a detailed simulation model that computes efficiencies as a function of operating speed and load for both devices. Conceptually, the general strategy is to downsize the engine so that the maximum power requirement is satisfied by the sum of engine and motor output. Relative to a series hybrid, the required electric motor size is much smaller, and costs can be lower. There are two possible operating strategies in the broad sense: (1) to use the electric motor for base (light) loads while using the engine to provide power at higher loads; (2) to utilize an engine for the light load and the electric motor for short-term peak loads. In the first approach, the engine is turned on and off depending on vehicle load requirements, whereas in the second it operates continuously.

VW has chosen the first approach and has used a small electric motor with 9 kW peak output to aid a diesel or gasoline engine. The weight of the motor without the clutch is 14 kg, and the motor is used exclusively at all loads below 7 kW, which corresponds to a cruise speed of 40 MPH on a level road. The engine is started instantaneously at higher power demand. However, the transitions from motor to engine power are quite difficult to accomplish smoothly across the range of driving conditions encountered. The VW Golf hybrid consumes 2.8 l of diesel per 100 km and 15.8 kWh of electric power on the Federal Test Procedure (FTP) urban cycle (Josefowitz & Köhle 1992). If the electricity was generated (for example) at 34 percent energy efficiency at the wall plug from primary fuel, the hybrid has a fuel consumption of 4 liters per 100 km diesel equivalent. This fuel use rate corresponds to a fuel economy of 58 MPG, about 35 percent better than that of the conventional Golf diesel, which has a city cycle efficiency of 43 MPG.

In the second operating strategy, the engine runs much as it does in a conventional car, and the electrical motor provides additional power during periods of high power demand—that is, during acceleration. As a result, a much smaller engine can be used without degrading performance. The disadvantage with this strategy is that the engine is operated at idle and light loads so that efficiency suffers. However, the need to start the engine instantaneously at high power demand is eliminated, and drivability is typically better while avoiding emission problems associated with hot restart. BMW has displayed a prototype 5-series car using this strategy, which attained a fuel economy of 28 MPG on the EPA combined cycle, a result not much better than for a conventional BMW 518i of equivalent performance.

We investigated two alternative specifications for midsize parallel hybrid vehicles. The first hybrid uses a 2-liter engine and a flywheel for energy storage, whereas the second uses a 1-liter engine with a battery for energy storage. Either type of operating strategy can be incorporated with the two specifications. We analyzed the fuel efficiency of these hybrid designs using a simple model, with the following results: the strategy of using the engine for peak loads could provide fuel economy gains of about 25 to 30 percent with the 2-liter engine plus flywheel specification; fuel economy gains would be 30 to 35 percent with the smaller (1-liter) engine plus battery storage. These estimates are relative to equivalent vehicles with conventional drivetrains, although the drivability and hot-restart problems are daunting. We estimate the fuel economy gains to be only half as much when the engine is on all the time, but emissions and drivability are much easier to perfect. The second strategy may make more sense when simplicity, reliability, and low cost are important. The percentage changes in fuel economy should be generally applicable to all size classes, given the inaccuracies inherent in our simple methodology. Fuel economy projections from existing HEV simulations provided by Chrysler (Asmus 1994) using a sophisticated simulation model are consistent with the estimates provided above.

Prices

We computed the incremental retail price equivalents for the types of series and parallel hybrid vehicles investigated using a methodology similar to the one employed for EVs. Battery and motor cost formulae were identical to those used for EV cost estimates. The generator was assumed to be less expensive than the motor because of its restricted operating speed range, and we estimated its cost at $25/kW (peak). Ultracapacitor and flywheel costs were based on DOE goals rather than real-cost estimates, and ultracapacitors were sized to be able to sustain peak power for at least one minute. Investments were estimated at $200 million (incremental) for an HEV facility to produce 100,000 vehicles per annum at 80 percent capacity in an earlier study (EEA 1995b).

From these inputs we estimated incremental prices relative to advanced conventional vehicles for HEVs of $3,170 with a bipolar lead-acid battery; of $6,100 with a flywheel; and of $8,300 with an ultracapacitor. The bipolar lead-acid battery is the cheapest solution since both flywheel and ultracapacitor are relatively expensive for energy storage, which became a limiting constraint in our analysis. Relaxing the energy storage requirements could make flywheels and ultracapacitors more competitive at the cost of performance repeatability.

Costs for parallel hybrids were not estimated in as much detail but appear to be lower than those for series hybrids. Costs are lowered for a hybrid having a continuously operating combustion engine because of the absence of a separate generator and the use of a small flywheel energy storage system, but are increased by the need for a larger engine and transmission. For a hybrid having an intermittently operating engine, the engine size is similar to that of the series hybrid, as is the battery size. The motor is smaller, and the vehicle does not need a separate generator, but these cost reductions are partially offset by the cost of a transmission. Hence, we expect the incremental RPE for a parallel hybrid to be about 25 percent lower than that for a series hybrid, but it could be even lower, depending on the specific strategies chosen.

Conclusions

Our estimates of the potential benefits of different technology combinations, summarized in Table 7-5, suggest a supply curve for midsize vehicle efficiency in 2015, holding performance constant.

Table 7-5

Summary Estimates of Potential Fuel Economy Improvements for Advanced-Technology Passenger Cars

	Fuel Economy (MPG)	Percent Increase[a]	Incremental Price[a] (1995$)
Advanced conventional (gasoline)	53.2	90	2,550
Advanced conventional (diesel)	59.0	111	2,870
Optimistic conventional (gasoline)	63.5	127	6,250
Electric vehicle (100-mile range)[b]	51.0	82	5,250
Advanced conventional (gasoline)	53.2	90	2,550
Hybrid vehicle with battery	65.3	133	5,700
Hybrid vehicle with flywheel	72.8	160	8,650
Hybrid vehicle with ultracapacitor	71.2	154	10,850

[a]Relative to a baseline 1995 midsize vehicle having a composite EPA test fuel economy of 28.0 MPG and a retail price of $19,500.
[b]Calculated for electricity generation efficiency of 33 percent at wall plug. Other assumptions regarding this efficiency are possible.

The incremental fuel economy and price estimates are given relative to a 1995 baseline midsize car rated at 28.0 MPG and costing $19,500 in 1995 dollars. We find that, for a price increase of 13 percent, an advanced conventional vehicle would achieve a 90 percent MPG increase, or a per-mile fuel use reduction of 47 percent. A relatively small further improvement in gasoline vehicles would come at a substantially greater cost. Electric vehicles of 100-mile range appear to offer an 82 percent energy efficiency improvement at a 27 percent price increase. Various hybrid electric configurations offer 133 to 154 percent MPG increases (57 to 61 percent consumption reduction) at price increases of 29 to 56 percent. The analysis points to an array of options available for the future, with each option providing different tradeoffs in technology risks and emission benefits. Hence, there may be market niches for all of these vehicles types.

References

AC-Delco. 1995. Private communications to Energy and Environmental Analysis, Inc.

Asmus, T. 1994. Presentation to the Office of Technology Assessment on HEV Attributes. Chrysler Corporation.

Bunch, D. 1992. *Demand for Clean Fuel Personal Vehicles in California*. ITS

Report No. UCI-FTS-WP-91-8. University of California at Irvine.

Bureau, N. 1994. Electric Peugeot 106 and Citroen AX Vehicles in Customer Hands in La Rochelle. Paper presented at the 12th EV Symposium, Anaheim, California, December 1994.

Burke, A.F. 1995. Hybrid Vehicles. In *Encyclopedia of Energy and Technology*, 1709–1723. New York: Wiley.

Business Week. 1995. Shocker at GM: People Like the Impact. January 23, p. 47.

Chattot, E. 1995. *The Continuing Development of a Charge Depletion HEV, Aftershock, at UC-Davis.* SAE Paper 95000.

Energy and Environmental Analysis, Inc. (EEA). 1994. *Documentation of the Fuel Economy, Performance and Price Impact of Automotive Technology.* Report to Martin Marietta Energy Systems.

_____. 1995a. *Automotive Technologies to Improve Fuel Economy to 2015.* Report to the Office of Technology Assessment.

_____. 1995b. *Characteristics of Alternative Fuel Vehicles: Inputs to the TAFVM.* Report to Martin Marietta Energy Systems.

GM. 1994. Preview brochure on Impact specifications. Detroit, Mich.: General Motors Corporation.

Josefowitz, W., and S. Köhle. 1992. The Volkswagen Golf Hybrid. Paper presented at 11th International EV Symposium, Milan, Italy, September 1992.

Lovins, A.B. 1995. Hypercars: The Next Industrial Revolution. In *Transportation and Energy: Strategies for a Sustainable Transportation System*, edited by D. Sperling and S.A. Shaheen. Washington, D.C.: American Council for an Energy-Efficient Economy.

Office of Technology Assessment (OTA). 1995. *Advanced Automotive Technology: Visions of a Super-Efficient Family Car.* Washington, D.C.: U.S. Congress, Office of Technology Assessment.

Scheurer, K. 1992. The BMW E-1: A Purpose Designed EV. Paper presented at 11th International EV Symposium, Milan, Italy, September 1992.

Sierra Research. 1994. *The Cost-Effectiveness of Further Regulating Mobile Source Emissions.* Report to the American Automobile Manufacturers Association (AAMA).

Chapter Eight

Keep On Truckin'—Sustainably?

K. G. DULEEP

On-highway trucks are estimated to account for about 30 percent of the total ton-miles of freight hauled in the United States and approximately 29 billion gallons of fuel consumption (both gasoline and diesel) in 1995. This chapter examines the potential growth in ton-miles of freight hauled by trucks from 1995 to 2015, as well as the resultant growth in fuel use under a baseline business-as-usual scenario. The analysis then identifies the potential for technological improvements to trucks and operational improvements to trucking to offset the projected growth in fuel use in the baseline scenario. The results of different scenarios determine if it is possible for trucking to be sustainable and identify the actions necessary to make it sustainable.

Truck Characteristics by Class

At the broadest level, heavy-duty trucks are defined by the Environmental Protection Agency (EPA) as trucks over 8,500 lb gross vehicle weight (GVW). The classification encompasses large pickups to tractor-trailer combinations with GVW in excess of 100,000 lb. The truck manufacturing industry has classified trucks into nine classes, with light-duty trucks labeled as Class I and Class IIA, which are not considered in this analysis. A somewhat more aggregate grouping is employed by Energy and Environmental Analysis, Inc. (EEA), which defines three subclasses of heavy-duty trucks:

- light-heavy trucks, covering industry Classes IIB through IV, or 8,501 to 16,000 lb GVW

179

- medium-heavy trucks, covering industry Classes V through VIIIA, or 16,001 to 50,000 lb GVW

- heavy-heavy trucks, covering industry Classes VIIIB and IX, or over 50,000 lb GVW

Although the light-heavy class dominates the fleet in registrations, with an estimated U.S. total of 6.396 million in 1995, these trucks are generally large pickups, vans, and delivery trucks used principally in local or intracity freight delivery operations or by light-commercial establishments providing building, maintenance, and repair services. Their contributions to intercity freight ton-miles is estimated to be quite small and is ignored in this analysis.

Medium-heavy-duty trucks are estimated to total 2.263 million vehicles in the U.S. fleet (EEA 1994) and are used in a combination of local intracity services and short-haul intercity operations. Gasoline versions of these trucks see greater local service, whereas diesel versions see more short- and long-haul service. About 80 percent of medium-heavy-duty trucks are diesel powered. Class VI, VII, and VIIIA diesel trucks are operated about two-thirds of the time in local (or intracity) use and only one-third of the time in short- or long-haul intercity use (Table 8-1). Since the typical average medium-heavy-duty diesel truck is driven about 20,000 miles per year, the net contribution of these trucks to intercity freight ton-miles is small.

Class VIIIB trucks account for the vast majority of intercity freight ton-miles, although their registration total is estimated at only 1.336

Table 8-1

Area of Operation of U.S. Truck Fleet by Gross Vehicle Weight (GVW) Class and Fuel Type in 1987

GVW Class/Engine Type	Local[a] (%)	Area of Operation Short-Haul[b] (%)	Long Haul[c] (%)
Class VI gasoline	84.4	13.8	1.8
Class VI diesel	66.1	27.8	6.1
Class VII gasoline	86.2	12.5	1.3
Class VII diesel	66.3	29.0	4.7
Class VIIIA gasoline	86.3	11.9	1.8
Class VIIIA diesel	63.5	24.4	12.1
Class VIIIB gasoline	25.4	32.9	41.7

Source: Bureau of the Census 1990.
[a]Local = greatest percentage of annual miles accrued within 50 mi radius of home base.
[b]Short-haul = greatest percentage of miles accrued between 50 and 200 mi radius of home base.
[c]Long-haul = greatest percentage of miles accrued beyond 200 mi radius of home base.

million units (EEA 1994). Three-fourths of these vehicles (all of which are diesel) are used in intercity operation, with an average annual use of about 66,000 miles (see Table 8-1). Since these trucks carry almost three times the payload of a typical medium-heavy-duty Class VII diesel truck, their total contribution to ton-miles of intercity freight is over ten times that of medium-heavy-duty trucks.

Total Freight Movement in the United States

Several studies have directly linked the total movement of freight to the U.S. gross domestic product (GDP) (FHWA 1987). Such correlations are obviously a simplification of the actual factors driving growth in freight as measured by ton-miles of intercity freight movement. Over the years, the composition and nature of the gross domestic product has shifted from manufactured goods to services; hence it would be logical to expect that freight ton-miles would be increasing at a pace slower than GDP.

Currently, annual data on total intercity movements are available from two sources, the Eno Foundation and the Bureau of Transportation Statistics. Of course, they both may rely on similar or identical sources for raw data to develop their estimates, and the general trends as well as the absolute estimates are not significantly different in these two sources. Some observers believe that both estimates may contain substantial errors, but no objective source of data is available to prove or disprove this hypothesis. Data on total ton-miles of intercity freight movement over the period 1970–1993 were utilized in our analysis.

Regression analysis of the two data sets for this period reveals the relationship between total ton-miles in billions and GDP in billions of constant 1987$ to be quite similar in the two sources (standard errors of coefficients are given in parentheses):

$$\text{Total ton-miles} = 0.4715 \, \text{GDP} + 559.7 \quad r^2 = 0.938 \text{ (Eno data)}$$
$$\phantom{\text{Total ton-miles} = }(0.0348) \phantom{\text{GDP} + } (85.6)$$

$$\text{or } 0.445 \, \text{GDP} + 646.7 \quad r^2 = 0.950 \text{ (BTS data)}$$
$$\phantom{\text{or }}(0.029) \phantom{\text{GDP} + } (72.6)$$

The Eno data for this regression is plotted in Figure 8-1. Given a 1994 GDP estimate of $5,344 billion (in 1987$), the computed ton-mile sensitivity to GDP shows an elasticity of 0.786—that is, ton-miles increase by 7.86 percent for a 10 percent increase in GDP. Greene (in Abacus 1991) investigated the dependence of ton-miles of intercity freight to GNP and suggested a model of the form:

Figure 8-1

U.S. Intercity Freight Movements in Relation to Gross Domestic Product (GDP)

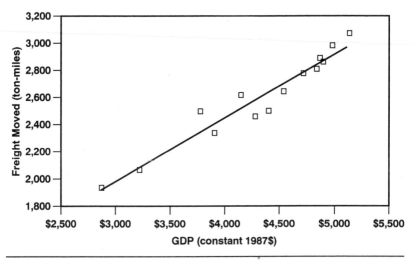

Source: Author's analysis of data from Eno Foundation (1993).

$$\text{Ton-miles} = -187.7 + [0.847 - 0.00542\,(t-1949)]\,\text{GNP}$$

In this model, the dependence on GNP declines over time, as indicated by the "(t −1949)." The above equation predicts 847 ton-miles increase per $1,000 GNP increase in 1949, but only 500 ton miles per $1,000 GNP increase in 2013. This decreasing sensitivity is explained by the view that the economy is "dematerializing." However, our analysis suggests that the elasticity is still quite high, possibly because exports and imports are becoming a larger share of GNP, with attendant increases in ton-miles. Indeed, the data from the last five years suggest even higher growth than in the previous ten years, and we have used an elasticity of 0.8 to estimate ton-mile sensitivity to GNP.

Trucking's share of total freight moved also appears to be growing, with the ton-miles carried by trucking from 1970 through 1993 rising from about 23 percent in the early 1980s to about 28 percent in 1991 (Figure 8-2). According to recent data from Eno, trucking's share for 1995 is estimated to be about 30 percent. This market share has come at the expense of pipeline and marine (noninternational) market share and is a result of the shifts in the market share of types of commodities carried. Hence, trucking ton-miles have been growing at a rate higher than is indicated by the total ton-miles regression above.

Figure 8-2

Shares of U.S. Freight Movements (Ton-Miles) by Mode, 1970–1993

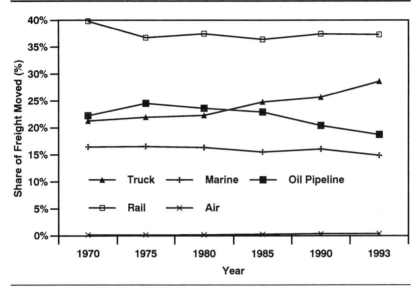

Source: Eno Foundation (1993).

Freight movements by commodity type are quite different for each of the different transportation modes. Pipelines and marine modes are used heavily for petroleum and chemical products, as well as natural gas (pipeline). Railroads typically specialize in high-density bulk commodities, such as coal, metallic ores, agricultural products, lumber, and chemical products, and in long-haul operations. Truck freight is not as easily depicted since detailed breakouts are not available, but it can be broadly characterized as manufactured products, low-density products, high-value-added products, or products being shipped to locations with no rail service.

One aspect of intermodal competition for freight that is important in the context of sustainability is the relative fuel efficiency of each mode. If one does not consider the type of freight carried, trucking is the least efficient of the modes. Oak Ridge National Laboratory average statistics on efficiency in terms of Btu of energy consumed per ton-mile estimate similar rail and marine energy intensities at about 400 Btu/ton-mile each, whereas trucking's energy intensity is estimated at 3,300 Btu/ton-mile. However, such estimates should not be used to assume that rail is much more energy-efficient for the same mix of goods moving between the same origin and destination points. For a controlled comparison, the efficiency depends on the route and the type of goods being carried; the rail-to-trucking energy efficiency ratio is certainly not 8:1, as indicated by the averaged fuel use statistics.

A typical modern Class VIIIB truck can carry a 30-ton payload with a fuel efficiency of about 6–7 MPG, which translates to 620–720 Btu/ton-mile for diesel fuel at 130,000 Btu/gallon. Studies by the Department of Transportation have shown that rail's fuel efficiency depends on the route circuity and how far the origin and destination are located from rail terminals.

Even under favorable circumstances, the fuel efficiency advantage of container-on-flatcar transport over truck transport is estimated to be on the order of about 40 to 110 percent (Abacus 1991). Indeed, this advantage has led to a mix of trucking and rail transport on long-haul routes; truck-trailer-on-flatcar and container-on-flatcar are the fastest growing segments of the rail freight market.

The above discussion suggests that shifting freight from truck to rail to improve fuel efficiency may not necessarily improve efficiency and that market mechanisms may be allocating freight movements to the most fuel-efficient mode, as fuel cost is a significant portion of total transport costs.

Trucking's Share of Freight and Fuel Consumption Effects

Heavy-heavy-duty trucks will consume an estimated 17.35 billion gallons of diesel fuel in 1995, whereas medium-heavy-duty trucks will consume a total of 5.65 billion gallons of fuel (4.68 billion gallons of diesel) (EEA 1994), an increase of approximately 17 percent over the values for 1990. This very high growth is partly related to the fact that the base year was a recession year. The Federal Highway Administration (FHWA 1994) reported that from 1987 through 1992, total heavy-duty truck travel declined by –0.26 percent/yr, but the trend has changed since 1992 with the economic recovery.

Future growth in heavy-duty truck vehicle-miles of travel (VMT) can be estimated primarily by utilizing the relationship of ton-miles to GDP growth. If increases in GDP average between 2 and 2.5 percent over 1990–2015, total freight ton-miles across all modes will likely increase by a smaller amount, which would result in a total increase in ton-miles of 49 to 64 percent over the 25-year period. Of course, trucking is actually increasing its market share of the total ton-miles of freight being carried, so its growth may be even higher. If historical trends continue, trucking could increase its market share from 26 percent in 1990 to about 35 percent in 2015, thereby increasing total trucking ton-miles by 100 to 120 percent over the same period. However, this increase translates into an annual growth rate of 2.8 to 3.2 percent, which is lower than the range recently observed.

An increase of trucking ton-miles by 100 to 120 percent would obviously cause a nearly proportional rise in fuel use, all else being constant. However, greater use of fuel-saving technology and improvements in operations could certainly counteract the effect of potential trucking ton-mile increases. Whether these two mechanisms are sufficient to completely counteract the projected increase in trucking ton-miles is the subject of this analysis.

Fuel Efficiency Improvements

Since the fuel crisis of the 1970s, there has been a substantial increase in the pace of introduction of fuel-saving technology. The absence of "official" EPA fuel economy numbers to rate truck fuel efficiency performance is partly compensated for by the fact that the Bureau of Census compiles a very detailed survey of in-use truck performance (the *Truck Inventory and Use Survey*, or TIUS) and obtains information on fuel economy that is measured or estimated. The 1987 TIUS data (Bureau of the Census 1990) have been extensively analyzed by EEA, and it is anticipated that the newly released 1992 TIUS will provide additional data and insight into truck efficiency.

The 1987 TIUS allows estimates of fuel economy by GVW class and vintage for vehicles up to ten years old but aggregates data for all older trucks (for confidentiality reasons). Class VIIIB diesel trucks show an obvious upward trend in fuel economy with more recent vintage (Figures 8-3, 8-4). Regression analysis of the data, controlling for engine horsepower and average payload, shows that medium-heavy-duty diesel truck fuel efficiency has increased at the rate of 1.5 percent/yr (see Figure 8-3), whereas heavy-heavy-duty truck fuel efficiency has increased at 1.2 percent/yr (see Figure 8-4). There were no obvious trends in horsepower in the 1977–1987 time frame, although recent anecdotal evidence suggests that horsepower is increasing in response to the relaxation of speed limits. Increased horsepower by itself does not have a large effect on fuel efficiency, but driving at 70 mph rather than at 60 mph does.

Future increases in the fuel efficiency of medium-heavy-duty and heavy-heavy-duty trucks have also been studied for the near term to 2001, using the actual 1987 baseline MPG from EEA's (1992) analysis

Figure 8-3

Average MPG of U.S. Class VII Diesel Truck Fleet by Vintage

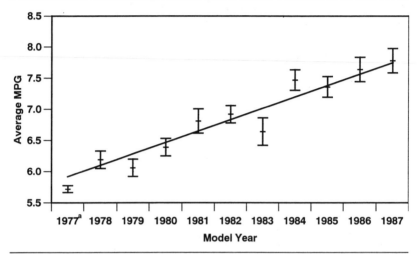

Source: EEA 1992. Based on 1987 TIUS data from Bureau of the Census 1990.
[a]Model year 1977 includes 1977 and pre-1977 models.

Figure 8-4

Average MPG of U.S. Class VIIIB Diesel Truck Fleet by Vintage

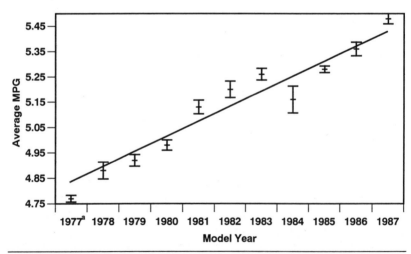

Source: EEA 1992. Based on 1987 TIUS data from Bureau of the Census 1990.
[a]Model year 1977 includes 1977 and pre-1977 models.

of the TIUS. Data for estimating these improvements were obtained from engine manufacturers and truck manufacturers. A more comprehensive description of these technological improvements can be found in EEA (1992). The results suggest that highway fuel efficiency will increase by 22 percent for medium-heavy-duty trucks (Table 8-2) and by 21 percent for heavy-heavy-duty trucks (Table 8-3), with smaller benefits in urban cycles. The composite efficiency increase suggests that the historical rate of 1.5, or 1.2 percent, per year improvement could be sustained to 2001. On the negative side, the increase in highway speeds from about 60 mph to 70+ mph is likely to decrease fuel efficiency 14 to 18 percent for the portion of truck VMT at high speeds.

Beyond 2001, however, the potential for continued increases in fuel efficiency is unclear. The diesel engine is already very efficient: modern diesels with high brake mean effective pressure (BMEP) are rated at overall peak efficiencies of 42 to 44 percent. Research programs sponsored by the Department of Energy (DOE) aim to raise efficiency levels to 48 to 50 percent, and technologies developed by these programs could be commercialized in the 2010 time frame. However, benefits from body technologies such as weight reduction and aerodynamic drag reduction are more likely to saturate since the relatively simple advances have already been made, and the more advanced body technologies could have significantly worse life-cycle cost/benefit ratios for the truck owner.

A second factor to be considered is the ever-increasing stringency of NO_x and particulate emissions standards; in the post-2001 time frame, it now appears that EPA will seek another 50 percent reduction in emissions of both pollutants relative to current standards. Hence, technology improvements may be used to reduce the emissions of criteria pollutants rather than to improve fuel efficiency, and the foregone gain could be relatively significant. In the absence of a detailed post-2001 technology study, EEA's conservative estimate, based on an understanding of current research, is that fuel efficiency improvements from technology improvements could drop to about half the current 1.2 to 1.5 percent rate in the 2002 to 2015 time frame (EEA 1992). A more optimistic scenario assumes that some of the DOE research in progress is successful and allows attainment of the 50 percent engine efficiency goal so that historical rates of fuel economy growth are continued to 2015.

Operational Improvements

Although technological improvements are one route to reducing fuel consumption, improvements in operations can also lead to the

Table 8-2

Potential Efficiency Improvements to Class VI/VII/VIII A U.S. Truck Fleet, 1987–2001

Technology	Market Penetration Increase (%)	Improvement in Fuel Economy	
		City (%)	Highway (%)
Weight reduction	100	0.35	0.15
Drag reduction			
Van body	45	0.15	3.35
Other	55	0.07	1.69
Rolling resistance	45	0.90	1.35
Engine improvements[a]	100	12.00	12.00
Drivetrain optimization	100	2.00	2.00
Electronic control	100	3.00	5.00
Lubricants	100	1.00	0.50
Total fuel economy improvement		19.47	26.04
Potential effect of 1998 NO_x standards		(−2.5)	(−4.00)

Source: Data based on EEA 1992.
[a]Weighted for light-heavy diesels in Class VI.

Table 8-3

Potential Efficiency Improvements to Class VIII B U.S. Truck Fleet, 1987–2001

Technology	Market Penetration Increase (%)	Improvement in Fuel Economy	
		City (%)	Highway (%)
Weight reduction (0.75%)	100	0.40	0.25
Drag reduction			
Van body	50	0.28	6.75
Other	35	0.07	1.60
Rolling resistance	65	1.85	2.90
Engine improvements	100	5.50	5.50
Turbocompound	10	0.30	0.50
Drivetrain optimization	na	1.50	2.00
Electronic control	100	2.50	6.00
Lubricants	100	1.00	0.50
Total improvement		13.00	26.00
Potential effect of 1998 NO_x standards		(−3.00)	(−5.00)

Source: Data based on EEA 1992.

equivalent movement of freight with reduced truck travel. The general operational improvements include

- coordination with rail

- reductions in highway maximum speed

- reduction in empty backhaul

- use of larger trucks

As discussed earlier, coordination between rail and trucking through use of trailer-on-flatcar or container-on-flatcar methods is increasing. Indeed, recent improvements in the overall efficiency and productivity of railways have resulted in better coordination with trucking in moving specific types of freight over long distances, rather than in competition for the same business. The current rates of such intermodal shifts are difficult to estimate in ton-miles, but the railways report significant growth in truck-rail combined operations (see Chapter 9). Continued growth of such operations will directly curb the increases in market share forecast for trucking, but no data are yet available to quantify these recent trends. As a guesstimate, this analysis suggests that even with increased cooperation in the future, trucking's market share, measured in ton-miles traveled, may rise from its 1990 figure of 26 percent to only about 30 percent by 2015, rather than the 35 percent estimated from continuation of historical trends.

Reduction in highway speed is known to have a significant impact on total fuel consumption. For example, reducing highway speed from 70 to 60 mph results in a fuel economy increase of 13.0 to 15.3 percent. However, reduced speeds also decrease truck (and driver) productivity; thus, at current low fuel prices, there is reduced incentive to control speeds. Many fleet trucks utilize electronic speed control devices or tachographs to keep speeds at between 62 and 65 mph, which is at, or slightly below, highway speed limits nationwide. However, highway speed data suggest that speeds higher by 8 to 10 mph are more common on noncongested freeways. Under a very optimistic sustainability scenario, it may be possible to increase the number of trucks at or below speed limits on noncongested freeways from the current 70 percent (FHWA 1994) to about 85 percent. If noncongested freeways account for about half of all highway driving for heavy-heavy-duty trucks, then a net fuel savings of 2.3 percent is an optimistic possibility. However, this reduction would not be relative to 1990 baseline conditions but would rather act as a control of potential increases over the baseline—that is, the optimistic scenario would merely restore speeds back to 1990 levels.

Empty backhaul constitutes a major share of total truck travel. Using 1987 TIUS data, EEA (1992) estimated the fraction of total VMT traveled without payload for truck classes VI–VIIIB (Figure 8-5). Surprisingly, the fraction of empty backhaul is similar across truck weight categories. It constitutes 30 ± 3 percent of total travel and consumes about 18 to 21 percent of total fuel used (since trucks have higher fuel economy under no-load conditions). Some observers believe that interstate trucking deregulation further reduced empty backhaul to about 22 percent and fuel used to about 13 to 15 percent by 1995. Deregulation of intrastate trucking should help reduce empty backhaul, as should more efficient communications, routing, and management practices. Optimistic estimates based on anecdotal information from truck fleet managers calculate that about one-third of empty-backhaul travel can be eliminated by 2015. However, increased competition and greater demands for timeliness may make it difficult to reduce empty backhaul very much, and experts consider one-sixth reduction to be a more realistic expectation. Hence, fuel savings under the optimistic case are about 6 to 7 percent—only about half as much in the realistic case.

The use of larger trucks, notably twin-trailer and triple-trailer combinations of various sizes, can also improve fuel productivity. Although twin-trailer combinations are currently legal everywhere on the interstate system, their use is relatively limited. The actual

Figure 8-5

Percentage of U.S. Truck Vehicle-Miles of Travel (VMT) Without Payload by Gross Vehicle Weight (GVW) Class, 1987

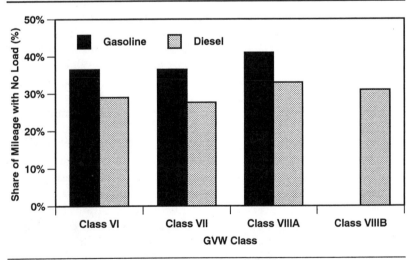

Source: EEA 1992. Based on 1987 TIUS data from Bureau of the Census 1990.

weight carried by a truck is set by the "bridge formula," which defines a maximum weight carried on any group of two or more axles as a function of the total number of axles and the distance between consecutive axles. The interstate highway system limits trucks to 80,000 lb GVW. State laws also determine the length of trailing units of a tractor-trailer combination. Although states must set a minimum trailer length of 48 ft for a single trailer, or 28 ft for twin-trailer combinations, they can set higher limits, and many western and Rocky Mountain states do allow longer trailers. The bridge formula caps the maximum weight of twin-28s with five axles at 91,500 lb, and of nine-axle twin-28s at 110,000 lb, but all trucks usually operate at 80,000 lb except under special permits. The longer "Rocky Mountain" doubles and "turnpike" doubles can be allowed to operate at even higher GVWs under the bridge formula but are also capped at 80,000 lb.

The current GVW cap of 80,000 lb constrains the productivity of twin-trailer combinations for those carriers that haul freight of high weight rather than high volume. However, even with the GVW cap, twin-trailer combinations can enhance fuel productivity significantly for carriers whose trucks "cube out"—that is, are volume limited. In terms of ton-miles per gallon for cube-out freight, EEA estimates fuel productivity to increase by 60 to 95 percent by 2015 (Table 8-4). However, safety considerations have not permitted more widespread use of these "doubles." Calculations performed for this analysis suggest

Table 8-4

Fuel Productivity Estimates for Size-Limited U.S. Truck Fleet and Potential Gains from Shifts to Longer Combination Vehicles

Truck Configuration	Fuel Productivity with Uncapped Bridge Formula (ton-mi/gal)	Potential Gain from Shifting to Rocky Mountain Doubles (%)	Potential Gain from Shifting to Turnpike Doubles (%)
5-axle tractor-semis	70.52	59.7	94.8
6-axle tractor-semis	70.24	60.4	95.6
5-axle twin-28s	80.70	39.6	70.2
7-axle twin-28s	79.84	41.1	72.1
8-axle twin-28s	79.36	41.9	73.1
9-axle twin-28s	78.87	42.8	74.2
Rocky Mountain doubles	112.64	na	na
Turnpike doubles	137.38	na	na

Source: EEA 1992.

that on a fleetwide basis, a penetration increase of 20 to 30 percent may be possible for double trailers, leading to fuel consumption declines of 8 to 14 percent. Another factor that may assist fuel consumption per ton-mile is that twin-trailer combinations are more speed limited than the usual five-axle tractor-trailer, so speeds over 65 mph are less likely for such vehicles.

Potential Emissions Reductions

Heavy-duty diesel trucks are relatively small contributors to the national total inventory of volatile organic compound (VOC) and carbon monoxide (CO) emissions, but they are significant contributors to total NO_x emissions and to fine particulate matter (PM-10). EPA's 1992 *National Air Quality and Emission Trends Report* estimates that all heavy-duty diesel trucks (8,500 ι lb GVW) account for only 1.3 percent of VOC and CO inventory but account for 8.6 percent of total NO_x inventory and 5.3 percent of combustion-derived PM-10 (Curran, McMullen, and Misenheimer 1993). (This estimate does not include fugitive dust, which dominates PM-10 emissions.) In 1990, the average value of fleetwide heavy-duty diesel vehicle emissions was about 7.0 g NO_x and 0.60 g PM per brake-horsepower-hour (BHP-hr).

EPA regulations are expected to reduce emission standards to about 2.0 g/BHP-hr for NO_x emissions and 0.10 g/BHP-hr for PM-10 in the 2004–2005 time frame. As older trucks are scrapped, average fleetwide emissions will decrease to these new standard levels by 2015, assuming that diesel emissions do not deteriorate significantly over the useful life of diesel engines, as is true now. The optimism that diesel engines can meet the stringent post-2000 standards stems from recent discoveries that control the combustion process better, such as electronic pilot injection and the possible use of exhaust gas recirculation. In addition, it is possible that the "lean-NO_x" catalyst may be developed for diesel engines. Such a catalyst could allow meeting NO_x standards without the fuel economy penalty resulting from engine calibration compromises aimed at decreasing engine-out NO_x emissions.

The post-2000 standards suggest that NO_x emissions per ton-mile could decrease by up to 80 percent, and PM-10 emissions per ton-mile by over 90 percent relative to 1990 levels. (Note that the reduction in engine work per ton-mile also affects tailpipe emissions.)

Prospects for Sustainability

The relationship between GDP growth and freight movements above suggests that trucking ton-miles could increase by 100 to 120 percent between 1990 and 2015. If technology, operations, and emissions stay constant, then both fuel consumption and emissions will increase in proportion to ton-miles.

However, given the potential decreases in emissions as a result of the 1998 and post-2000 standards, the heavy-duty NO_x emissions inventory will be only at 40 to 44 percent of 1990 levels and PM-10 emissions at 20 to 22 percent of 1990 levels after accounting for the growth in ton-miles. Hence it appears that trucking will meet the sustainability criteria for criteria pollutant emissions by a significant margin.

Meeting the stated sustainability criteria for greenhouse gases, and hence fuel consumption, seems to be a more difficult problem and also subject to more uncertainty. Fuel-efficient technology, intermodal shift to rail, reduction in empty backhaul, reduction in highway speed, and use of twin trailers will tend to offset the projected increases in fuel consumption relative to the baseline of 100 to 120 percent increase in ton-miles for the 1990–2015 period (Table 8-5). If each of these factors is assumed at its most optimistic level, it appears possible for all of these factors to actually reduce total fuel consumption for a growth of 100 percent in ton-miles, or to hold consumption flat for a growth in ton-miles of 120 percent. However, if we use the expected rate of improvement on all factors, then fuel consumption will grow by 29 to 42 percent by 2015. As a result, it does not appear possible to achieve sustainability in terms of fuel consumption without market intervention to maximize technological and operational factors aiding fuel conservation. However, the maximization of the factors offers the potential to meet the sustainability criteria for greenhouse gas emissions.

Table 8-5

Summary of Potential for Reducing U.S. Freight Trucking Energy Intensity: "Expected" and "Optimistic" Scenarios for 2015

	Expected (%)	Optimistic (%)
Fuel-efficient technology	−19	−25
Intermodal shift to rail	−13	−26
Reduction in empty backhaul	−2.5	−12
Reduction in highway speed	(+2.2)	0
Use of twin trailers	−8	−14
TOTAL[a]	−36	−55

[a]Multiplicative total of reductions available in fuel consumption.

References

Abacus Technologies. 1991. *Rail vs. Truck Fuel Efficiency.* DOT/FRA/ RRP-91-2.

Bureau of Census. 1990. *Truck Inventory and Use Survey, 1987.* Washington, D.C.: Government Printing Office.

Bureau of Transportation Statistics (BTS). Annual. *National Transportation Statistics.* Washington, D.C.

Curran, T.T., T.C. McMullen, and D.C. Misenheimer. 1993. *National Air Quality and Emission Trends, Report 1993.* EPA 454-R-94-026.

Energy and Environmental Analysis, Inc. (EEA). 1992. Analysis of Heavy-Duty Truck Fuel Efficiency to 2001. Report to EPA, Energy Policy Branch. Arlington, Va.: Energy and Environmental Analysis, Inc.

_____. 1994. The Motor Fuel Consumption Model, 15th Periodical Report. Report to Martin Marietta Energy Systems. Arlington, Va.: Energy and Environmental Analysis, Inc.

Eno Foundation. 1993. *Transportation in America.* Lansdowne, Va.: Eno Foundation for Transportation.

Federal Highway Administration (FHWA). 1987. *Trends and Forecasts of Highway Freight Travel.* Working paper 3. Washington, D.C.: Federal Highway Administration.

_____. 1994. *Highway Statistics, 1993.* FHWA-PL-94-023. Washington, D.C.: Federal Highway Administration, Office of Highway Information Management.

Chapter Nine

Integrating Steel Wheels into Sustainable Transportation

DICK CATALDI

When President Jimmy Carter signed freight transportation deregulation into law in 1980, the federal government stepped back and virtually let the market run the freight sector. Since fuel cost is a large fraction of the total cost of transportation, the entire freight sector has been working feverishly to conserve fuel while also meeting Environmental Protection Agency (EPA) exhaust emissions regulations. Freight railroads, the focus of this chapter, have probably accomplished the most in fuel conservation and, in addition, are the least polluting mode of freight transport even though they have not yet faced any EPA limitations. However, the entire freight sector is one system, and in planning for sustainability, the separate modes cannot be treated in isolation.

The various freight transport modes may be set in context by comparing their respective market shares and fuel consumption. Railroads move many more ton-miles of freight than other principal freight modes (trucks, waterways, and pipelines), carrying 38.3 percent of the total in 1993 (Figure 9-1), and use much less fuel—only 11 percent of the total freight sector fuel in that same year (Figure 9-2). Waterways and pipelines are also relatively fuel-efficient, whereas trucks used over 74 percent of the freight sector fuel in 1993. This comparison is not entirely fair, however, because trucks carry many lightweight commodities and often carry less-than-truckload freight. Trains, pipelines, and water transporters carry denser commodities on average. Still, it appears that better coordination among the transportation modes might help to meet overall sustainability goals.

Railroads were invented to provide faster, more reliable, and much cheaper overland transportation than could be provided by horses and canals, and the industry's history has been a continuous

Figure 9-1

U.S. Intercity Freight Market Shares, 1993 (Ton-Miles)

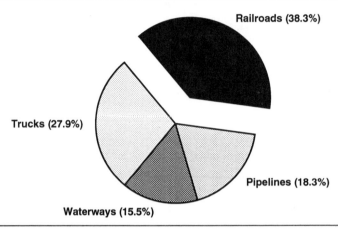

Source: *Railroad Facts* 1995, 32.
Note: Does not include air freight or natural gas and coal slurry pipelines.

Figure 9-2

U.S. Fuel Consumption by Freight Mode, 1993

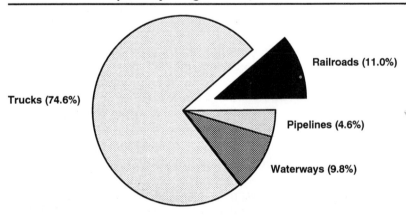

Source: Davis 1994, 2–24.
Note: Does not include air freight or natural gas and coal slurry pipelines.

evolution of improvements in productivity. With heavily subsidized highway and river competition and with trucks being naturally able to provide more reliable door-to-door service, railroads have had to be the low-cost providers of freight transportation. However, by moving away from boxcars to intermodal trailers and containers, railroads have also been able to improve speed and reliability so that they are now partners with trucking companies in "seamless transportation.

Since 1980, railroads have had a large increase in freight hauled while at the same time decreasing their fuel consumption (Figure 9-3), resulting in increased energy productivity as measured in net revenue ton-miles per gallon, one of the most important statistics in the railroad industry (Figure 9-4). Although these trends are good for the railroads, they are also helpful for the freight sector as a whole because in recent years, when it has been beneficial to them, truckers and bargemen have been moving freight off highways and waterways and onto trains. Such intermodal traffic almost doubled between 1984 and 1994 (Figure 9-5).

Railroad productivity had to improve because deregulation of freight rates allowed shippers to drive the price of freight transportation

Figure 9-3

U.S. Railroad Fuel Use and Revenue Ton-Miles, 1980–1994

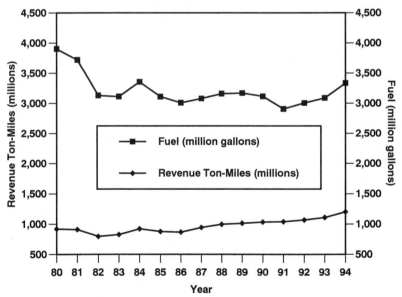

Source: Railroad Facts 1995, 40.

Figure 9-4

U.S. Railroad Energy Productivity, 1980–1994
(Net Revenue in Ton-Miles per Gallon)

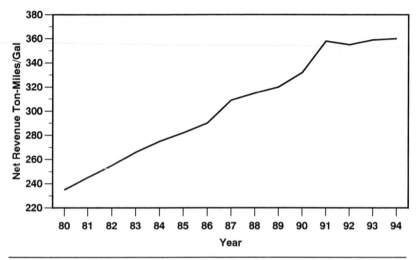

Source: *Railroad Facts* 1995, 40.

Figure 9-5

U.S. Intermodal Trailer/Container Loads on Rail, 1980–1994

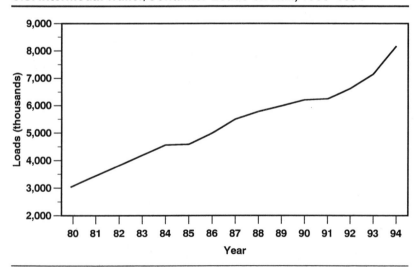

Source: *Railroad Facts* 1995, 26.

downward (Figure 9-6). The American economy has profited mightily from this reduction in transportation prices, yet railroads have improved their productivity so much that they make more profits today than they did in the early 1980s.

The lowered price of freight transportation seen in Figure 9-6 suggests another important message: the marketplace will not allow the freight transport sector to use technologies that are not worthwhile investments. Technologies that improve energy productivity or reduce exhaust emissions must pay for their capital cost in a short time frame. Although transportation companies are generally profitable, most of them do not make enough profit to pay for the cost of borrowing money. They cannot invest in sustainability unless it pays off handsomely.

How Did the Railroads Do It?

The railroads' huge improvement in energy efficiency since 1980 was accomplished through a systematic change in operations and through implementation of new technologies. The way that railroads operate their trains probably has had as great an impact on efficiency improvements as has the introduction of more advanced equipment

Figure 9-6

U.S. Railroad Revenue per Ton-Mile, 1984–1994

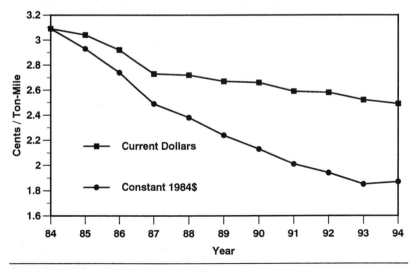

Source: Railroad Facts 1995, 31.

technologies. Communications technology may have played as much a role as engine and rolling stock technology.

Some of the more prominent technologies introduced since 1980 include the following:

- *Lighter-weight, higher-capacity freight cars.* The fleet average capacity of freight cars increased from 79.4 tons in 1980 to 89.5 tons in 1994 (*Railroad Facts* 1995, 52), an increase of over 13 percent. Average tare weight decreased slightly, with lighter-weight materials being offset by an increase in the size of cars. This improvement has reduced the total train resistance per unit of freight lading, but the fuel savings are specific to commodities and routes, and no national statistics exist for fuel savings.

- *Lower-resistance axle bearings.* New designs for roller bearing seals reduced the bearing portion of rolling resistance by 45 percent (Singh 1992, 113). This advance translates into a total reduction of fuel consumption of about 2 percent on trains fully equipped with these bearings.

- *Higher-horsepower, improved-efficiency locomotives.* The standard locomotive prior to 1980 had 3,000 hp for traction. In 1995, the standard was 4,400 hp, and 6,000 hp locomotives will start to come on-line in 1996. A variety of improvements in engine efficiencies and a reduction in other loads (for example, cooling fans, pumps, compressors) have improved overall locomotive fuel efficiency. A recent move from direct current (dc) traction motors to alternating current (ac) motors allows increased tractive effort and enables more horsepower to be applied to the rails. The resultant increased pulling power per locomotive reduces the number of locomotives needed to pull a given train, thus reducing total train weight. Union Pacific Railroad expects to save 65,000 gallons per year per 6,000 hp ac locomotive (*Car & Locomotive Yearbook* 1995). There will be over 1,200 ac locomotives in the national fleet by the end of 1995.

- *Wheel rail lubrication.* Applying grease to the gage face of the rails (the inside vertical planes of the rails where the wheel flange contacts the rail) reduces train rolling resistance by about 3 to 4 percent on tangent track and by over 10 percent on curves (Singh 1992). Depending upon train speed, track curvature, and grades, the fuel savings range from about 1 percent to 4 percent on trains equipped with lubricators.

- *Computer-assisted train dispatch control.* Most railroads are constrained in their ability to move traffic efficiently because of single-track territories and the need for trains to stay in formation in double-track territories. To move trains around each other means that one train often has to stop in a siding to make a "meet" or a "pass." Computers now help dispatchers to work with train engineers to calculate the most energy-efficient speeds for approaching the meets. Dispatchers can also now inform trains in sidings how long they will have to sit so that crews can shut down engines to save fuel. The resultant fuel savings are highly line-specific, and no statistics have been compiled to determine the industry-wide fuel savings of these train control methods. However, mainline locomotives consume about 5 gallons of fuel per hour while idling, and most trains have two to four locomotives. Every day, hundreds of trains spend over an hour idling in sidings, so the fuel savings due to reduced idling may be several thousand gallons per day.

None of these technologies is fully implemented. Some (for example, lower-resistance bearings) are just now starting to be implemented and will contribute to a continuing improvement in energy efficiency for many years.

Other, less technological changes have also improved productivity. Some of the more important changes include the following:

- *Improved utilization of freight cars and locomotives.* Railroads spend a great amount of money and use much energy in moving empty cars to where they are needed and deadheading locomotives around because of traffic imbalances. Antiquated rules governing the movement of empty cars have been changed to improve their use, and operations research optimization models now help distribute locomotives and empty cars to markets. Railroads cooperate more than they used to in so-called run-through trains, in which whole trains are passed from railroad to railroad without stopping. The fuel savings from these efforts may account for as much as a tenth of all fuel savings since 1980 but could only be calculated through complex simulation models, which have not been done.

- *Improved track quality.* Deregulation has allowed railroads to rationalize their route structures so that more traffic is handled on fewer routes and tracks. Even though the railroads now spend less money on track maintenance and signals, the remaining tracks are in better condition than they were in the 1970s. Improved track quality reduces train resistance because poor-quality track absorbs much energy; good-quality track also allows faster trains, which improve equipment utilization, thus further increasing energy efficiency. Track damping has been shown to account for as much as 0.8 lb/ton to 1.0 lb/ton train resistance.

Stiffer track can reduce that amount by more than half (Singh 1992), which would reduce fuel consumption about 1 to 2 percent, depending upon train speed and grades. Comparison data are not available for track stiffness, so it is not possible to attribute a specific fuel savings to track quality improvements. However, considering the poor track quality on probably more than half of the mainlines in the 1970s, the overall fuel savings probably approach 1 percent.

- *Enhanced training of locomotive engineers and dispatchers.* One railroad in the early 1980s found a 40 percent difference in fuel consumption on identical trains, attributable primarily to the train-handling techniques of different engineers. This finding led the railroad industry to upgrade their train simulators to include fairly accurate estimates of energy consumption and to put their engineers through intensive retraining, which continues today. Train dispatchers are also put through these courses so they are better able to work with their engineers for safe, reliable, and energy-efficient train operations (Eck et al. 1981). Canadian National Railways reported one extreme example of fuel savings using a train simulator with radically different train-handling techniques (Woodhouse 1985). One 9-mile run down a hill took 21.5 minutes and consumed 169.2 gallons of diesel fuel, whereas another run with the same 6,630-ton train took 22.3 minutes and consumed 71.7 gallons of fuel. The 58 percent fuel reduction seen in this simulation is not unusual for short distances but far exceeds the possible savings over the whole railroad. Railroads do not publish estimates of these railroadwide savings, but unsubstantiated claims tend toward 10 to 15 percent savings.

- *Increased use of intermodal freight transport.* The best freight service, from the shipper's standpoint, is provided by trucks that can reach any shipping dock at any desired time. However, the intercity portion of the freight movement does not have to be on asphalt for either speed or reliability. For the intercity part of the freight movement, railroads have learned how to provide reliable service at a lower cost to the trucking companies than the truckers can achieve by hauling trailers and containers themselves. The increase in the number of intermodal containers and trailers hauled by railroads since 1980 (see Figure 9-5) is much greater than the growth rate of the economy. Although intermodal freight is less fuel-efficient than boxcar traffic, it saves fuel compared with all-highway transport. A U.S. Department of Transportation study (DOT 1991) estimated that on a net ton-mile/gallon basis, intermodal freight (dock-to-dock, including highway drayage and rail) has a ratio ranging between 1.4:1 and 5.6:1 compared with all-highway freight in a variety of scenarios. In other words, even in the least favorable scenario, the rail-truck intermodal transport produced 1.4 times more net ton-miles per gallon of fuel than the competing all-truck transport.

Again, these changes are still far from fully implemented—especially the last one, as anyone who drives on an interstate highway can attest.

In summary, nearly all of the above changes, whether technological or operational, were instituted to save money or improve service quality; fuel savings were a secondary benefit. Fuel conservation works best when driven by economics. Additionally, a number of changes took place, some of which account for only a small percentage of reduction in fuel usage. However, these small reductions taken together are the reason for the railroad industry's impressive overall improvement in energy productivity.

Technologies for the Future

The railroad industry needs new technologies to continue to be competitive and to continue its drive toward sustainability. The most obvious need for research and development (R&D) is in prime movers and energy storage devices. Although the conventional diesel engine is a strong incumbent technology, we must always look at alternatives to see if something better can be brought into use. Several R&D programs are currently underway.

The Association of American Railroads (AAR), Argonne National Laboratory, and several manufacturers are studying the feasibility of flywheel energy storage devices. Flywheels should be well suited to railroad operations for several reasons. First, the volume and mass needed to store multimegawatts of power can be accommodated on trains. Freight trains would carry flywheel cars that have no prime mover and are coupled to more conventional locomotives. Second, trains presently give up an enormous amount of energy on downgrades and while slowing for curves and stopping points. Much of that energy is now absorbed by dynamic brakes, wherein the electric traction motors that drive the wheels are turned into generators and absorb energy to slow the train or to hold train speed on downgrades. Today, all of that electric power is literally thrown to the winds by running it through resistance grids (like a giant toaster) and then cooling the grids with air blowers. Third, the locomotive prime mover could be used more efficiently if it could be run at or near rated load all the time and the excess power stored in flywheels. Combined with a flywheel, the prime mover may not need to be as large as would be needed otherwise, which may reduce capital and maintenance costs along with saving fuel.

AAR and Argonne are also studying oxygen enrichment of diesel engines. This study is focused on membranes that separate a part of the free nitrogen from the air, resulting in an increase in the percentage of oxygen in the air. Placing such a membrane in the locomotive engine air filtration system seems feasible. With an increase in oxygen percentage, it is possible to increase the engine thermal efficiency and its power rating while decreasing smoke and particulates. Since both of the major locomotive engine manufacturers are presently working on increased power density (about 35 percent more power out of the same size and weight engine), oxygen enrichment may be worthwhile. However, this technology increases oxides of nitrogen (NO_x) in the exhaust, which will not be acceptable to EPA. Argonne is also working on a nitrogen-based plasma in the exhaust system (using the nitrogen from the membrane) that they hope will be a catalyst for NO_x reduction.

The use of fuel cells as energy storage devices is a long way from commercialization in transportation even though they are being demonstrated in some buses today. Locomotives would be obvious applications since they already have electric drive. AAR, western railroads, and locomotive manufacturers are working with California's South Coast Air Quality Management District and its Fuel Cell Implementation Task Force to study the feasibility of fuel cell locomotives. Carrying a large amount of a nonpetroleum fuel is technically feasible since some locomotives already have fuel tender cars with up to 100 tons of fuel. However, the fuel cell power density must be high, and the large amount of piping required for fuel cells would be subjected to much vibration on a locomotive. However, despite these drawbacks, railroads are pushing for the development of fuel cell technology.

Railroads have been studying alternative fuels for years. Several railroads and manufacturers are well into multiple-year prototype testing of natural gas–fired diesel-electric locomotives. Some developmental work still needs to be done before railroads can decide whether to commit to natural gas, but the technical feasibility looks good. Natural gas locomotives would be high-risk investments because of the high capital cost to get started and the uncertainty of the price differential between natural gas and diesel fuel oil. It is too early to predict whether natural gas will become a railroad fuel.

Nontechnology Changes

Although technology will help railroads and the whole freight transportation sector to meet sustainability goals, there is much more that can be done without technology.

Far and away the biggest potential tool for sustainability in the transportation sector is shifting more traffic off the highways and onto railroads. However, it must be commercially attractive to make this shift; it will not happen by decree. This is not to say that there is no place for government action. On the contrary, railroads and trucking companies are still vexed by many roadblocks to intermodal transportation, some of which could be eliminated or mitigated with governmental support.

The two biggest problems in intermodal transport are the location of, and access to, intermodal terminals. It is so difficult to obtain land, and then to gain all the permits necessary to expand a terminal or to locate an adequate terminal near a highway artery, that railroads simply locate terminals on land formerly used for switching yards. Such locations are rarely the right size and shape and are usually far from main highways. The roads leading to these terminals are rarely adequate, and there is no way to hold a long line of trucks inside the facility for processing. Too often, trucks must wait outside the terminal with their engines running, being victimized by thieves and bothering the local neighborhood with noise, diesel exhaust, and road damage.

Congress hoped to alleviate this problem with the Intermodal Surface Transportation Efficiency Act of 1991 (ISTEA), which provides funding for intermodal improvement projects. Unfortunately, many states and localities do not realize that freight transport is covered by the act. Intermodal freight facility siting and implementation simply do not fit into metropolitan planning as practiced in typical U.S. cities. A much greater effort can be made to consider freight efficiency and intermodalism within state and regional transportation planning.

Any legal or regulatory roadblock to intermodal integration should be studied in depth to determine whether there is any societal benefit to continuing the restrictions. If there is a benefit, it should still be weighed against the societal costs of inefficient transportation.

The railroads and trucking companies, as well as third-party transportation brokers, are all still learning how to integrate their marketing, operations, and communications systems to make intermodal freight more efficient and more attractive to shippers. These issues involve management and institutional problems; the key technologies needed (automatic equipment identification and communications systems) are already invented and at least partially implemented. In short, many opportunities exist for further efficiency improvement in the nation's rail and intermodal freight system. Exploiting these opportunities can provide economic benefits while leading to more sustainable transportation overall.

References

Car & Locomotive Yearbook and Buyers' Guide. 1995. Milwaukee: Progressive Railroading.

Davis, S.C. 1994. *Transportation Energy Data Book.* 15th ed. ORNL-6856. Oak Ridge, Tenn.: Oak Ridge National Laboratory.

Eck, H.C., A. Arakelian, N.W. Luttrell, W.R. McGovern, P. Rhine, W.G. Threlfell, and D.R. Yerkes. 1981. *Fuel Conservation in Train Operation.* R-506. Chicago: Association of American Railroads.

Railroad Fuels. 1995. Washington, D.C.: Association of American Railroads.

Singh, S.P. 1992. *Vehicle Track Resistance Research: A Summary Document.* R-800. Chicago: Association of American Railroads.

U.S. Department of Transportation (DOT). 1991. *Rail vs. Truck Fuel Efficiency: The Relative Fuel Efficiency of Truck Competitive Rail Freight and Truck Operations Compared in a Range of Corridors.* DOT/FRA/RRP-91/2. Washington, D.C.: U.S. Department of Transportation, Federal Railroad Administration.

Woodhouse, A.E. 1985. Fuel Conservation for Locomotive Engineers. *Annual Proceedings of the Railway Fuel and Operating Officers Association* 49: 249–53.

Chapter Ten

Commercial Air Energy Use and Emissions Transport: Is Technology Enough?

DAVID L. GREENE

The 1995 Asilomar Conference on Sustainable Transportation Energy Strategies addressed the question of whether technological improvements alone could be sufficient to achieve a sustainable transportation energy system. Four specific quantitative goals were adopted to define the otherwise ambiguous concept of sustainability:

- Reduce criteria pollutant emissions from on-road vehicles to low-emissions-vehicle (LEV) levels (and to lower levels in severely polluted areas) over their full life.

- Reduce greenhouse gas (GHG) emissions from light and heavy on-road vehicles to 1990 levels by 2015 (implying per-vehicle reductions of 25 to 30 percent by 2015).

- Reduce oil use in the transportation sector by 10 percent by 2005 and still further thereafter.

- Increase renewable fuel use to 15 percent of total fuel use by 2015 and to higher levels thereafter.

The first two goals apply to highway vehicles alone and therefore must be reinterpreted for air transport. I interpret the first to imply that emissions of criteria pollutants by commercial aircraft should be held at 1990 levels despite growth in air travel and that regulated emissions should meet Clean Air Act standards. The second is assumed to mean that air transport emissions of GHGs should be reduced to 1990 levels.

In fact, it will simply not be possible to achieve the above-listed transportation sustainability goals by concentrating on automobiles

207

Figure 10-1

U.S. Transportation Energy Use by Mode, 1993 and Projected to 2010 (Quads)

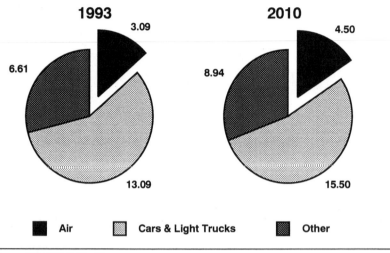

Source: EIA 1995, Table A7.

and light trucks alone. Even in the United States today, autos and light trucks account for only about 60 percent of total transportation energy use (Davis 1995, Table 2.10). The U.S. Department of Energy's Energy Information Administration (EIA 1995) predicts that light-duty-vehicle energy use will increase at an annual rate of 1.0 percent per year through 2010, whereas non-light-duty-vehicle transportation energy use will increase at nearly twice that rate (1.9 percent/yr). At these rates, by 2015, non-light-duty-vehicle transportation energy use will amount to 48 percent of the total. Ignoring commercial transport energy use will amount to ignoring half of the problem (see Figure 10-1).

It should not be surprising if the question "Is technology enough?" produces a different answer for different transportation modes. Differences in their rates of growth, together with inherent technological differences in energy conversion and fuel requirements, ought to result in varying abilities to meet sustainability goals with technology alone. Over the past 20 years, commercial air transport has achieved the largest improvements in energy efficiency among all transport modes, halving energy use per passenger-mile (Greene & Fan 1994, 15). At the same time, air travel has grown at by far the fastest rate, over 6 percent per year (Davis 1995, Table 6.2). As a result, air energy use has grown at about 2 percent/yr. Projections through 2010 anticipate a slowing of air travel growth, but only to about 5 percent/yr (Boeing 1995, 1; Douglas 1995, 15). Even the most optimistic estimates of aircraft efficiency improvements foresee improvements of only 3 percent/yr, far short of what would be necessary to hold energy use and GHG emissions in check, let alone return to 1990 levels by 2015. Moreover, government and industry experts agree that opportunities for substituting alternatives for petroleum-based conventional jet fuel in the next two decades are virtually nil. It seems clear that for the air mode, technology will not be enough.

Continued technological advances in propulsion, aerodynamics, materials, and design have allowed commercial air travel to achieve the largest energy efficiency improvements over the past two decades. A driving force behind this success has been massive technology research and development (R&D) financed by Department of Defense (DOD) and National Aeronautics and Space Administration (NASA) research budgets. Just as the commercial aircraft industry adapted the B-47 bomber to create the Boeing 707 and the DC-8 (Derbyshire, Jenkinson and Miller 1991), current research on laminar flow control and advanced composite materials for jet fighter aircraft will appear in future commercial jets. A recent report of the National Academy of Sciences (NAS) attests to this direct relationship between government-sponsored technology R&D and benefits to commercial industry:

At this point it is worth mentioning a program that exemplifies the type of joint NASA/industry cooperation that can have significant impact on the state-of-the-art and on the overall competitiveness of U.S. products. The Aircraft Efficiency (ACE) program was begun in the 1970s in response to the energy crisis and contained six separate programs aimed at producing real improvements in the efficiency of aircraft. One of the six ACE programs, the Energy Efficient Engine (E^3) program, had a goal of 12% reduction in engine fuel consumption. The goal was met and, most importantly, both GE and P&W have aggressively incorporated the component and systems technology that resulted from the E^3 program into their current generation of engines, including the GE CF6-80 and the P&W 4000 engines. . . . The Committee believes that this type of program can provide tremendous benefits to the U.S. aeronautics industry and should be pursued wherever feasible. (NRC 1992, 152)

Table 10-1

U.S. Aircraft Direct Operating Cost and Fuel Price

	$0.63/gal (1990$)	$1.20/gal (1990$)
Crew	13.3%	11.4%
Maintenance	14.4%	12.3%
Insurance	1.5%	1.3%
Fuel	18.6%	30.3%
Ownership	52.2%	44.7%

Source: NRC 1992, Table 2-1.

Energy efficiency improvements are also welcomed by the marketplace. In the past, fuel costs have exceeded 40 percent of airlines' direct operating costs and even today comprise 15 to 20 percent (Table 10-1). The market incentives to adopt cost-effective technology are strong.

A 25 percent improvement in fuel consumption would reduce airline operating costs by 5 percent at 1991 jet fuel prices of $0.63/gal and by almost 8 percent at $1.20/gal, a price last seen in 1983. Given that the net profit of a well-managed airline is about 5 percent of direct operating costs (NRC 1992, 43), there is a very strong economic incentive for commercial airlines to reduce fuel costs. Airlines will be quick to adopt cost-effective fuel economy improvements.

Technological Potential for Efficiency Improvement

Since the first commercial jet aircraft were introduced in the 1950s, the energy efficiency of air transport has improved enormously. Over the next 30 years, fuel burn rates in cruising mode decreased by 64 percent for short- to medium-range aircraft, and by 55 percent for long-range jets (NRC 1992, 42). Additional improvements in other areas allowed U.S. airlines to more than double their output of passenger-miles per gallon of fuel, from 13 in 1970 to 31 in 1992 (Davis 1995, Table 6.2). Seat-miles per gallon increased from 26.2 to 48.6 during this same period. The introduction of more technologically advanced aircraft was the main force behind the fuel economy improvement, but a 40 percent increase in aircraft size and a 30 percent increase in load factors (average seat occupancy) were also major ingredients (Greene 1992).

Considerable potential to further increase the efficiency of air travel remains. A recent study by the NAS concluded that over the next two decades,

> a reasonable goal . . . is a reduction in fuel burn per seat of about 40%, compared to current airplanes. A 25% reduction can be expected from improved engine performance and 15% from aerodynamic and weight improvements. (NRC 1992, 49)

Aircraft energy efficiency can chiefly be improved by increasing propulsion efficiency, reducing aerodynamic drag, and reducing airframe and engine weight. Of these, propulsion efficiency offers the greatest opportunities.

> Propulsion technology offers the greatest single contribution to the improvement of cruising economy and the environmental impact of commercial aircraft. The past three generations of gas turbine engines have incorporated increased turbine inlet temperature, increased compressor pressure ratio, increased bypass ratio, improved fan and nacelle performance, reduction of noise and emissions, and improved reliability that led to a continued dominance of the world commercial aircraft market. (NRC 1992, 149)

Propulsion Technology

Since its first use in commercial aircraft in the 1960s, the jet engine has evolved from turbojet to turbofan to high-bypass turbofan, with a 40 percent increase in energy efficiency (NRC 1992, 151). The early turbojet engines produced all of their thrust by means of the expanding hot air passing out of the core combustor. Current high-bypass engines achieve greater propulsion efficiency by sending five to six times as much air around the core turbine engine—air that is accelerated by fans driven by the core turbine (Greene 1992, 548). The bypass ratio of an engine describes the volume of air passing around the core turbine relative to the amount actually passing through the combustion turbine. Increasing the bypass ratio reduces specific fuel consumption (mass of fuel consumed per unit of thrust produced, generally measured in milligrams per newton-second) but requires an increase in engine diameter, thereby increasing engine weight and aerodynamic drag. Development of lightweight metal alloys, advanced aerodynamic designs for engines and fans, and advanced gearing systems was necessary to permit the fuel economy advantages of higher bypass ratios to be realized. Further increases in bypass ratios are possible but will require further advances in materials and engine designs. Modern engines are now less than 20 percent steel and about 65 percent lightweight metal alloys. Achieving the efficiency goals of advanced engine concepts is expected to require that 60 percent of their weight be composed of metal matrix and ceramic components.

In 1989 the NASA Lewis Research Center set efficiency goals for two new generations of jet propulsion technology that could be ready by 2005 and 2015. For the 2005 goal, current bypass ratios of 5–6 would have to increase to 8–10. At the same time, the cycle pressure ratio—that is, the ratio of the maximum turbine compression pressure to the ambient atmospheric pressure—would be increased from the current state of the art of 36–38 to the range of 60–75, and turbine inlet temperatures would be raised from 2,250° F up to 2,900°–3,000° F. These and other improvements in engine aerodynamics and weight should lead to a 15 percent to 20 percent reduction in specific fuel consumption (the current state-of-the-art specific fuel consumption is 0.54–0.56). By 2015, even higher temperatures (3,200°–3,400° F) and pressure ratios of 75–100, together with bypass ratios of 15–20, could lead to a 30 percent reduction in fuel burned (NRC 1992, 152).

Still greater gains (perhaps another 10 percent) are possible using unducted propfan propulsion systems. Propfans look much like turboprops but use eight or more highly swept blades, sometimes configured as twin counter-rotating propellers. Recent advances in propeller design have allowed aircraft to achieve speeds of Mach 0.65 to 0.85 with propfans (Greene 1992, 548). Higher cost and concerns about noise, vibration, and maintenance have thus far prevented commercial acceptance of propfan technology.

Advanced Aerodynamics

Aerodynamic efficiency can be represented by the ratio of lift (the force pushing an aircraft directly upward) to drag (the force opposing its forward motion). Reductions in aerodynamic drag on the order of 35 percent are possible by various improvements to the L/D ratio of current aircraft (Table 10-2).

At low speeds, airflow over a wing takes place in smooth layers (laminar flow). As speeds increase, an increasing proportion of the flow becomes turbulent, greatly increasing drag. The potential to reduce drag and fuel consumption by means of laminar flow control techniques is substantial.

The flow on most surfaces of an aircraft is turbulent. Laminar flow control (LFC), hybrid laminar flow control, and natural laminar flow are promising sources of skin-friction drag reduction on aerodynamic surfaces. Laminar flow nacelles

Table 10-2

Potential Aerodynamic Improvements for Commercial Aircraft

Application	Potential L/D Increase
Aspect ratio[a] increase (11–17.5%)	15%
Laminar flow control (upper wing and tail surface)	10%–12%
Airfoil development	2%–3%
Turbulence control	2%–3%
Induced drag	3%–4%
TOTAL	≈35%

Source: NRC 1992, Table 7-1.
[a]Aspect ratio is a general measure of the width (or chord) of an airfoil (wing) relative to its length (span).

are also being studied by NASA. Laminar/turbulent transition of the airflow next to the aircraft surface is delayed through a combination of pressure gradient tailoring of the wing and control such as suction through the skin. If full-chord laminar flow can be maintained in this fashion, fuel savings of up to 25% could be realized. (NRC 1992, 118)

This 25 percent upper bound on fuel savings from advanced aerodynamics is unlikely to be achievable in practice because of problems in maintaining surface smoothness in actual operation and difficulty in keeping suction grooves entirely free of debris. Estimates of what may be practically achievable by 2010 range from 10 to 20 percent (Greene 1992, Table 3).

Other opportunities to reduce drag exist. Riblets (tiny grooves made in the direction of airflow) have been found to reduce drag over the fuselage, where laminar flow control is very difficult (NRC 1992, 119). Winglets, wingtip extensions that alter turbulent flow at wingtips, advanced wing (airfoil) designs, and use of advanced computer techniques to simulate and refine aerodynamics all have potential to make small but significant additional contributions to drag reduction. The NASA goal of a 10 percent fuel savings from aerodynamic improvements to new aircraft by 2015 thus seems very reasonable.

Weight Reduction

A 1 percent reduction in the gross weight of an empty aircraft will reduce fuel consumption by 0.25 to 0.5 percent, the effect increasing directly with aircraft size (Greene 1992, Appendix). Substituting light-weight, high-strength materials in aircraft structures is particularly attractive because of the synergistic impacts of weight reduction (or increase). Weight added to the structure requires additional wing area for greater lift, additional engine power for the thrust to overcome the additional drag, and additional fuel to provide the same range, all of which add additional weight and create a feedback effect that ends up increasing (or decreasing) gross aircraft weight anywhere from 2 to 10 lb for an initial 1 lb increase (decrease) in structural weight (NRC 1992, 187). Today's fleet is about 97 percent metallic, with composites used for a very limited number of components, such as fins and tailplanes. Specialized military aircraft, jet fighters, and vertical take-off and landing aircraft are now 40 to 60 percent composite materials. Some believe that in the next century, commercial aircraft could be composed 80 percent of composites with equal or greater strength and an overall 30 percent reduction in empty aircraft weight (Greene 1992,

Figure 10-2

World Commercial Aircraft Fleet by Size Class, 1993 and Projected to 2013

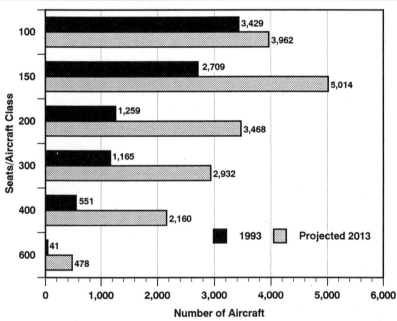

Source: Douglas 1995, 24.

551). If so, fuel consumption should decrease by 7.5 to 15 percent, depending on aircraft size. In light of this projection, the NASA goal of a 5 percent fuel burn reduction by 2015 seems technically achievable.

Operational Improvements

Growing air traffic and constrained airport capacity will be a worsening problem for the airline industry. Improvements to the air traffic management system, ground operations, and flight planning are underway, but experts in this area define success as preventing growing congestion from harming overall fuel economy (Greene 1992, 552). As airport congestion increases with increasing air traffic, airlines will respond by using larger planes. Manufacturers expect demand for smaller aircraft to stagnate while demand for larger aircraft grows rapidly (Douglas 1995, 24–25) (see Figure 10-2). The average number

Figure 10-3

U.S. and World Aircraft Size and Load Factor Trends and Projections, 1970–2015

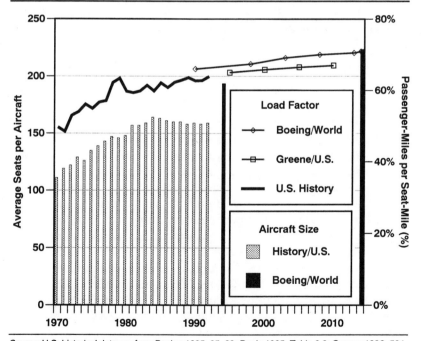

Source: U.S. historical data are from Boeing 1995, 25, 29; Davis 1995, Table 6.2; Greene 1992, 564.

of seats per aircraft is expected to increase by 15 percent, from 190 in 1994 to 220 by 2015 (Boeing 1995, 29).

Conventional wisdom used to hold that load factors could not practically be increased beyond two-thirds. Greene (1992, 564) assumed that U.S. load factors would increase to 66 percent by the year 2000 and gradually grow to 67 percent in 2010. Advances in fleet and crew management systems, however, have led major aircraft manufacturers to conclude that load factors of over 70 percent are achievable. Boeing (1995) projects worldwide load factors of 70.9 percent in 2014, while McDonnell Douglas (Douglas 1995) foresees 69.5 percent of seats occupied by 2013 (Figure 10-3). On average, McDonnell Douglas has load factors increasing at 0.24 percent/year, and Boeing at 0.30 percent/year over the next two decades. Increasing load factors improves energy efficiency per passenger-mile because the relative impact of an additional passenger on fuel consumption is less than one-tenth of the relative increase in load (passenger-miles).

Technological Potential for Reducing Conventional Emissions

According to estimates by the U.S. Environmental Protection Agency (EPA 1993), in the transportation sector, aircraft account for 1.4 percent of carbon monoxide (CO) emissions, 2.4 percent of emissions of volatile organic compounds (VOCs), 1.4 percent of nitrogen oxide (NO_x) emissions, and 4.4 percent of fine particulate matter (PM-10). These estimates, however, include only emissions in the lower troposphere (atmospheric boundary layer), below 3,000 feet of altitude. In this zone, aircraft emissions contribute to the formation of ozone and are regulated in the United States under the Clean Air Act. However, commercial aircraft burn most of their fuel and produce most of their emissions at cruising altitudes above the boundary layer. The environmental impacts of aircraft emissions in the upper troposphere and in the stratosphere are not well understood. Emissions of hydrocarbons and NO_x during ground operations, take-off, and landing contribute to ozone formation in the troposphere. NO_x emissions during cruising contribute to ozone depletion in the stratosphere (OTA 1994, 121; Vedantham & Oppenheimer 1994, 7–12). HC and NO_x emissions during cruising are not now covered by EPA regulations, but limits are likely to be established in future rulemakings required by the 1990 Clean Air Act Amendments (CAAA). Emissions of NO_x and even water vapor in the upper atmosphere may contribute to global warming, although their effects have not yet been established (Stolarski & Wesoky 1993, 6).

In this assessment, energy use and CO_2 and NO_x emissions will serve as indicators of the ability of commercial air transport to meet the sustainability goals. Only direct CO_2 emissions from fuel combustion are considered because of a lack of information on indirect or upstream CO_2 emissions. Delucchi (1991, Table 9) has estimated that fuel combustion accounts for 78 percent of full-fuel-cycle CO_2 emissions from heavy-duty vehicles using diesel, a middle distillate similar to jet fuel. The share for commercial jets is likely to be higher because of their more intensive use. Certainly, emissions of CO_2 by aircraft contribute to the buildup of GHGs throughout the atmosphere. Carbon dioxide emissions, of course, are directly proportional to energy use, assuming that conventional jet fuel continues to be the fuel of choice. Approximately 9.8 kg of CO_2 are produced per gallon of jet fuel burned.

Emissions of NO_x per gram of fuel vary greatly depending on the altitude, thrust level, engine design, and combustor type. Average indexes in terms of grams per kilogram of fuel burned have been estimated on the basis of average flight profiles and the quantity of fuel used.

Estimates for specific combinations range from 6 to 40 g of nitrogen oxides (as nitrogen dioxide) per kg of fuel.

Egli (1990) and Schumann (1993) propose an average index of 18. A recent analysis by NASA's Atmospheric Effects of Stratospheric Aircraft (AESA) project determines an index of 10.9 averaged over all fuel use. (Vedantham & Oppenheimer 1994, 39–40)

Reducing NO_x emissions in the future will be difficult because engine design changes to improve fuel efficiency, such as increased temperatures and pressure, tend, all else being equal, to favor the formation of NO_x. Nonetheless, aerospace engineers are confident that some reduction is possible. For example, NASA's Experimental Clean Combustor Program has demonstrated reductions on the order of 25 percent by designing turbines so that combustion occurs where the conditions are least favorable to NO_x formation. Laboratory tests have shown the possibility of producing less than 5 g of equivalent NO_2 per kilogram of fuel (Stolarski & Wesoky 1993, 4).

A preliminary goal for engine nitrogen oxide (NO_x) emissions is a reduction of 20% to 30%. (NRC 1992, 58)

The AESA project assumes a reduction in the aggregate NO_x EI [emissions index] of approximately 20% by the year 2015. . . . The AESA assumption may well be too optimistic for a base case without policy. (Vedantham & Oppenheimer 1994, 40)

A 20 percent reduction per kilogram of fuel consumed appears to be a reasonable estimate of what is technologically achievable by 2015. Note that as efficiency improvements reduce fuel use per passenger-mile, this will further reduce NO_x emissions.

Potential for Alternative Fuels Substitution

Substituting alternative fuels for conventional jet fuel is not likely to be a viable option for commercial aircraft over the next two decades. The potential to blend renewable fuels with kerosene jet fuel or to develop a renewable substitute is not evaluated here and may offer some potential to introduce renewable energy sources into the jet fuel market. If costs are higher and energy density lower, such fuels are likely to be resisted. High energy density, in terms of both weight and volume, together with ease of handling and storage, is critical to the practicality of a fuel for commercial jet aircraft. Kerosene jet fuel has among the highest volumetric energy densities of petroleum-based liquid fuels. Among alternatives that have been considered, propane and butane are next, having 75 percent of the energy content per gallon of jet fuel. But these fuels must be stored and transferred under pressure, adding to the complexity and cost of handling and storage, and they offer little in the way of environmental benefits (Hadaller & Momently 1993). The most promising alcohols, methanol and ethanol, have only 45 to 60 percent of the energy density of jet fuel, on the basis of either weight or volume (Table 10-3). To achieve the same range as a conventional jet carrying 775,000 lb of kerosene fuel, a methanol-fueled jet would need to store 1,760,000 lb of fuel, compromising both design and payload.

Table 10-3

Comparison of Properties of Alternative Jet Fuels

Fuel	Net Heat of Combustion (Btu/lb)	Net Heat of Combustion (Btu/gal)	Boiling Point (°F @ 1 atm)
Jet fuel (kerosene)	18,400–19,000	116,000–127,000	>100.0
Hydrogen	51,500	29,675	−423.2
Methane	21,500	76,193	−258.7
Propane	19,774	96,121	−43.7
Butane	19,506	97,973	31.1
Ethanol	11,550	76,000	172.9
Methanol	8,640	57,370	148.5

Source: Hadaller & Momently 1993, Table 10-1.

Gaseous fuels, such as hydrogen and methane, would have to be stored cryogenically in liquid form to achieve any reasonable energy density. Even so, liquid methane would have only 60 percent, and hydrogen less than 25 percent, of the energy density of jet fuel on the basis of volume. On a weight basis, however, methane has about 10 percent greater energy density and hydrogen has two and one-half times the energy density of jet fuel. Nonetheless, the problems of cryogenic storage and handling, as well as the greater volume necessary, pose severe technical difficulties for use of these fuels. As a result, aerospace experts do not foresee any significant substitutes for conventional jet fuel over the next two decades (Hadaller & Momenthy 1993). A recent study by the NAS expressed a similar viewpoint:

> There has also been much discussion regarding the use of exotic fuels such as liquid hydrogen or liquid methane to reduce fuel costs or noxious emissions. The Committee believes that such fuels will probably not be required in the period 2010–2020. (NRC 1992, 51)

In the more distant future, hypersonic aircraft flying at greater than four times the speed of sound (Mach 4) may create a demand for alternative jet fuels. (The speed of sound, Mach 1, is approximately 700 miles per hour.) Higher speeds require fuels with greater thermal stability, faster reaction (combustion) rates, and greater ability to absorb heat than traditional kerosene-type hydrocarbons. Specially processed conventional hydrocarbon fuels may be usable at speeds of Mach 3 to 4, but at speeds above Mach 4, cryogenic fuels may be required (Greene 1992, 552). Cryogenic methane may be usable at speeds of Mach 4 to 5. At speeds of Mach 8 and beyond, however, cryogenic hydrogen's fast reaction rate, stability, and heat absorption capability appear to make it the only option. Researchers on hypersonic flight have already begun experimenting with "slush" hydrogen, a 50/50 mixture of liquid and solid hydrogen offering greater energy density and heat absorption than liquid hydrogen. Perhaps by extending the boundaries of the technological frontiers in fuel handling and storage, research into hypersonic flight will create new opportunities to use alternative fuels in subsonic and supersonic commercial aircraft.

Projections of Travel, Energy Use, and Emissions Through 2015

Air travel is the fastest-growing major passenger transport mode. From 1970 to 1992, air passenger-miles traveled in the United States grew at an average annual rate of 6.2 percent, roughly twice the rate of growth of highway passenger travel. Although the rate of increase in air travel was the same in the 1980s as in the 1970s, industry analysts are convinced that future growth rates will slow somewhat as the industry becomes more mature throughout the world. McDonnell Douglas, for example, foresees an average worldwide growth rate of 5.7 percent/yr over the next two decades (Douglas 1994, 45). Worldwide domestic (within a country) travel is expected to grow more slowly than international travel: 4.6 percent versus 6.6 percent. Overall, Boeing (1995, Appendix A) analysts expect worldwide air travel to grow at an average of 5.8 percent/yr through 1999, and to slow to 4.9 percent/yr through 2014. McDonnell Douglas forecasters are slightly more bullish, anticipating a 5.9 percent annual growth rate through 2003 and 5.6 percent/yr from 2003 to 2013, in part due to a faster rate of economic growth: 3.5 percent versus 3.2 percent assumed by Boeing. For the United States, Boeing figures imply a 4.6 percent/yr growth rate through 1999 for combined U.S. domestic and international flights and 4.0 percent thereafter. The Energy Information Administration (EIA 1995, Table A7) expects a much slower expansion of total U.S. air travel: 3.9 percent/yr through 2010. Considering only domestic (internal) U.S. flights, Boeing predicts a 3.9 percent/yr average rate of increase to 2014, while McDonnell Douglas foresees a rate of 4.0 percent to 2013.

In-Use Fleet Fuel Economy Potential

The combined fuel economy improvement potential of propulsion, aerodynamic, and materials technologies has been assessed by the NRC (1992) and Greene (1992). The NRC (1992, 49) report estimates that a "reasonable goal" for new aircraft by 2015 is a 40 percent improvement in fuel burn per seat over current (1990s generation) aircraft. Greene (1992, Table 4) estimates the technological potential for fuel economy improvements in post-2000-generation aircraft at 42 to 110 percent, depending on degree of optimism in general and the market success of propfan technology. Given present low fuel prices, extensive use of propfans is not at all likely.

The rate of improvement of the in-use fuel economy of the U.S. and world aircraft fleets depends not only on the fuel economy potential of future aircraft, but also the fuel economy of existing aircraft and the rate of turnover of the stock. Because of their enormous value, aircraft have long lifetimes. In the United States, the decision to retire an aircraft is as likely to be due to environmental regulations concerning noise as to deterioration and maintenance costs. Worldwide, Boeing (1995, 27) estimates that passenger aircraft will be held at least 25 years before being permanently retired, and cargo aircraft at least 35 years. This means, on the one hand, that it takes decades for technology improvements to have their full effect but, on the other hand, that fleet fuel economy is improving today and will continue to improve as newer, more efficient aircraft join the fleet and older technology is retired.

Using a Federal Aviation Administration (FAA) projection of fleet turnover, Greene (1992) estimated a range of potential rates of fuel economy improvement through 2010. Today, the commercial aircraft fleet produces about 50 seat-miles per gallon (SMPG). The current, 1990s generation of newer aircraft delivers seat-miles per gallon in the high 60s and 70s (Greene 1992, 559). Thus, even with no new generation of post-2000 aircraft, Greene (1992) estimated that seat-mile fuel economy would improve to 65 SMPG in 2010, an average improvement rate of 1.3 percent/yr. Taking into account load factors increasing to 67 percent in 2010, passenger-miles per gallon would increase at 1.7 percent/yr. Advanced fuel economy technologies were assumed to be applied to create a "post-2000" generation of aircraft, to be introduced beginning in 2005. Adding a post-2000 generation of aircraft 70 to 80 percent more efficient than the 1990 generation boosted the annual SMPG gain to 2.5 percent/yr. Assuming that the existing fleet was aggressively retrofitted with more efficient engines produced a maximum growth rate of 2.8 percent/yr for SMPG. If the new generation of aircraft were only 40 percent more efficient, in line with the NRC's more realistic goal (given current low fuel prices), a rate of SMPG fuel economy improvement between 1.3 percent/yr and 2.5 percent/yr could be expected.

In its *Annual Energy Outlook 1995*, the EIA (1995, Table A7) projects aircraft efficiency improvements of 0.7 percent/yr through 2010 in their Reference Case, and as high as 2.1 percent/yr in their high-efficiency scenario. A study by the International Civil Aircraft Organization (ICAO 1992) predicted efficiency gains of 3.1 percent/yr through 2000 and 2.5 percent/yr thereafter for the world civil aircraft fleet. The rate of 3.1 percent/yr seems optimistic, given that the historical rate for the United States from 1970 to 1992 was 2.8 percent/yr, and that this period includes not only rapid technological progress and periods of very high fuel prices but rapid growth in the aircraft fleet, as well. Worldwide, however, air travel demand is growing more rapidly than in the United States, and this may partly account for the ICAO forecast's optimism.

2015 Scenarios

When projected rates of air travel growth from various sources are compared with projected rates of fuel economy improvement (Figure 10-4), it is immediately clear that no one expects efficiency gains to keep pace with the demand for air travel. To put the projections in historical perspective, U.S. air travel grew at an average of 6.2 percent/yr from 1970 to 1992. Moreover, the rate of increase in the second decade of that period was identical to that of the first. At the same time, fuel economy (SMPG) grew at an average rate of 2.1 percent/yr.

To illustrate the potential range of future fuel use and emissions, I constructed two scenarios to the year 2015. The high-efficiency scenario combines a relatively high rate of fuel economy improvement (2.5 percent/yr) with low rates of travel growth (3.8 percent/yr in the United States and 4.8 percent for the world). The low-efficiency scenario combines the EIA's assumed rate of fuel economy improvement of 0.7 percent/yr with consensus estimates of travel growth (4.2 percent/yr for the United States and 5.2 percent for the world). In both scenarios, it was assumed that load factors would steadily increase (at 0.24 percent/yr for the United States and 0.30 percent/yr for the

Figure 10-4

U.S. and World Annual Growth Rates of Air Travel and Seat-Miles per Gallon, Projected to 2015

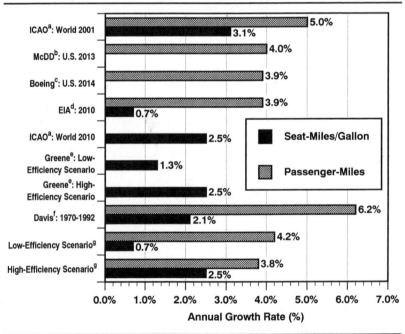

Source: [a]ICAO 1992; [b]Douglas 1994, 15; [c]Boeing 1995, Appendix A; [d]EIA 1995, Table A.7; [e]Greene 1992, Table 9; [f]Davis 1995, Table 6.2; [g]Chapter scenario assumptions.

world) to reach 67.5 percent for U.S. traffic and 71.1 percent for world-wide traffic in 2015 (Table 10-4).

By 2015, U.S. air travel is projected to more than double and world air travel to triple (Table 10-5). Even the most rapid rate of efficiency improvement will be unable to return GHG emissions to 1990 levels or to reduce oil use by 10 percent by 2005. The most pessimistic efficiency assumptions indicate a 17 percent increase in U.S. fuel economy

Table 10-4

Average Annual Growth Rates of Key Air Transport Forecast Parameters

	Low-Efficiency Scenario		High-Efficiency Scenario	
	U.S.	World	U.S.	World
Passenger-miles 1992–1999	4.6%	5.8%	4.2%	5.4%
Passenger-miles 1999–2015	4.0%	4.9%	3.6%	4.5%
Efficiency 1992–2015	0.7%		2.5%	
Load factor 1992–2015	0.24%	0.30%	0.24%	0.30%

Table 10-5

Projected U.S. and World Aviation Fuel Use and Emissions: Scenario Forecast Results for 2015

Item	1992 Base		2015 Low-Efficiency Scenario		2015 High-Efficiency Scenario	
	U.S.	World	U.S.	World	U.S.	World
Passenger-miles (billions)	493	1,333	1,274	4,253	1,166	3,896
Energy use (Quads)	2.14	5.80	4.47	14.70	2.72	8.96
Seat-miles/gal	48.6	46.8	57.0	54.9	85.7	82.5
Passenger-miles/gal	31.0	31.0	38.5	39.1	57.9	58.7
Load factor (%)	63.9%	66.4%	67.5%	71.1%	67.5%	71.1%
Fuel use (billion gal)	15.9	42.9	33.1	108.9	20.1	66.4
NO_x (10^6 metric tons)	0.52	1.41	0.88	2.91	0.54	1.77
CO_2 (10^6 metric tons)	155	419	323	1,064	197	648

Source: The basis for U.S. air travel activity is total domestic and international certificated route air carrier statistics, as reported by Davis (1995, Table 6.2). This includes neither military nor general aviation fuel use. The basis for world forecasts is total world revenue passenger-miles for 1992, as reported in Boeing (1995, Appendix A). Fuel use has been estimated for that year using the load factors and seat-mile per gallon numbers shown.

(SMPG) by 2015. Because load factors will increase at the same time, passenger-miles per gallon grow by 24 percent. As a result, energy use doubles in the U.S. low-efficiency scenario and is up more than 150 percent worldwide (Figure 10-5). As can be seen in Figure 10-5, the

Figure 10-5

U.S. Air Carrier Passenger-Miles and Energy Use: Trends and Projections, 1970–2015

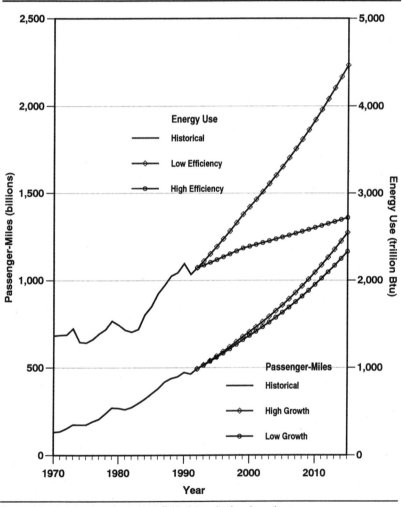

Source: Historical data from Davis 1995, Table 6.2; projections by author.

Figure 10-6

**World Emissions of CO$_2$ by Commercial Aircraft:
Trends and Projections, 1990–2015**

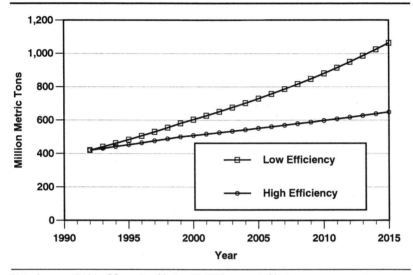

Note: Assumes 3.19 kg CO$_2$ per kg of fuel and 9.765 kg per gal of fuel.

low-efficiency scenario also assumes a slightly higher rate of growth in travel.

In the optimistic high-efficiency scenario, combining a slightly lower rate of travel growth with efficiency improvements that are likely only under much higher fuel prices (for example, propfan engines), the fuel economy of commercial aircraft increases 75 percent by 2015. Factoring in higher occupancy rates, a 90 percent energy efficiency increase is projected worldwide. Even this is unable to restrain the growth of energy use by the air mode. Jet fuel use is projected to increase 25 percent in the United States and 55 percent worldwide.

Because CO$_2$ emissions are proportional to fuel use (assuming no use of alternative fuels), CO$_2$ emissions grow worldwide in both scenarios (Figure 10-6). Even if renewable fuels were blended to displace 15 percent of jet fuel (consistent with the fourth sustainability criterion), CO$_2$ emissions would still increase worldwide, by over 30 percent in the high-efficiency scenario and by more than 100 percent in the low-efficiency scenario (corresponding changes for the United States alone would be approximately 10 percent and 75 percent).

The assumed 20 percent reduction in fleet NO$_x$ emissions rates holds total NO$_x$ emissions to a 4 percent increase in the United States

Figure 10-7

Global NO$_x$ Emissions by Commercial Passenger Aircraft: Trends and Projections, 1990–1995

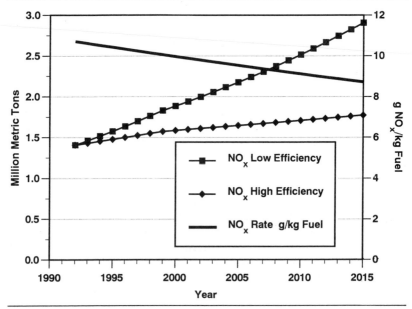

Note: The estimate of 10.9 g/kg of fuel is from Vedantham and Oppenheimer (1994), who believe it probably underestimated the true rate.

in the high-efficiency scenario and to a 70 percent increase in the low-efficiency scenario. Worldwide, however, emissions grow by 25 percent in the high-efficiency scenario and by over 100 percent in the low-efficiency scenario (Figure 10-7). Emissions of NO$_x$ increase less than CO$_2$ emissions because the emissions rate is specified per weight of fuel consumed. Thus, the decreasing emissions rate compounds the effect of increasing fuel economy. As noted above, improved combustion efficiency will be partly achieved by higher compression ratios and turbine temperatures. Such changes, other things equal, would tend to increase NO$_x$ emissions per pound of fuel. Thus, even the base case includes some amount of improvement in emissions technology.

Conclusions

Even under the most optimistic assumptions about energy efficiency improvement, air passenger transport will be unable to meet the 2015 sustainability goals with technological advances alone. Note again that we have not evaluated the potential to blend renewable fuels with conventional jet fuel or to develop substitutes in order to achieve the 15 percent renewable fuel goal. Nonetheless, this exercise serves to underline the critical importance of technological advances in determining the level of environmental impacts and oil consumption of commercial air travel. Oil use and CO_2 emissions are more than 50 percent higher in the low-efficiency scenario than when maximum technological progress is achieved. Almost all of this difference is due to technological advances leading to higher-fuel-economy aircraft.

Market forces, especially fuel prices, will be important as well. Higher fuel prices would create greater incentive to retire obsolete aircraft in favor of more energy-efficient models and would also reduce the demand for air travel via their impact on ticket prices. Higher fuel prices would also improve the cost-effectiveness of more expensive fuel economy technologies, such as the propfan engine.

Because technology is not enough to allow air travel to reach the Asilomar conference's sustainability goals, other modes and other measures would have to do more for the sector as a whole to meet them. Because it is such a rapidly growing mode of travel, air transport places a burden on other modes to make up the difference. The very great difference between the high- and low-efficiency scenarios, however, suggests that technology can make an enormous difference in the size of that burden.

References

Boeing Commercial Airplane Group. 1995. *Current Market Outlook.* Seattle. May.

Davis, S.C. 1995. *Transportation Energy Data Book: Edition 15.* ORNL-6856. Oak Ridge, Tenn.: Oak Ridge National Laboratory. May.

Delucchi, M.A. 1991. *Emissions of Greenhouse Gases from the Use of Transportation Fuels and Electricity.* ANL/ESD/TM-22, vol. 1. Argonne, Ill.: Argonne National Laboratory, Center for Transportation Research. November.

Derbyshire, T., W. Jenkinson, and D. Miller. 1991. Design Evolution in Jet Transport. *Aerospace America* 29 (9).

Douglas Aircraft Company, Economic Research Department. 1994. *World Economic and Traffic Outlook.* Long Beach, Calif.: McDonnell Douglas.

_____. Market Assessment. 1995. *Outlook for Commercial Aircraft.* Long Beach, Calif.: McDonnell Douglas.

Egli, R.A. 1990. Nitrogen Oxide Emissions from Air Traffic. *Chimia Technologie* 44 (11): 369–370.

Greene, D.L. 1992. Energy-Efficiency Improvement Potential of Commercial Aircraft. *Annual Review of Energy and Environment* 17: 537–573.

Greene, D.L., and Y. Fan. 1994. *Transportation Energy Efficiency Trends, 1972–1992*. ORNL-6828. Oak Ridge, Tenn.: Oak Ridge National Laboratory. December.

Hadaller, O.J., and A.M. Momenthy. 1993. Characteristics of Future Aviation Fuels. In *Transportation and Global Climate Change*, edited by D.L. Greene and D.J. Santini. Washington, D.C.: American Council for an Energy-Efficient Economy.

International Civil Aviation Organization (ICAO). 1992. *Outlook for Air Transport to the Year 2001*. ICAO circular 237-AT96. Montreal: International Civil Aviation Organization. August.

National Research Council, Aeronautics and Space Engineering Board (NRC). 1992. *Aeronautical Technologies for the Twenty-First Century*. Report of the Committee on Aeronautical Technologies. Washington, D.C.: National Academy Press.

Office of Technology Assessment (OTA). 1994. *Federal Research and Technology for Aviation*. OTA-ETI-610. Washington, D.C.: U.S. Government Printing Office. September.

Schumann, U. 1993. *On the Effect of Emissions from Aircraft Engines on the State of the Atmosphere*. Oberpfaffenhofen, Germany: Institut für Physik der Atmosphäre, Deutsche Forschungsanstalt für Luft und Raumfahrt.

Stolarski, R.S., and H.L. Wesoky. 1993. *The Atmospheric Effects of Stratospheric Aircraft: A Third Program Report*. NASA Reference Publication 1313. Hampton, Va.: National Aeronautics and Space Administration.

U.S. Energy Information Administration (EIA). 1995. *Annual Energy Outlook 1995*. DOE/EIA-0383(95). Washington, D.C. January.

U.S. Environmental Protection Agency, Office of Air Quality Planning and Standards. 1993. *National Air Pollutant Emission Trends, 1900–1992*. EPA-454/R-93-032. Research Triangle Park, North Carolina. October.

Vedantham, A., and M. Oppenheimer. 1994. *Aircraft Emissions and the Global Atmosphere*. New York: Environmental Defense Fund.

Potential of Leap-Forward Vehicle Technology: Automotive Industry Perspective

DICK KINSEY

The Partnership for a New Generation of Vehicles (PNGV) is a historic new partnership between the United States government and the U.S. Council for Automotive Research (USCAR), the latter comprising Chrysler, Ford, and General Motors. Suppliers, universities, and others are also involved (see Figure 11-1). This chapter offers a brief overview of PNGV and its goals, describes the types of technologies that may be available to meet those goals, and concludes with some thoughts on how the PNGV research program could potentially flow into the market.

PNGV Goals

PNGV is a precompetitive, collaborative research and development program with three interdependent goals (see Figure 11-2). Goal 1 is to pursue advances in manufacturing techniques that can reduce production costs and product development lead times for all automobile and truck production. Goal 2 is to pursue near-term advances in vehicle technologies that can lead to increases in the fuel efficiency and reductions in the emissions of conventional vehicle designs. Goal 3, PNGV's long-term goal, is to develop a revolutionary new class of efficient, environmentally friendly vehicle that achieves up to three times the fuel efficiency of today's comparable vehicle while retaining functionality, affordability, and safety. As technologies from goal 3 become commercially viable, industry will apply them to today's conventional vehicles.

Figure 11-1

PNGV Network

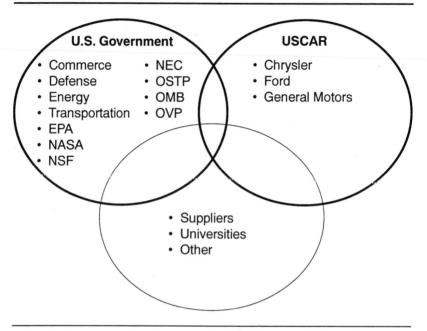

Note:
EPA = U.S. Environmental Protection Agency.
NASA = National Aeronautics and Space Administration.
NEC = National Economic Council.
NSF = National Science Foundation.
OMB = Office of Management and Budget.
OSTP = Office of Science and Technology Policy.
OVP = Office of the Vice President.
PNGV = Partnership for a New Generation of Vehicles.
USCAR = U.S. Council for Automotive Research.

Today's conventional vehicle is defined as the 1994 Ford Taurus, Chrysler Concorde, or Chevrolet Lumina and has the following specifications:

- capacity for five to six passengers

- 16.8 cu ft luggage capacity

- acceleration of 0 to 60 MPH in 12 seconds

- metro-highway driving range of 380 miles

- useful life of 100,000 miles

Figure 11-2

PNGV Research Goals

Goal 1: Manufacturing

Pursue advances in manufacturing techniques that can reduce production costs and product development lead times for all car and truck production.

Goal 2: Near-Term Advances

Pursue advances in vehicles that can lead to improvements in the fuel efficiency and emissions of conventional vehicle designs.

Goal 3: Long-Term: Next-Generation Vehicles

Develop a revolutionary new class of efficient, environmentally friendly vehicles to meet consumers' needs for safety, quality, performance, utility, and affordability and achieve up to three times the fuel efficiency of today's comparable vehicles.[a]

---

[a]1994 Ford Taurus, Chrysler Concorde, and Chevrolet Lumina.

Some of the specific assumptions related to the up-to-three-times fuel efficiency goal of a redesigned vehicle are that it

- be designed to Tier II emissions while complying with other Clean Air Act requirements.

- meet present and future Federal Motor Vehicle Safety Standards (FMVSS) while meeting equivalent in-use safety performance of the target vehicles.

- achieve a recyclability objective of at least 80 percent, up from 75 percent industry average today.

- maintain affordability.

- maintain manufacturability.

These criteria are not listed in any order of preference since they are all important to the customer. Clearly, for a new product to be acceptable in the market, especially the mass market, it must satisfy all of the customer expectations and provide value at least equivalent to the conventional product. The goal is for vehicles that result from the PNGV research program to be marketable to a high-volume segment for the social benefits of reduced fuel consumption, improved balance of trade, lower emissions, reduced global warming, and so forth.

Although this chapter focuses on goal 3, it is important not to lose sight of the fact that goal 1 is necessary to having an affordable product derived from the efforts toward goal 3. In addition, people

Figure 11-3

PNGV Goal 3 Timing

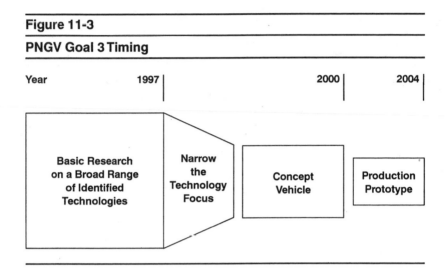

| Year | 1997 | | 2000 | 2004 |

are impatient by nature: they do not want to wait for the ultimate product from goal 3 but rather want to see results in regular doses along the way. Industry must therefore meet goal 2 by improving conventional vehicles as soon as practical.

Goal 3 Timing

In 1994, the PNGV technical team of government and industry participants identified technology areas in which basic research was needed in order to meet the PNGV goals. The process of selecting technologies and narrowing the technical focus is expected to continue through 1997. By then, the focus of technology development will have been narrowed down to only those candidate technologies that are sufficiently developed to meet PNGV vehicle requirements within the established time frame. As the technology focus is narrowed, the auto partners will develop concept vehicles to evaluate the engineering feasibility of incorporating potential technologies into total vehicle systems. Concept vehicles are expected to be developed by about the year 2000. By approximately 2004, production prototype vehicles will be developed that demonstrate the manufacturing feasibility of the technologies and their ability to meet rigorous performance criteria (see Figure 11-3).

Technology Challenges and Focus Areas

To provide an idea of the technology challenge facing the PNGV partners, it is useful to look at the distribution of input energy in a current midsize (family sedan) vehicle run on the metro-highway cycle (see Figure 11-4). Notice that 77 percent of the incoming energy is lost to engine inefficiencies. With other losses along the way, only about 11 percent of the input energy is available to actually propel the vehicle: 5 percent for rolling resistance and 6 percent for aerodynamic losses. Major advances must be made in numerous technologies simultaneously to achieve an 80 MPG vehicle.

The goal of creating commercially viable technologies capable of up to 80 MPG within a decade is very aggressive, especially when function and affordability must be maintained. The technology efforts are focused on several areas, including aerodynamics, accessory drives, and reduced frictional losses. Here we review three main areas:

- energy conversion
- energy storage
- reduced energy demand
- lightweight materials
- energy-efficient electrical systems

Figure 11-4

Where the Energy Goes in the Metro-Highway Cycle

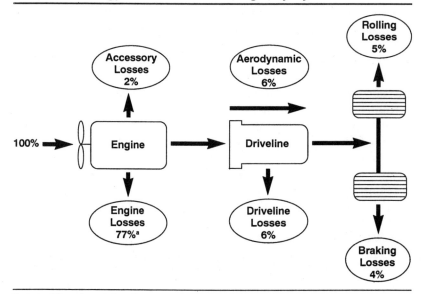

[a]Includes idle and coast-down losses.

Energy Conversion

Significant work is being conducted on energy conversion systems to meet the PNGV goals. The specific technologies being pursued are

- four-stroke, direct-injection (4SDI) engines
- turbines
- fuel cells

It is often said that electric vehicles (EVs) operate at a much higher efficiency level than vehicles with conventional internal combustion engines (ICEs). Motor and vehicle efficiency is only about 15.5 percent for a conventional vehicle, whereas the motor and controller efficiency is about 71 percent for an EV. However, when the picture is viewed from the perspective of the full energy cycle, the advantage of EVs becomes much less obvious. The full energy cycle starts from the base fuel feedstock. If we consider the energy at this point to be 100 percent, and presume that the energy source is petroleum, in a conventional vehicle cycle approximately 17 percent of the energy is lost before energy is input to the vehicle: some of the energy is lost in the gasoline refining process, and some is lost in transporting the gasoline to the refueling station (see Figure 11-5). With the EV cycle, 66 percent of the energy is used in the oil refining process, the power generation process, and the transmission of electricity over power lines before energy is even available at the "refueling" station. In addition, about 8 percent of the energy is used while "refueling" the vehicle. Thus, for vehicles with ICEs, about 87 percent of the energy is used before energy is available to propel the vehicle. For EVs, about 82 percent of the energy is used before energy is available for propelling the vehicle. This full-cycle analysis makes two points. First, the ICE operates at about 13 percent efficiency and the EV at about 18 percent—a difference of only about 5 percent. Second, increasing the efficiency of the ICE is a prime area for attention when pursuing fuel efficiency improvement of a non-EV.

The four-stroke, direct-injection (4SDI) compression-ignition engine is a promising energy conversion technology because it is a natural extension (albeit enormously challenging technically) from port-injection gasoline engines. Current gasoline engines operate at only about 32 percent peak thermal efficiency, whereas 4SDI engines operate at about 43 percent peak efficiency (see Figure 11-6). Important PNGV goals for the 4SDI engine are to increase peak thermal efficiency to about 46 percent and to reduce NO_x and particulate matter emissions to Tier II levels. It is noteworthy that the efficiency on a transient driving cycle will be less for all of the energy conversion devices being pursued. (Note that all peak thermal efficiencies

Figure 11-5

Full-Cycle Efficiency: Internal Combustion Engine (ICE) Versus Electric Vehicle (EV)

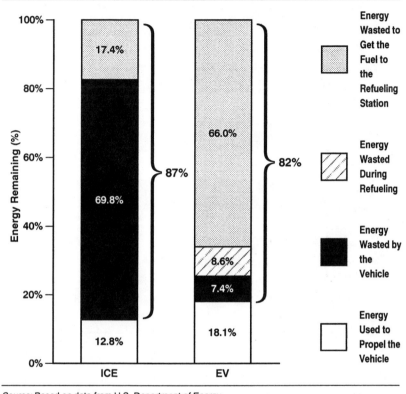

Source: Based on data from U.S. Department of Energy.

of energy conversion devices discussed in this chapter are based on Ford estimates.)

Turbines are of interest to PNGV because of their high power density, high reliability, low emissions, and ability to run on a variety of fuels. However, turbine efficiencies for low-power applications, like those required for PNGV, are inadequate today—only about 30 percent. To overcome this drawback, research is oriented toward high-temperature turbines that may achieve thermal efficiencies near 42 percent, focusing on the use of ceramics that can withstand high temperatures (2,500° F).

Another energy conversion device that may play a role in meeting PNGV goals is the fuel cell, an electrochemical device that converts

Figure 11-6

PNGV Energy Conversion Candidates

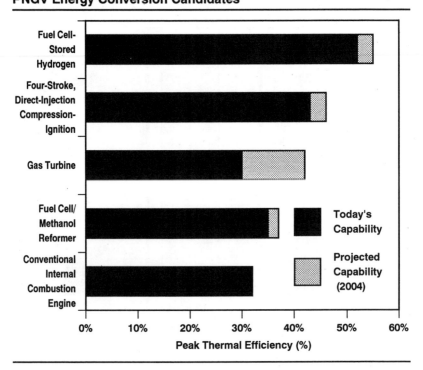

chemical energy directly into electrical energy. In a typical fuel cell system, hydrogen and oxygen (from air) react to produce electricity. The process requires a hydrogen source, which can be a hydrogen tank or a hydrogen-containing fuel with a reformer to extract hydrogen from the fuel. Fuel cells using stored hydrogen potentially have high vehicle efficiency; full-cycle efficiency still needs to be assessed. Fuel cells currently have vehicle peak thermal efficiencies of about 52 percent and are expected to achieve efficiencies greater than 55 percent in the 2004 time frame. Fuel cells with an on-board methanol reformer have 35 percent peak thermal efficiency today and are projected to improve to 37 percent. With a petroleum reformer, the efficiency is 30 percent today, with improvement to 32 percent projected. Fuel cells have been used for years in the space program because of their high efficiency and reliability in providing high power. More recently, fuel cells have become commercially available for use in applications such as on-site power generators and are currently being demonstrated in an urban bus environment. For fuel cells to be used in an automobile application, improvements must be made in size, weight, cost, and fuel storage/reformation.

Hybrid Propulsion

All of the fuel converters discussed above (4SDI engines, gas turbines, and fuel cells) may be combined with electric drive motors and efficient energy storage devices to form hybrid propulsion systems. A hybrid propulsion system incorporating efficient conversion technologies may provide the opportunity for better energy management and utilization. Hybrid vehicles also require energy storage devices for several reasons. In today's cars, energy dissipated during braking can account for about 4 percent of vehicle energy losses; much of this braking energy can be recovered with a regenerative braking system in which kinetic energy is recovered and stored for later use. In addition, a considerable amount of energy that is available during either deceleration or idling could also be stored for later use, such as when the driver wants to climb a hill or pass another car. With the series configuration of the hybrid electric vehicle (HEV), the energy storage device allows the energy conversion device to run at more nearly optimum conditions, at which the efficiency is greatest (see Figure 11-7). Candidate technologies being investigated include high-power batteries, ultracapacitors, and flywheels.

Figure 11-7

Series Hybrid Electric Vehicle Configuration

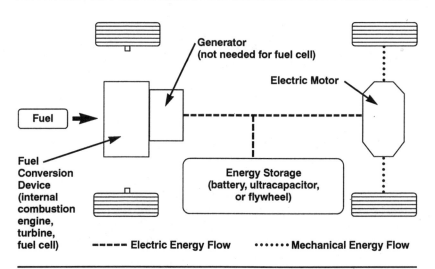

237

Energy Storage

The specifications for HEV energy storage devices needed to store braking energy are much different from those being developed for EVs. These devices are used primarily for power management and are required to store much less energy; however, they must operate at very high power levels. Furthermore, HEV energy storage devices could be discharged and charged many times per drive. Therefore, cycle life becomes extremely important.

Candidate battery technologies include nickel–metal hydride, lithium-ion, and lithium polymer. Batteries for PNGV vehicles must provide a very high power-to-energy ratio—more than a factor of 10 increase over batteries now under development for EVs. The needs are for high efficiency—perhaps using bipolar cell construction—and for novel manufacturing processes applicable to very thin electrodes.

Ultracapacitors—an emerging high-power technology—are electrochemical energy storage devices in which the charge storage takes place at the electrode/electrolyte interface. Ultracapacitors are characterized by a high power density and high charge/discharge energy efficiency. The key technical challenges are to improve the ultracapacitor's low energy density, which is on the order of 10 to 15 percent of that of batteries, and to reduce costs. Ultracapacitors cannot meet PNGV energy storage goals by themselves. They may, however, enable the goals to be met in combination with an advanced battery. Ultracapacitors can peak-shave the discharge and regenerative pulse power demands on the battery. This implies a less challenging power-to-energy capability for the battery and could extend the battery's life. Significant benefits are envisioned for this approach, despite the added challenge of integrating the two technologies into a single system.

Flywheel systems represent another energy storage option for hybrid propulsion systems. They work by electricity causing the rotor in the flywheel to spin at high speeds. When energy is needed by motors that drive the wheels, the rotational energy in the rotor is changed into electricity. This energy can be stored for a long time since the rotor is spinning in a vacuum on magnetic bearings. Flywheel systems have demonstrated suitable specific energy and power in commercial transit buses. Several experimental vehicles have been built using flywheels for automotive applications. Additional research and development efforts should focus on increasing the specific energy and reducing the cost of flywheel systems. Further, research and development offers the potential to reduce material costs, provide lightweight containment, and simplify overall system integration.

Lightweight Materials

PNGV needs to find a way to cost-effectively process and fabricate the lightweight components necessary to significantly reduce vehicle mass and thus improve fuel efficiency. Mass reduction is a proven way to obtain improved fuel economy in vehicles. For every 10 percent reduction in the mass of the vehicle, over 5 percent improvement in fuel economy is expected. The improvement is even greater when the powertrain is sized for the lighter vehicle body. The challenge is to reduce mass while maintaining a safe, affordable structure. To address these challenges, major efforts are required to make feasible the following technologies:

- enhanced processing and manufacturing techniques for lightweight metals

- processing and manufacturing techniques for high-tech, lightweight, high-strength materials, such as polymer and metal matrix composites and structural ceramics

- recycling technology for in-plant and scrapped vehicle waste

- robust analysis and design methodologies for optimized designs and reduced engineering development time

Initial research and development activities may focus on technologies such as:

- improved high-strength steels and more efficient usage of steel

- low-cost sheet aluminum

- damage-resistant aluminum components for primary structure and body panels

- low-cost aluminum, magnesium, and titanium casting technology

- glass- and carbon-fiber composites for primary structure and body panels

- joining technology for lightweight metal and composites, including adhesives

- advanced ceramics for engine weight reduction, friction reduction, and improved thermal performance

- glazing materials as substitutes for glass

Energy-Efficient Electrical Systems

Major advances have occurred in power electronics, motor design, motor controllers, and permanent magnets. These improvements have led to the development of alternating current (ac) powertrains for electric vehicles that offer advantages such as reduced size and weight and improved efficiency. Research and development work will be done to improve the overall efficiencies of the regenerative braking mode and the electric driveline, which includes three main components: the inverter, the motor, and the transmission. Another great challenge is to achieve large reductions in manufacturing costs of the electric drivetrain. Research and development activities, including cost reduction efforts, are focused on the following areas:

- lighter-weight replacements for power conductors

- improved magnetic materials for more efficient and compact actuators and motors

- high-power-density electronics for power conditioning and control

PNGV Phase-In

The goal of PNGV is to research a product that customers will select on a high-volume basis when offered for sale to the public—a marketable product. If, in fact, the technologies and the PNGV program are successful, commercialization should follow as a natural progression.

Some have said that the auto industry is wed to the current designs and will stick with internal combustion engines, steel bodies, and conventional drive systems forever. One need only look at the gradual transition that has been taking place in vehicle bodies to see that when and where alternate materials make sense, they are being phased in. Examples are the Lincoln Continental, which now utilizes plastic body panels for the fender, hood, and deck lid; and the Ford Ranger/Explorer, whose instrument panel cross-vehicle beam is made of plastic composite. This same logic can be applied to other aspects of the vehicle. Although the auto industry has an enormous amount of capital invested in engine and transmission plants, these plants are periodically being refurbished, remodeled, and replaced, providing the opportunity for transition to other technologies. However, the phase-in schedule must make business sense and minimize risk and premature obsolescence.

The extent of infrastructure change is greatly dependent on the technologies adopted and will have varying impact on the auto and nonauto sectors. For example, although a change from steel to aluminum bodies will have a significant impact on the auto companies' stamping and assembly plants, this impact will be far less than if the change were to composite materials. However, the impact on the material industries would be significant with either new material. Conversely, going from gasoline internal combustion engines to turbine engines that can use multiple fuels, including gasoline, will have a major impact on the auto industry and minimal if any effect on the fuel supply industry.

Conclusion

PNGV has the potential to greatly improve several major societal concerns:

- global warming
- air quality
- energy security and the associated balance of trade

Much work needs to be done by many parties for the PNGV goals to be attained. Reduced government funding for high-risk research is a major concern in maintaining the timetable. If the product is right for the marketplace, then the wise companies—those wanting to stay in business—will offer it to the public.

Chapter Twelve

Transition to New Sources of Energy Using Sustainable Energy Strategies

ROBERTA J. NICHOLS

Development of vehicles to operate on nonpetroleum fuels began in earnest in response to the energy shocks of the 1970s. Although petroleum will remain the predominant transportation fuel for many years to come, supplies of petroleum are finite, so it is not too soon to begin the difficult transition to new sources of energy. In the past decade, the composition of the fuel utilized in the internal combustion engine (ICE) has been recognized as a major factor in the control of automobile tailpipe emissions and the rate of formation of ozone in the atmosphere: hence, the introduction of reformulated gasoline. Even further improvements in air quality can be realized, however, through vehicles that operate on natural gas, propane, methanol, or ethanol. Moreover, battery-powered vehicles and hydrogen-oxygen fuel-cell-powered vehicles have no tailpipe emissions at all. However, as long as gasoline remains plentiful and inexpensive, introduction of these alternative-fuel vehicles will present major technical and economic challenges to the auto and energy industries, as well as to the entire country.

Many lessons have been learned already, but more are sure to lie ahead. One of the major barriers to progress in the past has been short-term policies that change or disappear before they can be implemented. The key to success in making the transition to new sources of energy is a long-term policy that creates an environment in which sustainable goals to meet this need can be realized.

Background

Two major factors drive the use of alternative fuels into the marketplace: (1) the recognition that many of the nonpetroleum fuels have the potential for improving air quality beyond the reductions in ozone emissions projected for the use of reformulated gasoline in the United States; and (2) perhaps even more important, the recognition that the supply of petroleum in the world is finite and that someday, even if it is 50 or 100 years away, we will need to rely on new sources of energy, such as our abundant reserves of coal.

In the near term, some of the alternative-fuel technologies, such as the electric vehicle (EV), will give us more flexibility in the choice of energy used to generate electricity at the power plant, with no tailpipe emissions from the vehicle in the urban environment. Many issues must be resolved, however, if any of the alternative fuels are to become competitive in the marketplace.

Major Market Barriers

Market research conducted by the automotive industry and others has shown over and over that the average consumer is wary of investing in major or unproved technological changes. There are always a few innovators eager to be the "first on the block" with the latest technology, but, in general, consumers take a wait-and-see attitude toward any technology that deviates very far from their previous experience. In the case of alternative fuels, consumers no longer remember the long gasoline station lines of the 1970s. In fact, gasoline seems to be everywhere in abundance, as evidenced by the "cheap" prices, whereas it is difficult to find any alternative-fuel stations at all. In short, it is hard to compete with the economics of gasoline in the United States, both in terms of fuel costs and in terms of the purchase price of alternative-fuel vehicles. In this respect, however, we seem to be out of step with the rest of the world, where fuel prices are several times as high as in the United States, primarily because of higher taxation.

Future Transportation Fuels

The primary alternative-fuel candidates for the ICE are the gaseous fuels, such as natural gas (primarily methane) and liquefied petroleum gas (LPG) (primarily propane), and the liquid fuels, such as methanol, ethanol, and biodiesel fuel. In the near term and midterm, reformulated gasoline and diesel fuel will also play a major role in improving air quality.

244

Another gaseous fuel, hydrogen, could become a major alternative-fuel candidate if hard evidence for global warming were to appear, since no carbon dioxide is associated with the combustion of hydrogen. In the near term, however, hydrogen is too valuable to the petrochemical industry to be competitive as an ICE fuel. Its best use appears to be in the fuel cell. Fuel cell technology has made great progress in the last decade, with major reductions in cost bringing it into the realm of possibility, but the technology is still very much in the research stage of development.

How to store hydrogen for fuel cells is still an open question. One of the storage methods under study is to carry hydrogen in the form of methanol and to reform the methanol to produce hydrogen on-board the vehicle. The development of an infrastructure for methanol for flexible-fuel vehicles (FFVs), or eventually the dedicated methanol vehicle, could be important for fuel cell vehicles in the future.

EVs must still find a better (longer-life, lower-cost) battery with more energy density than the lead-acid cell if they are to satisfy the needs of more than a small percentage of vehicle operators. In any case, EVs are best suited for the urban environment, with its limited driving range and its large need for reductions in tailpipe emissions.

Cost Considerations

A 1992 car and light-truck buyer survey reported the top three reasons for vehicle purchase as (1) durability and reliability, (2) a well-made vehicle, and (3) a good engine and transmission. The price of the vehicle ranked fourth, but price probably would have a different ranking if the cost were significantly different from that of conventional vehicles or expectations. It is well known that operating costs are especially important to fleet operators.

The use of nonpetroleum liquid fuels in the ICE probably will have the broadest application and the most penetration in the private sector since this technology has the least departure from today's vehicles and therefore has the least additional cost and risk for the consumer. Gaseous fuels have an operating cost advantage, however, at least presently, for high-mileage fleet operators, but if the vehicle is a dedicated one, the resale value is a concern. The average consumer will have a difficult time amortizing the higher cost of the natural gas vehicle against the lower cost of the fuel because the vehicle is not driven enough miles per year. Also, the high cost of a fast-fill natural gas refueling station makes it unlikely that one will be found on every corner, again making natural gas a fuel more likely to be used by fleet operators with central refueling. These issues are less of a barrier for

LPG because of the lower vehicle cost and the lower refueling station cost, but the ultimate penetration of LPG is probably limited by the fact that it is a by-product commodity.

At present, cost is a major issue for the EV. Not only is most of the vehicle system new technology, with a higher cost, but when the need to periodically replace the battery is factored in, the operating cost does not even begin to compete with that of gasoline except in France and Italy, where gasoline is quite expensive. In addition, unless an advanced battery with substantially better energy density than lead-acid is commercially available, the limited driving range of the EV will limit interest on the part of consumers.

The Commercialization Process

If an automotive manufacturer decides to take a promising new technology beyond the research stage, it must be a good business decision because the manufacturer has an obligation to its shareholders. First and foremost, the decision should be customer-driven because consumers will only buy what they want to buy. Secondly, the technology must be well developed, with a long history of prove-out testing, because premature introduction can seriously hurt the market: it takes a long time to recover from a bad experience. In addition, the technology must have the ability to penetrate the retail market, not just be sold to fleets, in order to become widespread and broad based enough to build the necessary supporting infrastructures and to develop competitive economics.

Almost all of the changes in the auto industry in the past have been evolutionary, but the shift to nonpetroleum sources of energy is much more revolutionary, thus putting these programs at high risk for success. Government support, with long-term commitments and sustainable policies, is needed to bring these programs to market. Any major change requires a lengthy period before showing any noticeable result. If policy is always shifting, chaos results, with a terrible waste of resources.

Getting started is the hard part. Because there is not an immediate need to give up gasoline, making the transition to alternative fuels is a slow and difficult process. Incentive legislation and policies, not mandates, are needed to jump-start the market. Not only must the technology be reliable and affordable for the customer, there should be incentives for all of the stakeholders: the customer, the auto industry, the fuel industry, and the government.

Incentives

Incentives to encourage the purchase and use of alternative-fuel vehicles can be both monetary and nonmonetary. Examples of monetary incentives are reduced registration fees; sales and use tax exemptions or reductions; investment tax credits; no toll fees; reduced parking fees; reduced insurance premiums; credit trading, both mobile and stationary; personal property tax exemption; reduced loan fees/loan guarantees; and in the case of the electric vehicle, lease of the battery instead of purchase.

Taxation of fuels should be on an energy basis, but a new-fuel tax exemption or reduction at market start-up would greatly encourage the consumer to give up gasoline. The reduction in revenue and the cost of the monetary incentives should be offset by an increase in gasoline tax since the United States is out of step with the rest of the world in this respect anyway.

Nonmonetary incentives for owning an alternative-fuel vehicle can also be powerful. Examples are being able to use the high-occupancy-vehicle (HOV) lane even if there is only one person in the vehicle; special parking places; exemption from transportation control measures (TCMs); special-recognition license plates; public recharging stations for the EV, as well as ones at work; and support from the dealer and utility at the time of EV purchase in meeting the vehicle's recharging needs at home. Many additional actions could give the consumer a much higher level of confidence in the new technologies. For example, there should be a requirement that all vehicles must meet current emission and safety standards, including aftermarket conversions, and there should be uniform standards for measuring such items as driving range and performance. Unwarranted shipping, tunnel, and other road restrictions for alternative-fuel vehicles should be removed, and a nationwide program to train and certify emergency personnel and service technicians should be implemented.

California has already put some of these incentives in place, but even more are needed. For example, California has an investment tax credit for purchase of a low-emission vehicle (LEV), but unfortunately this legislation sunsets too soon to help the introduction of EVs. Also, the cap on the total dollars of credit that can be given per year limits the number of eligible vehicles to a maximum of 750 per year. Legislation was introduced that would have provided a sales tax exemption, but with California's current economic conditions, it did not find the necessary support. The alternative-fuel vehicles do have a higher value than 1 (a gasoline vehicle counts as one vehicle) in the TCMs put in place in Los Angeles, with the EV counting for the most (5). Exemptions from other TCMs are under consideration as well.

The federal Energy Policy Act of 1992 (EPACT) has also put some of the needed incentives in place. For example, the investment tax credit for purchase of an EV (up to $4,000) and the income tax deductions for other alternative-fuel vehicle purchases are good motivators for the consumer to at least consider such a purchase. If the new technology is reliable, affordable, and purchased voluntarily, rather than forced into the market, satisfied consumers will soon be telling their neighbors about its attributes.

Mandates

Mandates are a poor way to introduce new technology. As soon as there is a mandate to do something, one must also say when that something must start. However, the technology may not be ready or affordable by that date. A good example of this issue is California's zero-emissions-vehicle (ZEV) sales mandate. When the legislation was put in place in September 1990, introduction of the EV by 1998 looked difficult, but not impossible. However, each year that has gone by since 1990 has made the level of anxiety go higher because it is now clear that the needed advanced-technology batteries with higher energy density and lower lifetime costs are not going to be available in this time frame. It will be well past the turn of the century before the advanced battery technologies will be ready for mass production. Industry needs the flexibility to delay introduction of any new product until all of the issues are resolved. Otherwise, the customer will not be satisfied, and the long-term market will not develop.

Lessons Learned

Ford made a serious commitment to the development of alternative-fuel vehicles as a result of the energy crisis of the 1970s and continues to support these programs today, even though it has been an uphill battle all the way. Late in 1980, despite a deep recession, Ford decided to put a propane or LPG passenger car into production; production began in 1982. Canada had some monetary incentives in place that gave the purchaser in Ontario province an instant payback of the $700 incremental increase in price. Even in the United States, with the lower cost of the fuel, the consumer could amortize this additional cost in about two to two and a half years, driving at 12,000 miles per year (with a 25-gallon fuel tank, the driving range of an LPG vehicle was equivalent to that of its gasoline cousin). However, by 1984, gasoline prices had fallen, and LPG vehicle sales also fell, to the point where Ford had to give up production.

The build and public display of a dedicated compressed natural gas (CNG) vehicle in 1982 resulted in great interest on the part of the American Gas Association (AGA) in a 1,000-unit demonstration program for CNG vehicles, particularly since the performance of this vehicle was rather remarkable when compared with that of most aftermarket conversions. The CNG vehicle had a 200-mile range and an acceleration time even better than its gasoline counterpart's. Ford responded with the build of 1984 Ranger trucks dedicated to operation on CNG, again with superior performance; however, at $20,000 per unit, only 27 units were actually leased by the AGA member utilities.

A similar story can be told for the dedicated methanol Escorts that were built on the production line in 1983 with an incremental cost of $2,200. The success of a 40-car fleet in Los Angeles in 1981 caused the state of California to ask if Ford would produce 1,000 units at the factory. When the orders actually came in, however, only 501 went to California, with another 81 delivered to experimental programs elsewhere in the world.

Much was learned from these early experiences. The customer wants, and expects, the vehicle to be transparent in operation—that is, to present no discernible differences—when compared with gasoline vehicles, including the cost. Ultimate sales volumes are heavily dependent on economics, no matter how good the technology. In fact, development of technology is relatively easy compared with development of the market.

Good research results do not mean the product is ready to go to market, as can be seen in the length of time it took to bring the flexible-fuel vehicle to production. The first experimental FFV was built in 1983. Production started in 1993, although still in limited quantities, because Ford wanted to be sure that all of the technical issues had been resolved and, given previous experiences, was apprehensive about the real size of the market. Between the first research vehicle and production, 705 FFVs operated in demonstration fleets. These FFVs, along with 630 dedicated methanol vehicles, accumulated more than 50 million miles of experience with methanol. Nevertheless, fuel quality in the field remains an issue. In addition, the slow growth in the number of refueling stations has been detrimental to pursuit of more aggressive production plans. In 1996, however, there was a ramp-up in the number of units produced because the market now sees the FFV as a reliable product. In 1997, production is completely open: Ford will build as many units as anyone orders, with shipment anywhere.

One of the key events that brought the FFV out of research and into the production development process was the passage of the Alternative Motor Fuels Act (AMFA) of 1988. This act is an example of how powerful the right kind of incentive legislation can be. The AMFA is based on logic in that it recognizes that the Corporate Average Fuel Economy (CAFE) legislation was put into place to conserve petroleum and that, therefore, if a vehicle does not consume petroleum, it should receive a CAFE benefit. The AMFA does not cost the government money, other than the commitment to help develop the market by purchasing alternative-fuel vehicles, but it provides the auto industry the opportunity to comply with CAFE with new product whenever some of the cost of that new product can be justified by the offsetting CAFE benefit. The fact remains that this new product is part of the long-term effort to make the transition to new sources of energy, desirable in the near term because of the improvements in air quality to be realized, and unavoidable in the long term because of the finite supply of petroleum.

Conclusion

Forecasts for the future are difficult. However, a vision for success should include the realization that the transition to new sources of energy is required for the long term. Much patience is needed because the process will be, and should be, slow and methodical. Development of the technology is the easy part. Introduction of, and adherence to, a long-term policy that supports nonbiased development of the marketplace is critical to achievement of this vision; special interests should not be allowed to drive the market. There is no perfect fuel, and moreover, in contrast to our dependence on petroleum-based fuels in the past and present, multiple fuel choices are more likely in the future. One thing we know for sure is that customers will let us know which ones work the best for them.

Is Technology Enough?
A Synthesis of Views Expressed
at the Conference

BARRY MCNUTT, LEW FULTON, AND DAVID GREENE

A major purpose of the Asilomar Transportation, Energy, and Environment conference series is the exchange of information: data, methods, and inferences. Another is to advance the collective understanding of the nature of the policy issues in transportation and energy. In an effort to address this second purpose, a new element was added to the 1995 Asilomar conference: a final session in which the remaining participants (about half of total conference participants) attempted to reach consensus on the question raised in the conference title, "Sustainable Transportation—Energy Strategies: Is Technology Enough?" and on the related technology and policy issues. This effort (however foolhardy it might appear, given the contentious nature of the issues and the divergent views of conference participants), was designed to serve several purposes:

- First, in response to concerns about lack of conclusiveness that had been raised after previous conferences, the organizers aimed to develop conclusions that most participants could support and to gauge quantitatively the extent of that support.

- Second, the session would present an opportunity to address the key question raised by the conference—"Is Technology Enough?"—in a way that collectively and simultaneously involved all conference participants. The 1995 Asilomar conference was the first that posed a specific, carefully defined question as its theme.

- Third and least—or most—importantly, depending on one's perspective, a structured, consensus-seeking wrap-up session seemed like an activity that, in addition, to the "open mike" session,[1] could add fun and interaction to the conference and also help us to understand differences and similarities in our positions.

Surprisingly for many of us involved, the effort may have actually achieved most of the goals.

The Consensus Process

The organizers of the final session invoked typical consensus-building techniques of

- strawman propositions (developed by members of the conference organizing committee at the end of the technical sessions)

- voting by the participants to express varying degrees of agreement or disagreement with the strawman propositions

- a collective effort to reword the propositions to garner greater, if not unanimous, support from the participants

- a facilitated discussion of the issues raised

Barry McNutt served as session moderator. To start the process, David Greene provided a brief summary of the conference's technical presentations to set the stage for the strawman propositions and the consensus-building exercises. Jan Sharpless of the California Energy Commission acted as facilitator for the exercise.

The following five points of possible consensus were offered to the session participants and briefly explained by the moderator:

1. The current menu of technology is/will be adequate to reach the conference goals.

2. Current programs and policies will not bring these technologies into use to the degree needed to achieve the goals.

These two points treat the conference topic—namely, whether technology alone will be enough to achieve the sustainable transportation goals as defined for the conference.

---

[1]The "open mike" session is a three- to four-hour moderated, but free, exchange of views by Asilomar participants. Everyone who signs up at the beginning of the evening is given a five-minute opportunity to speak on any topic related to the conference.

3. Buy-in to the level and timing of the conference goals has not been achieved, but we do agree on these directions:

- reducing greenhouse gas emissions
- reducing priority air pollutants
- reducing oil imports
- increasing renewable fuels

This point was offered for discussion because a number of the conference participants did not agree with the definitions and measures of "sustainable transportation" used by the conference organizing committee.

4. Consumers are being left out or not adequately involved in the debate over goals, policies, and technology. "We" need to shift our focus from the analysis and policy development community (ourselves) to consumers in terms of understanding their views on appropriate policies.

5. Consensus on the right policies is not possible. Differences of opinion are real and not likely to disappear.

The fourth and fifth points address issues that developed during the conference. Some conference participants had suggested that not enough attention was being given to the views of consumers and that our failure to hear consumers out would doom policies to failure. On the last point, the strength with which positions were held and expressed (particularly in the open-mike session) suggested that consensus on policies might be impossible.

After a brief introduction to the consensus building process and the strawman propositions, the facilitator and participants engaged in the task of trying to reach consensus on each of the points. Voting was conducted on a scale of 1 to 5, with higher numbers indicating stronger disagreement:

1 = Strongly support but don't want to see any wording changed

2 = Support but would like wording changed

3 = Can live with it as is but neither strongly disagree nor support

4 = Disagree but could support it if wording were changed

5 = Strongly disagree and could not support

The voting allowed all involved to better understand where other participants stood on the issue and to judge whether wording changes were headed in the direction of greater consensus.

Results

Conference participants eagerly joined in the initial voting process, in suggesting new wording, and in subsequent voting. Although the debate itself was more valuable than its outcome, here we will summarize mainly the outcome.

Point 1   The current menu of technology is/will be adequate to each of the conference goals.

This point was reworded to read: *"The current menu of technology, as discussed at the Asilomar conference, has the potential to meet the conference goals, including timing and level."* Conference participants were particularly adamant about making a distinction between technology potential and realized benefits. The reworded statement was supported (levels 1 and 2 on the voting scale) by more than 50 out of the 60 participants present.

Point 2   Current programs and policies will not bring these technologies into use to the degree needed to achieve the goals.

This point was supported, without any rewording, by all but 2 of the 60 participants voting.

Point 3   Buy-in to the level and timing of conference goals has not been achieved, but we do agree on these directions:

- reducing greenhouse gas emissions
- reducing criteria pollutants
- reducing oil imports
- increasing renewable fuels

This point engendered much discussion. In the end, participants agreed to strike renewable-fuel use per se as a goal whose direction they could support. This outcome is interesting for a conference focused on sustainability. A distinction was also drawn between oil imports and oil vulnerability. The final wording, supported by 52 and opposed by 3 participants, read: *"With regard to the conference goals, we agree on the desirability of reducing greenhouse gases, criteria pollutants, and oil vulnerability."*

Point 4   Consumers are being left out or not adequately involved in the debate over goals, policies, and technology. "We" need to shift our focus from the analysis and policy development community (ourselves) to consumers in terms of understanding their views on appropriate policies.

Point 4, as presented, was largely rejected by the conference and was refocused on the need to better understand consumer requirements and behavior in our technical and policy assessments. Little support was given to the thought that consumers were not adequately involved in the policy development process. In fact, some participants offered the thought that consumers were too involved and that catering to their every whim stopped any progress. The final wording, supported by 43 and opposed by 3 participants, read: *"Within the Asilomar conference context, we need to give more attention to consumer information/education and to understanding consumer preferences and responses to policies."*

As an aside, we note that our failure to give such attention to consumer information and preferences has led to considerable negative reaction to various technical programs, including, most recently, the reformulated/oxygenated gasoline programs. These programs represent stereotypical technological fixes to criteria pollutant problems that should have been relatively invisible to consumers. However, consumer attitudes toward small price changes and a faint fuel odor, combined with media attention, created substantial resistance in some areas. Better consumer education and information might have helped. In any case, such recent experiences do not bode well for the acceptance of other, more visible technology and policy changes, such as mandated alternatively fueled vehicles.

Point 5 Consensus on the right policies is not possible. Differences of opinion are real and are not likely to disappear.

There was not enough time in the final session to work completely through this fifth point, and there was strong opposition to its original wording. Several important points did arise during the discussion: (1) Some suggested that it would be better to change the word *opinions* to *interests*, thereby putting the focus on stakeholders, not just policy analysts. (2) Some pointed out that the word *right* was wrong: policies are neither right nor wrong; it is just that some work and others don't. (3) Some emphasized that we achieve agreement all the time—without actually reaching consensus—on policies such as the Clean Air Act and the Energy Policy Act, making the issue of "reaching consensus" somewhat moot in a practical context.

On this last point, it is worth noting that our society and government work on the basis of compromise and agreement, not consensus. Much of our progress is made with the support of a narrow majority.

This discussion of "right" policies and the role of "consensus" provided an ending point for both the session and the conference. Perhaps consideration of these concepts will serve as a useful starting point for pursuing further discussions at the next conference.

The issues raised in the wrap-up session lead some of us to conclude that real progress in achieving sustainable transportation will have to be based on very good and nearly transparent technologies. (*Transparent*, in this case, refers to technologies that would involve no change in consumer perceptions and behavior.) A significant minority of people will always object to changing their behavior for what are fundamentally public, not private, benefits. Alternatively, policymakers can try to get more widespread public buy-in to the seriousness of the problems (that is, educating individuals and interests to accept that the problems faced are, in fact, problems for them). There might then be an acceptance of significant changes that go beyond technology to respond to the problems. Another part of this buy-in is an acknowledgment that government can be trusted to "do the right thing" and that any perceived sacrifices are considered a necessary and unavoidable part of solving the problem. This issue was outside the scope of this conference, even as it relates to technology, but is worth considering for future conferences.

Wherever one stands on these issues, the point of the conference was to explore one approach (technology change) to solving the stated problems. The purpose of the final session was to see if the participants could come to "consensus" (really, reasonable agreement) on one or more points related to the topic. We think that the conference was successful on both counts. In summary, the 1995 Asilomar conference can be said to have come to some important conclusions regarding the *adequacy of technology* and the *inadequacy of policies*, the desirability of certain sustainability goals, and the need for greater attention to consumer needs, education, and behavior regarding both policies and technologies.

About the Editors

JOHN M. DECICCO is a senior associate with the American Council for an Energy-Efficient Economy (ACEEE), where he directs the organization's transportation efficiency program. His work focuses on energy efficiency in the transportation sector, including assessments of ways to improve the efficiency and lessen the environmental impacts of motor vehicles. Dr. DeCicco has coauthored ACEEE's recent studies on automotive fuel economy, incentives for improving transportation efficiency, and the economic and job creation benefits of energy efficiency improvement. He has been active in analyzing and advancing regulatory and market incentive programs for improving vehicle efficiency and reducing travel demand, and has assisted in the development of policy proposals at the state and federal levels. His other projects include the environmental aspects of energy use, and he has published on a variety of energy and environmental issues. Dr. DeCicco received a Ph.D. degree in mechanical engineering from Princeton University in 1988, where he was associated with the university's Center for Energy and Environmental Studies.

MARK DELUCCHI is at the Institute of Transportation Studies–Davis. He holds a B.A. and an M.Arch. degree from the University of California at Berkeley, where he studied engineering, economics, planning, and architecture. He received a Ph.D. degree in ecology in 1990 from the University of California at Davis, where he did research on rail transit systems, alternative transportation fuels for motor vehicles, and emissions of greenhouse gases from the use of electricity and transportation fuels. After receiving his doctorate, Dr. Delucchi spent a year at the Center for Energy and Environmental Studies at Princeton University, evaluating the performance and economics of hydrogen fuel-cell vehicles. In 1992 he returned to ITS-Davis, where he is researching social costs of motor vehicle use in the United States, the environmental impacts of using public transit, and electric vehicles.

About the Authors

DICK CATALDI brings over 25 years of transportation engineering research experience to his work as a senior program manager for locomotive research at the Association of American Railroads (AAR). He began his career in the Industrial Engineering Department of the

257

Pennsylvania Railroad as a co-op student, moved to Norfolk & Western Railway's Mechanical Maintenance Department, was a consultant to the U.S. Postal Service on facility design and transportation logistics, and was later a consultant on track maintenance equipment for the Federal Railroad Administration. He joined AAR's Research & Test Department in 1980, where he managed a series of wind tunnel tests in the Energy Research Program. He took over diesel engine research in 1985 and became director of the Energy and Locomotive Research Program in 1990. Mr. Cataldi received a B.S. degree in industrial engineering from Virginia Tech in 1970 and did graduate work in systems engineering at the same school. He is a member of the American Society of Mechanical Engineers (ASME), the Society of Automotive Engineers (SAE), the Locomotive Maintenance Officers Association, and the American Railway Engineering Association.

K. G. DULEEP is director of engineering at Energy and Environmental Analysis (EEA), where he manages automotive practice. He specializes in fuel economy and emission control technology and strategy issues, as well as in alternative-fuel-vehicle technology. EEA's automotive group provides a range of analytical services to federal and state agencies, auto manufacturers, fuel suppliers, and foreign governments, principally related to technology forecasting, regulatory development and compliance, and emissions/fuel economy modeling, and Mr. Duleep has developed an international reputation for his work on automotive technology cost and performance modeling. Prior to joining EEA, he worked at the Bendix Fuel Injection Systems Group, where he assisted in the development of the first domestic "closed-loop" fuel injection system for the Cadillac, as well as the first low-cost "throttle-body" fuel injection system used in the Renault Alliance. Mr. Duleep holds an M.S. degree in engineering from the University of Michigan and an M.B.A. degree from the Wharton School.

LEW FULTON is currently a Visiting Scholar at Independent University Bangladesh, where he teaches in the School of Environmental Science and Management and is also conducting research on reducing vehicle emissions in Dhaka, the fastest-growing large city in the world. Dr. Fulton's background includes ten years' experience in the fields of transportation and energy research and policy analysis. From 1992 through 1995, he worked as an economist and industry specialist at the U.S. Department of Energy, Office of Policy, where he supervised a number of policy studies, including reports to Congress on the potential impacts of telecommuting on transportation energy use and emissions, and the costs and benefits of widespread alternative-fuel use in the U.S. light-duty-vehicle sector. In addition, he has provided policy analysis for several major federal government initiatives, developing transportation policy options for the Climate Change Action Plan in 1993 and analyzing policy options for the Policy Dialog Advisory Committee to Assist in the Development of Measures to Significantly Reduce Greenhouse Gas Emissions from Personal Motor Vehicles (the "Car Talk" committee) in 1994–1995. Dr. Fulton holds a Ph.D. degree in energy management and environmental policy from the University of Pennsylvania.

JOHN GERMAN is with the Environmental Protection Agency (EPA), Office of Mobile Sources, National Vehicle and Fuel Emissions Laboratory in Ann Arbor, Michigan. His background includes rule-making development—as for cold-temperature carbon monoxide standards, on-board diagnostics, and revisions to the Federal Test Procedure—as well as work on factors impacting emissions, fuel economy technology and modeling, travel demand projection models, computer models of modal emissions, nonroad emissions inventories, and strategic planning. Before coming to EPA in 1986, Mr. German spent 8 years in powertrain engineering at Chrysler, working on a wide variety of fuel economy issues. He holds a B.S. degree in physics from the University of Michigan and got halfway through an M.B.A. degree program before coming to his senses. Although he insists he is not really an engineer, after 20 years of functioning as one, no one pays any attention to his disclaimers. He has a wide variety of interests and will work on almost anything he thinks is interesting, in addition to promoting teams, empowerment, and improved science.

DAVID L. GREENE is a senior research staff member of the Oak Ridge National Laboratory (ORNL) Center for Transportation Analysis, where he has worked since 1977, establishing ORNL's Transportation Energy Group in 1980 and its Transportation Research Section in 1987. Dr. Greene has contributed over one hundred publications to the professional literature and has given congressional testimony on transportation and energy issues. He is editor-in-chief of the U.S. Department of Transportation's new *Journal of Transportation and Statistics,* and his recent book, *Transportation and Energy,* was published by the Eno Foundation for Transportation in 1997. Dr. Greene is active in the Transportation Research Board (TRB) and the National Research Council and has served as chairman of TRB's Energy Committee and of the Section on Environmental and Energy Concerns. He is a recipient of TRB's Pyke Johnson Award and two Distinguished Service citations. He holds a B.A. degree from Columbia University, an M.A. degree from the University of

Oregon, and a Ph.D. degree in geography and environmental engineering from the Johns Hopkins University.

RICHARD J. KINSEY is manager of the Fuel Economy Planning and Compliance Department at the Ford Motor Company, where he is responsible for compliance of the company's products with current and future fuel economy requirements, evaluation of proposed standards and test procedures, and liaison with federal and state agencies on such matters. Mr. Kinsey joined Ford Motor Company in 1963 and has held positions in manufacturing engineering, product design engineering, automotive safety compliance, and emission certification engineering. Before assuming his present position in 1993, he was manager of Ford's Certification Engineering Department, Certification Engineering and Compliance Programs, where he was responsible for controlling, maintaining, and testing Ford's certification test vehicles and engines to ensure that all products sold complied with federal and state emissions and fuel economy standards, and for federal and state agency liaison activities relative to Ford-submitted test data. Mr. Kinsey holds a B.S. degree in mechanical engineering from Lawrence Institute of Technology and an M.B.A. degree from Michigan State University.

LEE LYND is an associate professor of engineering at the Thayer School of Engineering, Dartmouth College, where he directs an interdisciplinary research program focused on new technologies with potential to make strategic reductions in the cost of converting biomass into ethanol and other commodity products. He is also active in analyzing the efficacy of biomass-based processes in current and future contexts. Dr. Lynd is co-founder and director of Process Development for Independence Biofuel, Inc., and associate editor of *Biotechnology and Bioengineering*. He was a representative of the biofuels industry on the Policy Dialog Advisory Committee to Assist in the Development of Measures to Significantly Reduce Greenhouse Gas Emissions from Personal Motor Vehicles (the "Car Talk" committee). He holds a B.S. degree in biology from Bates College, an M.S. degree in bacteriology from the University of Wisconsin, Madison, an M.S. degree in engineering from Dartmouth College, and a D.E. degree in engineering from the Thayer School of Engineering at Dartmouth. Dr. Lynd is a recipient of the National Science Foundation Presidential Young Investigator Award and a two-time recipient of the Charles A. Lindbergh Award in recognition of his efforts to promote a balance between technological development and environmental preservation.

BARRY D. MCNUTT is a policy analyst with the U.S. Department of Energy (DOE), Office of Energy Efficiency and Alternative Fuels Policy, where he is responsible for end-use demand analysis projects covering all sectors of the economy; development of new analytic techniques; and development and analysis of policies regarding petroleum conservation, transportation efficiency, alternative fuels, and reformulated gasoline. He has been with the Policy Office since the formation of DOE in 1977, and earlier worked with the Federal Energy Administration and the Environmental Protection Agency. Mr. McNutt represents DOE at many national and international meetings covering transportation, energy, and fuels issues. He is a member of the Society of Automotive Engineers (SAE) and the author of numerous technical articles and policy papers addressing transportation energy use, fuels, and fuel economy. He holds a B.A. degree and a B.S. degree in mechanical engineering from Rutgers University.

MARIANNE MILLAR MINTZ specializes in transportation energy forecasting and policy analysis for the Center for Transportation Research at Argonne National Laboratory. Since joining Argonne in 1977, she has devoted her energies to a wide range of transportation energy issues. She has developed forecasts of transportation energy demand and estimated potential impacts of energy conservation measures in the United States and for such other countries as Argentina, South Korea, Portugal, Jamaica, and Tunisia; she has studied the effects of transportation control measures, policies to reduce global warming, new technologies, and alternative fuels and has evaluated the market potential of new fuels and energy technologies; she has analyzed vehicle ownership and transportation patterns of different ethnic and demographic groups and the differential impacts of transportation policies on those groups; and she has evaluated the discrepancy between on-road fuel economy and estimates obtained from federal tests. Ms. Mintz is an active member of the Transportation Energy Committee of the Transportation Research Board, a recipient of two Argonne Pacesetter awards, and the author or coauthor of more than 50 publications. She obtained her master's degree in 1973 from the University of California at Los Angeles, where she specialized in public service systems.

ROBERTA J. NICHOLS has been an engineering consultant since retiring from Ford Motor Company in 1995. At Ford, her primary responsibility was development of alternative-fuels vehicles, including alcohol (methanol and ethanol), natural gas, propane, and electric vehicles. She is the holder of three patents on the flexible-fuel vehicle (FFV), which went into production in 1993, and is author of more than 50 technical papers. Prior to joining Ford in 1979, Dr. Nichols worked for 22 years in the space programs at the Aerospace Corporation and the Space Technology Laboratory of the Douglas Aircraft Company. She holds a B.S. degree in physics from the University of California at Los Angeles, an M.S. degree in environmental engineering from the University of Southern California (USC), and a Ph.D. degree in engineering from USC. Dr. Nichols received the National Achievement Award from the Society of Women Engineers in 1988 and is a fellow of the Society of Automotive Engineers (SAE) and a member of the National Academy of Engineering.

MARC ROSS is a professor of physics at the University of Michigan and a part-time senior scientist in the Information Sciences Division at Argonne National Laboratory. After working on the theory of fundamental particles for 20 years, in 1972 his interests shifted to energy and environmental problems. In 1974 he codirected the American Physical Society's landmark study on the efficient use of energy. Dr. Ross's present research focuses on energy use and its environmental implications from the perspectives of physics, economics, behavior, and policy. At Argonne, his work is concerned with understanding and forecasting industrial energy consumption and emissions in order to evaluate public policies that influence industrial performance. His university research focuses on energy use and emissions of vehicles and on the design of alternative vehicles. His current work on automotive emissions involves analysis of data from measurement programs using dynamometers, as carried out by the Environmental Protection Agency, manufacturers, and states; and analysis of data from remote-sensing programs carried out by the California Air Resources Board and others. Dr. Ross holds a Ph.D. degree in physics from the University of Wisconsin.

MARGARET SINGH is a transportation systems planner with the Center for Transportation Research at Argonne National Laboratory. Prior to joining Argonne, she worked as a campus transportation planner for a consulting firm and as a transit planner for the Chicago Transit Authority and the Northeast Illinois Regional Transportation Authority. Since joining Argonne in 1978, Ms. Singh has worked on a wide variety of transportation energy projects but in particular has focused on alternative-fuel vehicles (AFVs) and electric vehicles (EVs), assessing their costs and benefits. She has also analyzed the energy, oil use, and greenhouse gas benefits of various reformulated gasoline formulations; projected AFV fleet markets; and evaluated emergency evacuation plans of communities surrounding nuclear power plants. She has authored or coauthored approximately 50 papers and reports on AFVs, EVs, and other transportation technologies and has served several terms on the Transportation Research Board's Alternative Fuels Committee. Ms. Singh has a master's degree in urban planning from the University of Illinois.

TOM WENZEL is a scientific engineering associate at Lawrence Berkeley National Laboratory. His research concerns the analysis of large datasets of in-use vehicles in order to identify, and to develop effective policies to reduce, the remaining sources of vehicle criteria pollutant emissions. He also is involved in an effort to develop improved techniques to model emissions from high-emitting vehicles, as part of the National Cooperative Highway Research Program modal emissions model project managed by the University of California at Riverside's Center for Environmental Research and Technology. He has coauthored several papers on in-use vehicle emissions, as well as a report on pay-as-you-drive auto insurance. Mr. Wenzel holds a master's degree in public policy from the University of California at Berkeley.

Index

involvement in and education on
sustainable transportation, 254-55
See also market barriers
container loads of rail freight in U.S.
(graph), 198
conversion technology for ethanol, 111-13
summary of process parameters
(table), 112
conversion to alternative fuels and
alternative fuel vehicles. *See* AFVs;
alternative fuels; biofuels
corn ethanol
production costs, 85-86
and subsidy policy, 124
See also cellulose ethanol; ethanol
Corporate Average Fuel Economy
(CAFE) standards
automotive emissions regulations
impact, 67-68
future uses, 100, 250
cost effectiveness of ethanol use and
production, 130
cost estimates
AFV transition costs, 143-54
of alternative fuels, 245-46
electric vehicles, 165-69, 246
ethanol cost effectiveness, 130
ethanol production, 84-88, 101-3, 109-
13, 116-17, 122, 130
of fuel economy and biofuel
combination, 98-99, 101-4
of fuel economy technology, 82-84, 158-
59
hybrid electric vehicles, 176
See also fuel price; price
crops for cellulose ethanol production,
116-21
CRP (Conservation Reserve Program),
projected role in ethanol production,
119
cryogenic fuels for jet aircraft, 219
cycle development studies (for
automotive emissions), 52-53

D

data gathering for emissions system
malfunctions, 31, 37-39
DeCicco, John, 257
on reducing automotive emissions, 75-
108
on technology and the Asilomar
conference, 1-20
Delucchi, Mark, 257
on technology and the Asilomar
conference, 1-20
Department of Defense (DOD) air
transport efficiency R&D, 209-10
Department of Energy (DOE) studies

compared with actual AFV costs,
143-54
diesel engine oxygen enrichment, 204
diesel trucks. *See* trucks (heavy-duty)
diesel vehicles
diesel engine oxygen enrichment, 204
electric vehicles compared with, 164-66
emissions standard predictions, 192
losses within overall energy chain
(graph), 164
low-emissions models, 162
See also rail freight; trucks (heavy-duty)
direct-injection engines (four-stroke),
234-35
dispatch (for rail freight)
computer-assisted, 200-201
dispatcher training, 202
distribution costs for alternative fuels,
147-48
DOD (Department of Defense) air
transport efficiency R&D, 209-10
DOE (Department of Energy) studies
compared with actual AFV costs,
143-54
drag reduction for aircraft, 212-13
driving behavior and emission impacts,
54-65
air conditioning operation, 59
fuel consumption impacts, 66-68
soak distributions and trip patterns,
59-63
graphs, 61, 62, 63
speed and acceleration, 25-26, 54-58
graphs, 55, 56, 57, 58
survey methodology, 52
Duleep, K. G., 258
on fuel economy, 157-78
on heavy-duty trucks, 179-94

E

economics. *See* cost estimates
economy. *See* fuel economy
ECS (emissions control systems)
malfunction. *See* emissions control
systems (ECS) malfunction
EEA (Energy and Environmental
Analysis, Inc.) fuel economy
technology study, 157-78
advanced conventional vehicles, 159-
62
hypothetical midsize car (table), 161
technology used in, 160-62
electric vehicles, 162-76
performance requirements, 158-59
efficiency. *See* fuel economy; fuel
economy and biofuel combination
EIA (Energy Information Administration)
air transport growth projections, 220

269